Practical Property Development
and Finance

Practical Property Development and Finance

Godfrey Bruce-Radcliffe
Partner
Hobson Audley Hopkins & Wood, Solicitors

LAW & TAX

© Pearson Professional Limited 1996

Godfrey Bruce-Radcliffe has asserted his right under the Copyright, Designs and
Patents Act 1988 to be identified as the author of this work

ISBN 075200 2171

Published by
FT Law & Tax
21-27 Lamb's Conduit Street
London WC1N 3NJ

A Division of Pearson Professional Limited

Associated offices
Australia, Belgium, Canada, Hong Kong, India, Japan, Luxembourg, Singapore,
Spain, USA

First edition 1996

All rights reserved. No part of this publication may be reproduced, stored in a retrieval system, or transmitted, in any form or by any means, electronic, mechanical, photocopying, recording, or otherwise, without the prior written permission of the publishers.

No responsibility for loss occasioned to any person acting or refraining from action as a result of the material in this publication can be accepted by the author or publishers.

A CIP catalogue record for this book is available from the British Library.

Printed in Great Britain by Hartnolls, Cornwall

Contents

About the Author	ix
Preface	xi
Table of Cases	xv
Table of Statutes	xv
Table of Statutory Instruments	xvi

1	**The Players**	1
	Public sector	3
	English partnerships	4
	Single regeneration budget	5
	Set aside	6
	Ultra vires	6
	Private sector	6
	Insolvency	7
	Joint venture companies	8
	Jointco in use	9
	Interaction	12
	Partnerships and limited partnerships	13
	Full company on stage	14
	Checklist	16
2	**The Site**	18
	Contracts	18
	Negotiated approach	18
	Conditional element	20
	Options and pre-emption	21
	Public authority co-operation	22
	Other public authority options	23
	English partnerships	24
	Third party rights	26
	Nuisance	28
	Restrictive covenants	29
	The environment	30
	Checklist	32
3	**The Professional Team and Contractors**	34
	Duplication of roles	37

	Appointment	40
	Consequence of termination	41
	Collateral warranties	42
	Building contract	43
	Sub-contracts	45
	Commitments to third parties	45
	Assignment and novation of appointments	46
	Defects liability insurance	48
	Overview	49
	Checklist	50
4	**Development Cost**	52
	True development cost	53
	Landowners and institutional purchasers	53
	Funder's view	55
	Purchasers and tenants	57
	Principal players generally	57
	Forward funding	59
	Notional interest	60
	Other interested parties	61
	Fund costs	62
	Other relationships	63
	Overview	64
	Checklist	64
5	**The Construction Process**	66
	Consents and approvals in the construction context	67
	The construction programme	69
	Building contacts–the tendering process	71
	Licence to go on site	73
	Procuration of construction versus implementation *per se*	75
	General building obligations	77
	Development periods	78
	Management contracting	79
	CDM	79
	Approval of works	80
	Supervision–defective works	80
	Supervision–generally	82
	Insurance and indemnity	84
	Buildings insurance	84
	Period of insurance and contractor's insurances	85
	Insuring the overage	86
	Reinstatement in course of works	87
	The insurers	87

	Indemnity clauses in development agreements	88
	PI cover	89
	Overview	90
	Checklist	92
6	**Timing and Completion of the Development**	**94**
	Preliminary stages	94
	Certificates and draw downs	95
	Completion of the building contract	97
	Interim certificates	97
	Partial possession by the employer	98
	Practical completion	99
	Defects liability	99
	Final certificate	101
	Certification under development agreements	101
	The landowner/local authority	101
	The bank	104
	Investing institutions	106
	Tenants	108
	Delay and delay clauses	109
	Checklist	111
7	**Letting and Letting Policy**	**113**
	Lawyers and agents	115
	The needs of the players	116
	The landowner	116
	The investing institution	119
	Overage provisions	120
	Mix of uses in the context of overage	122
	The bank	123
	The tenant	127
	Letting agents	127
	Checklist	131
8	**Funding**	**133**
	Security	134
	Development agreements and major interests	135
	Alienation	136
	Bank funding	139
	Non-recourse	142
	Profit sharing mortgages	143
	Institutional funding	144
	Forward funding	144
	Financial formulae	146

Profit erosion	147
Default versus overage	148
Forward purchase	148
Leaseback	149
Overview	150
Checklist	151

9 Default and Disputes — 153

Default	155
The landowner	156
The bank	158
Forward funding	159
Forward purchase and tenants	161
Third parties	161
Default of major players	162
Disputes	162
Arbitration	163
Experts	164
Alternative dispute resolution (ADR)	165
Other kinds of dispute procedure	166
Overview	167
Checklist	168

10 Epilogue — 170

Negotiation	170
Public versus private sectors	172
Site as a tool of the trade	174
Taxation	175
VAT	176
Stamp duty	177
Corporate and partnership taxation	178
JV features	178
Negotiating strength and bargaining power	179

Index 183

About the Author

Godfrey Bruce-Radcliffe is a solicitor of more than 25 years standing. Throughout almost all of his professional career, he has specialised in commercial property with particular emphasis upon development and finance.

In November 1994, after nearly 18 years as a partner in the City law firm D J Freeman, Godfrey Bruce-Radcliffe joined another City firm, Hobson Audley (now Hobson Audley Hopkins & Wood), as Head of Property. He has lectured widely on development related topics and is a familiar conference speaker. He has also been an occasional visiting lecturer at the University of Westminster and, in particular, to its school of Urban Development and Planning.

In the early 1990s, at its invitation, Godfrey Bruce-Radcliffe participated as a consultant to a research project being conducted by the school into joint venture media. This was sponsored by the Crown Estate and the Continuing Professional Development Foundation. The fruits of this research led, in turn, to an important book in the Longman Transactions series entitled *Property Development Partnerships*. That book was co-authored with its originator Clive Darlow BSc M Phil (*Cantab*) FRICS FSVA, a senior lecturer in the School of Urban Development and Planning of the University of Westminster, and with Stuart Morley BSc MA Dip TP FRICS, formerly a lecturer at the University of Westminster and now a partner and head of research at Grimley International Property Advisers, and John Boff BA, a tax associate at D J Freeman.

Sadly, Clive Darlow died in March 1995, and so this book is also written as a tribute to him, and in recognition of his enthusiasm for the world of development and finance, and the inter-relationships between the public and private sectors in the development scene.

Godfrey Bruce-Radcliffe's many years of experience of development gives *Practical Property Development and Finance* the benefit of a thorough understanding of the development process, and the contractual and other legal relationships by which that process is controlled and regulated. The preceding book, *Property Development Partnerships*, is also, therefore, an ideal background to the material which this book, in particular, now presents.

Preface

The recession, even now not 'recent', had its perceptible beginnings in 1988, if not earlier. The previous decade had seen an unprecedented expansion of development activity. Following the property crash of 1974, insolvencies of secondary banks and the realignment which rapidly followed, the market had recovered, by 1978, some of its composure.

Notwithstanding the minor recession in 1981, the development industry soon regained its momentum. Those who were experienced in development took full advantage of the market available to them. Modest names became famous and appeared invincible in the wake of the Thatcher revolution. How different they appear today.

By 1988, in the wake of the stock market crash of 1987 and the bold fiscal strategies which followed, an economic bubble appeared which was soon to burst. The property industry raced on and flung itself over the precipice, believing that here was a bottomless pot of gold, only to find, instead, that it had fallen into a bottomless pit!

Moreover, the manpower available to finance the investment market had become so stretched that immediately prior to the recession the most sophisticated and financially substantial transactions were being thrust into place by people who, in some cases, had very limited experience. The fire of recession in the property industry was being fuelled long before the players realised the enormity of the disaster which was to befall them. The events of 1990, and the years which immediately followed, are now history.

It is arguable whether the recession in property terms (whether viewed from a national, European or even global standpoint), has yet run its course. The development market is subdued at present, but this book is not about such conundra. However, an inevitable consequence of the recession is that those engaged in development, developers themselves, their financiers, the providers of land, all those involved in the development process, including not least their professional advisers, are now lacking a vital dimension.

A good many years have gone by in which, for many, the experience of development has not been available. Those whose chosen professions might traditionally have assumed an understanding of such matters have not, in the event, enjoyed the experience which the future will surely demand. In particular, many surveyors and solicitors who qualified from 1989 onwards are—through no fault of their own—not yet competent to deal with new development. History has literally passed them by.

It would be a pity if a re-emerging market were claimed exclusively by those whose mistakes, as well as their experience, contributed so handsomely to the economic consequences with which we now live. Those who stand ready to challenge their forebears need as much knowledge as they can gain, as they assess and set about that re-emerging market.

Traditionally, whether one was a surveyor or a solicitor, one would learn the practicalities by working alongside senior professionals until one had learned the basics of the development process. Surveyors, as a profession, are not number crunchers, still less are solicitors. Yet these two professions in particular have guided themselves, their immediate clients (including banks and financiers as well as landowners), in formulating development proposals which ultimately emerged as investments of a certain kind. The legacy is not entirely a proud one, but the purpose of this book is to bridge, however slightly, some of the experience gaps of recent years.

Accordingly, solicitors and surveyors in particular, as well as members of other professions (particularly those who have qualified since the onset of recession), together also with their clients and others involved in the development process, may yet recoup a little of the essential experience which they have been denied, particularly if they are coming to development for the very first time, by considering the issues which this book endeavours to set down in a simple and straightforward manner, as a manual for those for whom the development process is relatively unfamiliar. An assumption must be made that they are at least technically competent in the various mechanisms and processes which their chosen professions demand of them, and that what is now lacking is an appropriate context in which practical experience can be acquired. This book is, therefore, quite intentionally not in any sense a legal reference work, neither does it seek to instruct in the basic professional skills which are a necessary precursor to embarking on a career in this field.

It is also to be hoped that those for whom development has been a familiar and happier playground will find that within some of these pages their better (as well as bitter) experiences will be relived. It is further hoped that for those for whom this is a relatively new subject, not only the text but also the checklists appearing at the end of each chapter will strike a chord, and that these will motivate the newer or younger development professional towards an ordered and disciplined approach to development projects.

This book is emphatically not intended to be a detailed commentary. Equally emphatically, it is not intended to be a general overview. It is specifically intended to identify, separate and compare basic development principles from the standpoints of the different players with the view to assisting those involved in the detail of the development process to reach workable agreements.

Finally, in the absence of the usual lengthy acknowledgements to fatten the book, it only remains for me to thank my secretary, Tracey Mann, who has endured preparation of the text and its many and varied amendments, and also my partners for their kind indulgence.

Godfrey Bruce-Radcliffe
30 October 1995
London EC4

Table of Cases

D & F Estates v Church Commissioners [1989] AC 177; [1988] 2 EGLR 213;
15 Con LR 35 154
Murphy v Brentwood District Council [1991] 1 AC 398; [1990] 3 WLR 414;
[1990] 2 All ER 908, HL; revsg [1990] 2 WLR 944; [1990] 2 All ER 269;
(1990) 134 SJ 458, CA; affg 13 Con LR 96 154

Table of Statutes

Arbitration Act 1950 164
Arbitration Act 1979 164
Community Land Act 1975 24
Companies Act 1985 6
Development Land Tax Act 1976 .. 24
Environment Act 1995 32
Estate Agents Act 1979 127
Financial Services Act 1986 .... 14, 143
Highways Act 1980—
 s 157 26
Insolvency Act 1986 .... 7, 8, 140, 141
 s 9 8
Land Registration Act 1925—
 s 70 175
 (1) 125
Land Registration Act 1986—
 s 4(1) 124
Landlord and Tenant (Covenants)
 Act 1995 .... 15, 120, 125, 149
Law of Property Act 1925 .. 8, 30, 140
 s 84 30
 s 146 158
Law of Property (Miscellaneous
 Provisions) Act 1989—
 s 2 21
Leasehold Reform, Housing
 and Urban Development Act
 1993 .... 4, 26
 Part III 25
 s 162 25

Leasehold Reform, Housing
 and Urban Development Act
 1993—contd
 s 167 26
 s 170 26
 s 171(2) 26
 Sched 20 25
Limited Partnerships Act 1907 14
Local Government Act 1972—
 s 123 3
Local Government and Housing Act
 1989—
 Part V 179
London Buildings Acts 28
Partnership Act 1890 13
Perpetuities and Accumulations
 Act 1964—
 s 9 21
Planning and Compensation Act
 1991 3
Prescription Act 1832 27
Property Misdescriptions Act
 1989 127
Town and Country Planning
 Act 1971—
 s 52 3
Town and Country Planning Act
 1990—
 s 192 3

Table of Statutory Instruments

Construction (Design and Management) Regulations 1994 (SI No 3140) 79

Local Authorities (Companies) Order 1995 (SI No 849) 6

1 The Players

'I'll have my bond; I will not hear thee speak:
I'll have my bond, and therefore speak no more'.
Shylock, The Merchant of Venice: Act III, Scene III

Poor Shylock, a man who knew exactly what he wanted, determined his bargaining position and pursued that course, to the exclusion of all other, to its fateful conclusion. The problem with deals is people. Every player is motivated by a particular objective. The advantage he seeks will usually have financial overtones, possibly a socio-political dimension as well, otherwise identified in gentler times as *pro bono publico*.

The purely political dimension should not be underestimated, whether it is derived from planning legislation, derivative PPG guidance, perceived needs of regeneration, various forms of government encouragement, etc. A revitalised public sector may, in time, recreate some of the municipal endeavours and achievements of the 19th Century, things we have taken for granted and which have shaped our lives for so long.

The players in the development process are not driven by ambition alone: they are also channelled by a variety of constraints whether financial, of custom, legal, political, and so on.

It is, therefore, supremely important for every player, in devising his agenda, not only to identify his own position, but also to appreciate the motivations and needs of (and constraints upon) the other players in the piece. In addition, those who negotiate a contractual relationship should not fail to grasp one fundamental principle which encapsulates the underlying thesis of this book, that is to say, that every player entering into a contractual commitment must examine that commitment not only in terms of his and others' willingness to perform, but also in terms of parallel and subsidiary transactions and the players in those transactions, and whether the giving (and sometimes more importantly the taking) of one commitment may in some way frustrate another. If insistence on one kind of commitment will inevitably frustrate the provision of another, it may lead ultimately to collapse of the project.

The most common difficulties may be identified within development agreements the regulation of which may make the exercise impossible to fund, or create such uncertainty or impose such burdens as to discourage a pre-let tenant commitment. More subtly, however, a freestanding subsidiary contract, for example a construction contract, may give rise, if not to frustration then, perhaps, to pricing fluctuations if the development obligations imposed by, say, a landowner whether private or public, are inimical to the proper conduct of the construction process.

There is an irresistible tendency for every player to regard his role as central, and thus privileged. It is only human nature, but while this may be true in the sense that the deal cannot happen without his particular contribution, it is equally true that neither can the deal happen without his co-operation. Contribution and co-operation go hand in hand, and such a notion ought to be a *sine qua non*. Unfortunately, many negotiations are beleaguered by a false sense of co-operation which in reality hides a measure of *naiveté* and self-indulgence, if not intransigence. A successful negotiation, therefore, recognises the respective roles of the principal players and the nature of their dependence upon subsidiary players from the many points of view (principal or subsidiary) which may have to be accommodated.

These ideas affect not just principals—they reach down with equally penetrating consequences to those who are providing support services, not only contractors and the providers of materials but also the professional disciplines concerned. They are, in their own way, just as much players as their principals and, in turn, they may similarly misconstrue the nature of their roles. For surveyors and solicitors who, in the very nature of their work, are intimately bound up in identifying, expressing and articulating the contractual relationships into which their principals will enter, they will do well to perceive the limitations of their own knowledge and understanding which are necessarily circumscribed, not only by their professional training but also by the very nature of the experience which the practice of their respective professions affords them.

One difficulty for many professionals entering the frame, particularly solicitors, is that the principal players may have been in dialogue for some time. However much optimism one would like to share, to fail to cater for downside consequences is prospectively negligent, however little one's input was appreciated at the outset. Assessment of one's own clients' knowledge and ability is often not easy, but the inexperienced need to learn how to remain detached and objective while still retaining the client's confidence. It is a technique which can never be learned to perfection, and one which must be consciously practised from the day one is first allowed the conduct of a development until retirement from the scene.

Public sector

The public sector has an inevitable role to play in every development situation. At the very least, within the political and legal dimensions, responsibility is devolved upon a local authority as planning authority and also in such areas as building regulations and a wide variety of statutory constraints, the conduct and policing of which usually devolve upon local authorities. It is a constitutional *sine qua non* that the political dimension is circumscribed by the law as it stands for the time being, and zealous pursuit of political ideals, whatever one's persuasion, is fraught with danger.

Nevertheless, statutory roles need to be distinguished carefully from principal roles, even though the latter may in turn be governed by statutory constraint. As every solicitor should know, for example, if someone is given an indication, say by a planning officer (and given clear case law, the mistake is rarely made) that a particular process does not require planning permission and even if that view is expressed in writing, the local authority as planning authority is *not* estopped from exercising its power as planning authority if, in the event, permission is required. Accordingly, the distinction between, say, a local authority as landowner and the same authority as planning or highway authority is fundamental, and must not be confused. (There have been vital changes in planning laws on this issue. If one was proposing to use premises for a certain purpose, a determination would have been available under the Town and Country Planning Act 1971, s 53. Because no special form of application was required it was possible to argue that a planning officer's innocent letter was precisely such a determination. The Planning and Compensation Act 1991 has introduced a new s192 of the Town and Country Planning Act 1990 by recreating s 53 in a more positive and recognisable form. Moreover, as regards past use, the recent planning legislation has also overhauled provisions relating to established use certificates and, in particular, has introduced the concept of a certificate of lawful use over a period of at least ten years.)

It is essential for those dealing with local and other public authorities to recognise and remember one principle of common law which also affects every mortal soul, which is that one is free to do exactly as one pleases, except if it is against the law. As a corollary to this, the effect of the law may be to discourage a person, if not from doing something, then from doing it in a certain way. For local authorities in particular, dealing with land assets at an under value, ie at a consideration less than the best that can reasonably be obtained will not be permitted (except with the consent of the Secretary of State under s 123 of the Local Government Act 1972).

Local authorities will be particularly sensitive at times, because of their statutory benefits and constraints, to questions such as value to be derived, and also security. It is frequently the latter which imperils a negotiation not least because of the impact it may have on others' ability to deal.

In the case of a development agreement with, for example, a private sector developer, a (local authority) landowner must afford to itself the ability to retrieve the situation if the developer fails. The imposition of stringent development obligations backed by default procedures, and retention of legal possession during the development period, will clearly satisfy these fears but, at the same time, may produce pressures on other players with whom, perhaps, the landowner is not in direct contractual relationships. A bank providing finance, almost certainly using the development agreement as security, will not be able to proceed if it is not itself in a position to retrieve the developer's default. (An agreement leading to grant of a major interest, whether of the freehold or a long lease, is generally perceived as good security, so long as it meets essential tests as to the ability to remedy a default before it is too late and as to the ability to deal with it in order to recoup losses and to facilitate achievement of its and a bank's objectives.) Again, the tenant of an anchor pre-let may be similarly dismayed.

In considering the public sector one should also look beyond local authorities to various other statutory bodies such as development corporations which are expressly charged with facilitating the development process in certain designated areas. Other statutorily based bodies, whether transport orientated or public utilities have undergone, and continue to undergo, the process of privatisation, but still retain many of the characteristics of their public sector forebears through statutory constraints imposed upon them.

English partnerships

Perhaps the most remarkable new public sector body to be created in recent years is English Partnerships, known by its statutory name as 'The Urban Regeneration Agency', the provision of which is comprised in Pt III of the Leasehold Reform, Housing and Urban Development Act 1993. There was, in fact, never any logic in placing this legislation in a statute otherwise devoted to leasehold reform. It sits in isolation, and should be treated as such accordingly.

English Partnerships is a unique body which has the ability to impose its will throughout England, overriding both public and private sector interests and performing, subject to the guiding hand of the Secretary of State, virtually any of the available roles of any of the players in the development scene including the provision of financial assistance (which, it is stated quite clearly, can be 'in any form').

It is, however, expressly not authorised to provide housing except by way of existing stock in furtherance of its objects, which are in essence the regeneration of land in England. Neither can it acquire an interest in a company which would make that company a subsidiary, nor can it dispose of land at an undervalue.

Although subject to statutory constraints of its own, the essential characteristic of English Partnerships is that it may, upon application by anyone interested, or on its own initiative, facilitate or direct development, either by private agreement or by overriding the interests of others, including often where others may be discouraged by statutory constraints imposed upon them.

No doubt some will see English Partnerships as a threat but, equally, others will see it as an opportunity. It has subsumed English Estates and it has effectively taken over certain grants, including City grant and derelict land grant; but the grant system itself is evolving, and with the removal of these as identifiable grants, one must look to the legislation for English Partnerships to see how its powers to provide financial assistance are regulated. It is also necessary to be aware of guidance notes issued from time to time in order to ascertain any areas in which it is concentrating its energies.

Single regeneration budget

Treasury funding is heavily influenced by the wider issues raised by the single regeneration budget of which English Partnerships' funding forms part. However, in considering viability of a scheme in terms of what financial benefit may be derived from the public sector, and in particular government based grants, regard should be had to the statutory powers available to provide financial assistance in conjunction with the various European grants which are available for a variety of purposes depending, in particular, upon location and purpose.

Therefore, it is entirely feasible for a development scheme to be conceived and implemented according to all the practices and methods of the private sector by wholly public sector entities, so long as the statutory constraints and inhibitions are thoroughly understood, and followed with care (see **Ultra vires** below).

So far as UK government grants are concerned, and in particular those administered through the single regeneration budget, these may be sought through regional government offices which combine various ministries for the purpose. These grants and, by contrast, the encouragement towards inward investment enshrined in the private finance initiative, suggest that co-operation between the public and private sectors is here to stay, whatever political party is in power.

Set aside

When dealing with local authorities one should pay close attention to difficulties created for them by what are known as the 'set aside' rules which govern the application of receipts of money and under which a local authority will be permitted to utilise only part of those receipts for its own immediate purposes. There have been periodic relaxations and one must look to the rules as they stand for the time being. As the law presently stands, developers and others in the development process should be equally sensitive to a local authority's need to structure a deal in a certain way, to ameliorate the impact of these rules, as to the latter's need to understand that there are taxation and other considerations which bear precisely on the viability of a scheme in the hands of a private sector developer and, as much also, the way in which it should be structured.

Ultra Vires

It should be remembered that, when dealing with the public sector and in particular local authorities, the corporate covenant of a local authority is not a bottomless pot of gold any more than a blue chip PLC. As development lawyers are well aware, a contractual commitment which is beyond the powers (*'ultra vires'*) may be no commitment at all so that, for example, a guarantee may be worthless and there will be no recourse. (There are certain saving provisions for companies under s 35 of the Companies Act 1985 as amended.)

Again, if a local authority deals by, or through, a related company, or a company in which it has an interest for the purpose of development, that in itself may signal difficulties in identifying the propriety of the local authority's involvement. Granted that certain regulations, particularly the Local Authorities (Companies) Order 1995 (SI No 849), are presently in force, the area continues to be politically sensitive, and those negotiating with the view to local authority participation in a development scheme should look closely at the particular time to the constraints then in force, whether statutorily based or otherwise, and take advice accordingly.

Private sector

XYZ Ltd is a development company. A company is a statutorily contrived medium for the conduct of business. Its essential characteristic is that it is a legal person and, therefore, within the confines of its objects and powers it can contract and deal in the same way as a human.

It is a convenient medium for trading because it can combine the interests of a number of people, including other companies, in one single entity. Those interests will be represented by shareholdings of varying kinds and status. A company, by implication, is also capable of committing a criminal act and is thus liable to penalty. One cannot send a company to prison but one can impose the death penalty, through the process of liquidation (bankruptcy thus being a term applicable to a state of insolvency in people rather than companies). Responsibility for a company's affairs throughout its life devolves upon its board of directors (who may in turn incur personal penalties—non-executive directors, beware!).

Insolvency

A variety of statutorily contrived measures confers differing status upon a company which is insolvent, and in any such event a company's contractual position may be affected, perhaps fundamentally. For example an administrator appointed under the Insolvency Act 1986 is empowered not only to run the business, but also to operate a moratorium in relation to a company's debts. A liquidator can, by contrast, disclaim onerous contracts. An administrative receiver under a debenture can run the business of a company, but by reason that the security afforded is the whole, or substantially the whole, of the company's assets, can also ensure through enabling provisions of the 1986 Act that an administrator cannot be appointed (see below) and so on.

Those dealing with a company will, therefore, need to be satisfied as to its financial ability to perform (including whether security already given would, if enforced, frustrate that ability) and also whether, by the powers comprised in the objects set out in its memorandum of association, it has the ability and is permitted to engage in the particular activity, and in any event that it is empowered to give the kind of security that the deal requires. If not, there may be an avoidance of commitment, and legal remedies made difficult to pursue.

Lawyers involved in the development process are necessarily on enquiry as to the status of each of the players. Often, a company will be created specifically for a particular scheme. This is not just a matter of trading convenience but will almost certainly be required by a bank providing finance. The reason for this lies in the nature of the security which can be offered.

In the case of a company providing the whole or substantially the whole of its assets by way of security, the lending bank is afforded the opportunity, in case of need, to appoint an administrative receiver who, if the appointment is made in time, can over-ride the appointment thereafter of an administrator who might otherwise be appointed at the instance of the company itself or its directors or of one or more creditors. (The overriding power lies with the appointor of an administrative receiver whose consent is required for appointment of an administrator under s 9 of the Insolvency Act 1986.) By contrast, a receiver appointed under express powers deriving from the Law of Property Act 1925 has no such powers. Indeed if he wants to dispose of the charged asset, the terms of the legal charge must also give him the express power so to do, in effect, as agent and attorney for the borrower.

The term 'receivership' is loosely used, and often misused, and in particular habitually confused with liquidation, but the structure of a private sector developer goes to the root of the requirements of any bank lender, particularly in consequence of the Insolvency Act 1986, which gave birth to administrative receivers, administrators and other kinds of insolvency status.

Joint venture companies

A limited company may be set up as an appropriate medium for a joint venture in order to present a unified front to, say, a landowner (perhaps a local authority), a banker, or perhaps another landowner participating in the development, tenants, contractors, professionals, etc. The joint venture agreement, essentially a shareholders' agreement, may prescribe for a variety of functions to be carried out by the respective participators. Often, for convenience, there is a shareholders' agreement to deal with structural matters concerning the joint venture, and then a separate joint venture agreement which is more focused on the development itself.

For those who negotiate the terms of a joint venture it is essential that they take accounting, taxation and legal advice. The objectives of the joint venture, the division of responsibility, controlling mechanisms, the derivation of profit, etc can be dealt with in a variety of ways and determine the ultimate structure.

It is essential that principals and their consulting surveyors start from a base of understanding their objectives, instead of dictating the structure. To try to deal with each in parallel is likely to inhibit the negotiations. Until that lesson is learned, it is impossible for professional advisers (particularly solicitors) to be used to full effect. Worse, it may reflect a lack of experience on the part of the player in question and raise the question in the minds of others (quite rightly) whether this is a company or other body with whom one should be doing business.

A classic example of how *not* to set up a joint venture arose in the case of a public sector housing body looking to reclaim large tracts, indeed hundreds of acres, of derelict and in part contaminated land, for redevelopment. They knew they did not have the resources, neither did they have the technical skills, all of which would have to be imported. They had even identified a joint venture partner and were now seeking initial advice as to how *both* parties might together be advised as to the structure of their relationship. They had thus not grasped that there were different, conflicting, interests at work, and that although successful development might be their apparent common aim, success for each of them would ultimately be measured in wholly different ways. So, although it was possible to make constructive comment as to a framework under which they could pursue their respective agendas, the interests of each side, ie those very agendas could not be served by more detailed advice from one source, and it would have been foolhardy to undertake any such role (save to provide a backdrop to an insistence upon each side taking independent advice in the truest sense).

In one sense there is no such thing as a joint venture company, whether limited by shares or by guarantee. A company is a company is a company. The players participating in that company, however, may enjoy the fruits of that relationship in a number of different ways, for example, two landowners joining forces to exploit their combined sites. One of them is an experienced developer (perhaps XYZ Ltd above) who has been conducting a site assembly exercise; the other is a successful trading company whose site could have been simply acquired by the developer. However, the trading company is interested in more than just a fair price, more than just perhaps a share in possible future profits: what it wants is a far more active role which it will be able to perform with the aid of appropriate professional advice. More to the point, its covenant strength, if lent to the scheme, will give credibility to any proposal for development loan finance and much comfort, not only to prospective tenants but also, perhaps most particularly, to the consortium of financial institutions which, it is hoped, will buy the completed development. The institutional purchasers, having satisfied themselves that, apart from the lead tenant, there will be sufficient financial strength to finance voids on completion of the development (whether through payments of interest, a notional lease at a market rent or an actual lease) will thus be encouraged to maximise their initial price, albeit subject to a counter-balancing dilution of overage (if that is what the deal includes), which may be paid upon subsequent lettings for the first time of the void portions.

Jointco in use

The following scenario suggests how, for example, different kinds of profit may be derived. Developer and trader each sell their respective sites to 'Jointco'. The developer's carrying costs have immediately been expunged. The developer, (XYZ Ltd) having suffered in the recession, had difficulty in maintaining these costs: the developer consists of brains rather than brawn. Under the shareholders' agreement the trader has agreed to lend to Jointco the necessary cash to assemble the site. It does so on terms more favourable than if bank finance had been procured (albeit that in practice what it is doing is no doubt itself borrowing from its own bankers under existing wider overdraft facilities, which are not onerous in relative terms and which in context are seen to be favourable). Therefore, through sheer strength of covenant the trader is helping the deal to 'stack up'. The trader takes security from Jointco on the combined site to service the loan meanwhile. Incidentally, both the developer and the trader have each created subsidiaries to enter into the joint venture agreement, thus containing their exposure to the minimum, commonality (and personal liability in certain circumstances) of directors apart.

It will be seen, therefore, that the prospective profits from the development are already conceived in different ways. First, the participators have sold land to their own creature, Jointco. Perhaps they are already making some initial profit because the original site acquisition for each of them happened early in the recession, at a time of rock bottom land values.

Another way of extracting profit is by way of share dividend as and when there is income to justify it. This being a trading venture, and provided all contractual prophecies are fulfilled, a dividend should ensue when the completed investment is sold on to institutional investors and may continue to arise thereafter during the initial letting programme in the event of receipt of overage payments under an institutional development finance agreement.

Under the shareholders' (joint venture) agreement the developer must also perform various development functions under controlled conditions, and the trader offers its covenant in support of financial commitments. Various other obligations are parcelled out between them. In case of default, there is a contractual mechanism for re-apportionment of dividends and also, *in extremis*, for buy-out of the other's interests (see Chapter 9). There is further provision within the agreement for project management fees for the developer during the course of the development, again on terms which will effectively be a first charge on profits including a bonus fee based upon the investment value derived. This fee, being a cost to the joint venture, has a natural in-built priority to other kinds of derivation of profit but is, of course, not secured as such, save perhaps by guarantees (if any) given by Jointco's participators.

In due course, a lead tenant is found, ie a tenant the fact of whose occupation, and through income to be derived from letting to that tenant, makes the scheme viable not only in terms of financial security, but also in terms of making the development relatively more attractive to other prospective tenants of the void portions. The deal is, therefore, perceived as essentially bankable and a bank, or a consortium of banks headed by a lead bank, is prepared to lend on the strength of a combination of factors. First, there is the successful pre-let of one of the principal units. Secondly, although Jointco is itself not a company of substance (having been created specifically for the purpose of the exercise) it has the strength of the trader's covenant offered by way of guarantee to the bank. Thirdly, these same attributes have enabled Jointco to agree for the sale of the completed development to institutional investors: thus, provided the development is built and lettings are achieved, there will be an onward sale at an agreed price and the bank will be repaid.

The objective is to see that this happens. It cannot happen if the contribution of any one player is frustrated by protective measures exacted by another, perhaps under a separate and not immediately related contract. The key, as always, is interaction.

As will be seen later, XYZ Ltd as 'developer' will, in this process, have attracted a variety of contractual commitments, and Jointco will have provided the necessary interface. XYZ Ltd will make sure that those commitments are to be honoured by each of the participators in the shareholders' agreement. Moreover, those particular commitments will demonstrate the need for the various players to recognise that not all their aspirations can necessarily be met in the way that they want and that, for their ultimate objectives to be achieved, some accommodation is required.

As it happens, XYZ Ltd, in assembling its contribution to the particular site, could secure a major portion of it from the local authority only by agreeing to provide certain municipal facilities. The local authority was also concerned about the maintenance and upkeep of the remainder of the buildings on that part of the site it was providing. Thus, instead of selling a freehold to the developer, it entered into a development agreement whose fulfilment would be the grant of a headleasehold interest. Such agreements can be perfectly acceptable as security for funding purposes so long as they meet certain criteria (see also Chapter 8) and the benefit of the agreement was made expressly capable of funding (by affording a bank providing finance as mortgagee the ability to exercise its power of sale under controlled conditions).

In this small but important twist, it does not necessarily follow that the developer would have been able to assign the agreement to Jointco. It may possibly have negotiated so as to procure that the agreement be with Jointco in the first instance on the strength of other covenants available.

Alternatively, the developer's part of the site may have been seen as a viable entity in its own right and the developer may have become committed at a much earlier stage. If the local authority cannot be required to grant the headlease direct to Jointco in due course, this presents the possibility of an assignment at the time with its attendant stamp duty ramifications, quite apart from whether the tenant's covenants in the lease are such (for example because the lease contains a rental commitment) as to make it necessary to permit alienation in favour only of an approved assignee or underlessee. An institutional purchaser is more likely to be acceptable as an original lessee.

Interaction

In the final analysis, XYZ Ltd, with or without a 'Jointco' as principal development vehicle, ends up with a parallel series of agreements with the principal players (as distinct from participants in Jointco), each comprising development obligations governing such matters as planning, consents, the construction process, supervision of construction, timing, letting, etc. There are, therefore, related provisions contained in each of the development agreement with the local authority, the loan agreement from the bank, the agreement for forward sale to the institution and also with the lead tenant under the agreement for lease. It must be noted, therefore, that a series of major contractual commitments must be entered into by the developing entity (and through the joint venture (if any) in turn implemented by the developer) and, in particular, they must each be assembled in such a way that there is a fall-back position in case one or more of the relevant players asserts its authority or takes protective measures—perhaps on one narrow and isolated issue—and thus endangers the structure.

If the local authority attempts to repossess (its portion of) the site, the bank precipitately exercises its power of sale, the institutions withdraw, or the lead tenant threatens to pull out, in any such case because of some specific breach by Jointco or the developer, or by the trader if its guarantee is called (which as an issue in itself does not perhaps *immediately* touch the other players), mechanisms must be contained within each of those agreements whereby, even though an aggrieved player is not a party to that agreement, eg the bank in relation to the pre-let agreement between Jointco/XYZ Ltd and the tenant, the position can be fully retrieved.

It will be retrieved in the last mentioned case because the bank has taken the power to remedy the wrong in the loan documentation; it will have incorporated into the documentation provision for the appointment of an administrative receiver together with an attorney clause so that the receiver can act fully on behalf of the developing entity, or the bank simply steps in the receiver to remedy the breach. (Hence the desirability of ensuring in principal development agreements that notification of breaches should reach down not only to the developer but also to any relevant bank, financier, etc as a condition of enforceability. If this is not done, the particular agreement may on (wider) analysis be shown to be unbankable. Neither should this necessarily be seen as irksome by the landowner. It ensures that those who stand to lose the most if the development does not proceed can be alive to difficulties as soon as they arise.) The pre-let agreement, on the other hand, will preferably have contained an express condition whereby, although the tenant could resile upon notice in case of a developer's default, it would not do so until it had given not less than so many weeks' notice to any (bank) mortgagee of the site particulars of whom had been notified to it and, no doubt, the bank would have seen to it that this was done.

Therefore, the watch word is 'interaction'. Every agreement in the development process, every contractual commitment, must reflect the other essential elements of the process involving parties who are not themselves party to the commitment in question. This fundamental theme also reaches right down to relationships with professionals and contractors so that, again, in case of default or difficulty those relationships can be preserved or, if the contractors or professionals themselves are at fault, so that suitable replacements can be engaged on terms which are also acceptable to (or can require to be accepted by) the other major players in the piece.

Partnerships and limited partnerships

Unlike companies, in England and Wales partnerships have no separate legal personality. 'Partnership' is a popular term in 'regeneration-speak'. It is not usually intended to connote its narrower legal meaning.

True legal partnerships are what they are, ie a collection of two or more legal persons who are jointly bound. In a partnership, a partner can accordingly bind his partners. There are inevitable tax consequences too. A partnership for tax purposes is essentially transparent so that liability for taxation reaches down to the partners individually. It may be of small comfort to an individual partner but partnerships, like any other kinds of joint venture vehicle, are marriages of convenience and it is really a matter of how and where the players perceive their interests to lie. There is, of course, no reason why a partnership should not own, as one of the partnership assets, a limited company which can be used as a conduit for the business of the partnership and, again, it may suit the players to structure their relationship in this way.

Nevertheless, the Partnership Act 1890 continues to stand the test of time to the extent that formal agreement does not provide.

A derivative entity is the limited partnership, which is governed by the Limited Partnerships Act 1907. Under such a partnership, the partners can limit their liability to a nominal level so long as there is at least one general partner who bears the liabilities of the partnership accordingly. This may well suit an arrangement where the limited partners are, effectively, sleeping partners who want clear contractual commitments from their active partners but who do not, in turn, want to be exposed to the consequences of the actions of the active partners. A limited partnership can of course use a company, which itself is a creature of the limited partners, as the general partner to satisfy the rules: the practicality is that as an exercise in ringfencing it appears to be neat; as a credible and credit worthy entity it may be less than desirable where the deal is prospectively driven by covenant strength. The limited partnership is not a medium one has become used to meeting in a development situation: perhaps its time has yet to come. There are Financial Services Act implications, however, which may preclude use of such a vehicle in context.

From a banker's point of view, any partnership has the disadvantage that it is not able to give security of a kind affording the bank an ability to appoint an administrative receiver, but the inclusion of a company in the assets of the partnership means that a debenture can at least be given by that company over its assets. Therefore, at one level partnership property becomes corporate property. In turn, neither does a partnership have to file accounts at Companies House but, if all the partners are companies, then recent regulations to satisfy European requirements prescribe for the filing of accounts. Again, as with a conventional corporate joint venture, there is no reason why the partners should not be represented in the partnership by (probably, but not necessarily, wholly owned) subsidiaries of each of the players.

There can be joint ventures within joint ventures, within joint ventures—each with different characteristics and pressure points. The skill to be deployed is how to recognise the progressive impacts of the relationships and to accommodate them in the component parts of the structure.

Full company on stage

The development process draws together as wide a variety of players as it is possible to imagine—both public and private sector and, in the case of the latter, whether trading for profit or as investors. In the case of a joint venture the relationship between the players in that the joint venture on the one hand, and the other players on the other, are further characterised by the possibility of one or more joint venture partners dispensing with his interest. He will be inherently unable to dispose of his contractual commitments, for example as a guarantor. (By contrast, not every benefit under a contract can necessarily be assigned. If the contract in question is, legally, personal only it must be made expressly assignable and this may be regulated by express provisions accordingly.) A burden, ie a contractual obligation, is not assignable as such. A person shifting his responsibility can oblige another to perform it, under a separate contract, and can even seek an express indemnity for that person's failure. He should do so because nothing in that exercise relieves him of his original obligation (unless he attains a release or unless the particular contract provides that the person assigning the benefit is automatically released, say upon the assignee entering into direct contractual commitments to the other party or parties). This is inherent in the doctrine of privity of contract (leases are contracts and it was this particular difficulty which for so long underlay the consequences for original tenants of assignments of leases. Modifications to this principle, so far as tenancies are concerned, but not otherwise, are now enshrined in the Landlord and Tenant (Covenants) Act 1995).

The players within the joint venture may also wish to impose restrictions on dealing upon each other, say, with their shares in Jointco until a certain stage or stages can be reached. There may be buy-out provisions, particularly in case of default or dispute within the joint venture, and these can cause problems of their own where the bargaining position of the individual players is unequal. In the case of a developer represented by skill rather than financial muscle it is clear that certain safeguards must be employed (see Chapter 9). In any case, a bank or financial institution providing finance for the development will be concened with the identify of the participators in the joint venture vehicle, and buy-outs may be prohibited.

It should, therefore, be appreciated from the outset of a development transaction that the various players are approaching the matter from different standpoints. Their interests are as diverse as their contributions. Their priorities and needs must be understood as also the statutory and other legal constraints within which they are working. One has become used, on countless occasions, to witnessing needless wrangling in a negotiation because one player, of whatever variety, has persisted with a requirement or a series of requirements which stand four square within the needs of the player concerned but immediately place difficulties in the way of unrelated relationships.

Inevitably, this is counter-productive. The good negotiator will be able to explain not only the difficulty that this raises but also how, in the long run, it is contrary to the interests of the offending player. He will also be able to suggest, through his wider knowledge and experience, what steps each of them may take to get over the difficulty so as to arrive at a suitable solution, perhaps without the need for compromise.

Never under-estimate the need for local government officers, whose brief has been endorsed by an appropriate committee, to justify modifications, if not to their senior officers then to the relevant committee itself and that, if a committee has handed down a particular direction, the need to work out a plan of action which meets that direction. Local authorities also work under increasingly tight financial constraints, and this is reflected not just in what they do but how they do it. Again, banks and institutions have yet to re-acquire the bad habits of the seventies and eighties respectively (although there is evidence that they are trying hard), but the new found spirit of co-operation between the public and private sectors augurs well for co-operative ventures.

Checklist

1. Identify the prospective players.
2. Identify subsidiary relationships.
3. What are their statutory bases?
4. What legal inhibitions are there on their ability to contract? Include in this the tax status of the players as well as other statutorily imposed constraints, whether public bodies, companies, etc.
5. What are the respective financial strengths? What other bargaining positions are in play?
6. In the case of a joint venture what special protections will the financially weaker player require, particularly if his skills are being exploited?
7. In the case of corporate vehicles, and in particular special purpose vehicles, what guarantees are likely to be required and from whom, and why?
8. If the 'player' is characterised by a joint venture, how will this be structured? How will profits and losses be shared?
9. How may disputes or defaults within the joint venture impact upon underlying relationships with other players? In that case, what measures will the other players require to ensure that the joint venture remains an entity with which they can properly deal during the course of the development? What fallbacks are

available for them in order to avoid a formal dispute? (NB see Chapter 9)
10. How will similar considerations impact upon the relationship between the principal players?
11. For every contractual relationship entered into, how will it impact upon other contractual relationships both in terms of performance (and prospectively also default, see again Chapter 9)? In particular, will proper compliance with one contractual commitment adversely impact on another, or prospectively do so if that other relationship has yet to be consummated?
12. Can a player afford to enter into one major contractual commitment before entering into a parallel commitment? Have all the parameters been thoroughly explored and what is the analysis of risk? What is the agenda of the player seeking the commitment?

2 The Site

> 'I will not be afraid of death and baine
> Till Birnam Forest come to Dunsinane'
> *Macbeth, Macbeth: Scene III, Act IV*

Unfortunately for Macbeth, no sooner had he uttered those fateful words than the wood indeed began to move and his number was up, so to speak. (It was not, of course, the wood but MacDuff's army on the move.)

The problem with sites is that, as night follows day, they adjoin other sites of whatever kind and therein lie the seeds of conflict. The question then arises, if something is done with a site, what will the consequences be for third party interests? Site assembly is not normally thought of as controversial: the potential is, however, both intriguing and enormous. Third party interests are but one single facet: first, therefore, what of the site itself?

Contracts

It is a *sine qua non*, one tries not to lose one's site as did Macbeth his kingdom, (or indeed one's head as he lost his!). If one is a developer of substance, the assembly of a site may be no more than painful. If it is an entire site, and one is able to risk taking a view on planning, for example because the proposed development and its use are consistent with the local plan, and well within known density levels and other factors, it may be possible to acquire the site on a speculative basis. It is even better if it already has outline planning permission and has been marketed as a whole with a specific use in mind. The principal difficulties of site acquisition lie more in areas such as the planning prospects being in doubt, or, even when there is no shadow of a doubt, the need to assemble component parts of the site in an unencumbered form from a number of unconnected interests.

Negotiated approach

Unconditional contracts apart, the attainment of certain objectives, which will make it worth the developer's while, necessarily assumes some conditional element. If the developer is negotiating on a number of fronts he may still do so on an open contract basis if he is able to line up his exchanges of contracts simultaneously. However, even the simplest contracts are far from being free from risk. In such circumstances the developer will almost certainly be advised to conduct a full title investigation for each parcel of land, or interest, prior to contract, to secure that all his interests are protected by registrations in the appropriate registers, ie land charges or land registry, to ensure that alienation provisions in leases can be properly met (and that the vendor is suitably bound to ensure that they are), that mortgagees' consents are obtained, etc.

Anything that should not be left to chance, but must be, points to the need for conditionality or the undertaking of risk. Developers are used to risk; the question is essentially one of assessing it and then containing it, in the case of the latter particularly from a legal standpoint. The first candidate for risk assessment is whether completion of each of the other contracts should be made expressly conditional on completion of the first. If stealth is required, the downsides require careful assessment.

The conveyancing exercise, properly conducted by the developer's solicitors, should seek to ensure that, come what may (and provided that the developer himself can proceed) he must ultimately secure the entirety of the site and its component parts, but clearly it would be naive to assume that this must follow.

In an imperfect world there may be any number of reasons why the component parts of a site cannot be acquired all at once. A site may in any case have to be acquired over time. If the parts so far acquired can be developed alone, the developer's concerns will be confined largely to the viability of the project within the confines of the limited site. If some part of the site is vital to the viability of the whole, he will need to proceed with caution. The attitudes which may be struck by prospective vendors will be driven largely by questions of bargaining position as much as initial valuation, and it is a matter of judgment the extent to which one discloses one's hand as to the development possibilities. Particularly, a prospective vendor may also see the opportunity to take a more pro-active role, and in that case it may be advisable to consider offering him an incentive such as a share in future profits. Indeed, he may for example, be the trader mentioned in Chapter 1.

One can, for example, present a vendor with the notion that a conditional contract be entered into. In the wider scheme of things, one might be saying, there is a greater site to be developed and the viability of the exercise is dependent upon negotiation with, say, a local authority landowner, the obtaining of planning permission, the construction of highways, perhaps modification of an existing roundabout and so on. All of these matters are bound up with the prospects of success and, above all, timing. The scheme may seem attractive but the prospective vendor may believe that his interests would be better served by selling his site in isolation for a specific development within its confines, or by joining forces with others.

It is helpful if developers and their advisers enlist the aid of their solicitors at an early stage. A solicitor experienced in development may well be able to suggest appropriate contractual mechanisms which will assist the developer in juggling his negotiations towards ultimate acquisition of the site on the basis that he really wants. Moreover, disclosure of the developer's intentions will trigger the mind of the experienced solicitor to raise specific enquiries which should be raised of prospective vendors and of relevant public authorities. (Beware the client who keeps his cards close to his chest and who may, perhaps subconsciously, be hiding his own limitations or lack of technical knowledge.)

Conditional element

The counter-balance to the vendor's eye for a deal, in terms either of an excessive price for his interest or of pro-active participation in prospective development or the prospective sharing of profit, may be the justification of a more relaxed approach to conditionality upon assembly of other parts of the site, planning, etc by offering others also a share in future profits. The wide variety of joint venture techniques is explained in Property Development Partnerships to which reference is made in the introduction to this book. Ultimately, however, one is likely to be working towards a profit sharing mechanism of some kind. This has the particular advantage for the developer that he may be afforded the opportunity to contain his initial acquisition cost. Carrying costs are expensive and, even if translated into development cost under a bank or other financing facility, this in turn bears down upon ultimate profitability. Lighten the load where possible and the real profit in due course may be enhanced accordingly.

A profit share agreement is perhaps the simplest form of joint venture. It implies a formula based on successful development, letting and disposal, or deemed disposal if the investment is retained. This, in turn, gives rise to an overage payment, or added value, for the vendor. It is a useful tool where values are uncertain and the prospects of profit more so. A worried borough valuer may, for example, be able to fix a current value in order to obtain approval for disposal, but the wisdom of disposing will be the better perceived if he can show that the council can benefit further from the developer's skill and the council's encouragement.

The problem with profit share agreements is security, or rather the lack of it. The taking of security on the land itself will almost certainly make the scheme unfundable thereafter, and so a compromise is called for. In the case of a good covenant (for example, Jointco backed by a major trader's guarantee—see Chapter 1), this may alone suffice. If the prospects of overage are seriously good, but the covenant weak, a more conventional development agreement may be called for, leading to grant of a major interest in due course. This is at least prospectively bankable. If the scheme is to be pre-sold to a fund under a forward funding agreement (see Chapter 8), the fund's covenant may also be forthcoming.

Profit share mechanisms should always be used with care. The securing of future profits, for example by legal charge, may seem an obvious answer. As suggested earlier, the practical reality is that this will in turn impact adversely on the fundability of the project. In every development scenario, the question the developer must constantly ask himself is 'Is it bankable?' Sensibly, the other players in the development process must recognise this as the ultimate immovable object, of which failure to recognise can only impair their own interests. Chapter 8 considers these issues in more detail.

It is a necessary corollary of interaction that squeezing the last drop, particularly in the delicate process of site assembly, is potentially self-defeating. In any case, experience shows, time and time again, that the more complex the development, the more straightforward the relationship between the players must be.

Options and pre-emption

Options are perhaps one of the most readily recognisable mechanisms for juggling one or more uncertainties before a transaction can go live. Few solicitors are unaware that, in order to cope with the provisions of the Law of Property (Miscellaneous Provisions) Act 1989, s 2, under which both vendor and purchaser must now, in effect, sign the same or identical forms of contract, the exercise of an option can still be triggered by a unilateral act, eg purchaser's notice of exercise, so long as the giving of that notice is made a condition of the contract. Only one first instance decision of the High Court has been required to clarify this point, but it has also established the principle that an option is really no more than a certain kind of conditional contract; this notwithstanding that an option remains a recognised legal creature and subject to an express limitation period for exercise (21 years) under the Perpetuities and Accumulations Act 1964, s 9 (contrast an option contained within the body of a lease, say for renewal, which is not subject to such a time constraint).

From a vendor's point of view, and in particular to give added certainty to his own circumstances, and whether subject to conditions, he may wish to impose a 'put' option. The notion of put and call options is by no means confined to the world of stocks and shares. However, unlike a call option which is registrable by a purchaser, a put option exists in contract only and, once exercised, is accordingly enforceable as such. It is, therefore, implicit that unlike a call option, a put option cannot represent an interest in land, and cannot be recognised by any form of registration (although an accountant may argue that in certain circumstances it may require reflection in the accounts of a company (the 'puttee,' to invent a new term) as a contingent liability).

Finally, an option should be carefully distinguished from a right of pre-emption under which a vendor may still retain the right to dispose elsewhere but, if he proposes to do so, he must give notice to the purchaser of that intention and thus give the purchaser the opportunity to complete his purchase on the express terms of that right. He will not normally be able to avoid complying with the pre-emption conditions if the purchaser has taken the precaution of registering his interest. If the purchaser fails to do so (just as with an option) the site may be sold free of the right of pre-emption although the vendor may find himself personally liable in damages *in lieu* of specific performance. A developer's solicitor may be properly expected to be alert to the need to make appropriate registrations to secure the intended outcome.

A right of pre-emption is not usually seen as an effective developer's tool, however, given the inherent uncertainly of acquiring land by this means although, if market conditions suggest that a vendor is likely to want to deal in any event, it is not to be ruled out entirely. Options, by contrast, are a useful tool, and the offer of a suitably attractive option fee, linked to a period which does not tie an owner's hands for too long, may assist greatly in the developer's endeavours to assemble a site.

Public authority co-operation

Developers in difficulty with site assembly may well consider calling in aid the assistance of appropriate public authorities backed by statutory powers available to them. Designation of an area within a local plan for particular development or regeneration may be the precise motivation which has brought the developer to consider the possibilities of site assembly. It may be that the local authority itself owns some of the land or has in mind re-establishing highways with the view to development, or is simply in the business of encouraging developers to take an interest in certain land.

The local authority may be seeking bids from developers who can show that they have the necessary skills and financial backing. This may signal the need for the developer to go a considerable way towards securing the requisite financial backing and co-operation of other third parties as necessary, at an early stage, albeit conditional upon the outcome of the bid. Attendant upon this may be a commitment to enter into certain statutory agreements with the local authority in terms particularly of planning and highways, as part of the planning negotiation.

Preparation of bids can be a costly exercise and, whether public or private entity, the entity seeking the bid should consider being prepared to meet some or all of the bidding costs of shortlisted developers. In the case of very major schemes some authorities as well as other land owners are now at last prepared to recognise the cost of preparing bids and, for example, to meet certain costs of shortlisted bidders.

In such collaborative exercises, the opportunity may also be afforded for the developer to utilise the statutory powers of the local authority in the process of its own site assembly. In the case of a friendly (or at least non-hostile) local authority the use of compulsory purchase powers, or at least the threat of them, may be a convenient method of securing vital component parts of a development site. This being so, the developer may also find that he is afforded a stronger negotiating position in relation to other land owners. Care should be taken by co-operating local authorities to ensure by appropriately worded documentation that they do not, and are not seen to, fetter their discretion and in particular that statutory inhibition is not compromised.

Other public authority options

Conversely, a developer may perceive that, if only he can secure the entirety of the development site, he ought reasonably, at least, to achieve the desired planning permission without opposition, save planning grounds themselves, and any attendant facilities necessary for successful development of the site. (Certain statutory notices are required to be given to those with major interests in the site.) If he cannot achieve the co-operation of the local authority or of relevant landowners various alternatives still remain open to him. The securing of a local authority's co-operation carries with it a prospective assumption that, in some way, the local authority will be recompensed for the cost of acquiring component parts of the site, as part of the compulsory or negotiated purchase of the relevant land; and where the local authority has in mind regeneration of a particular area, it will already have set about 'packaging' a site by earmarking various interests for compulsory acquisition, so as to deliver the assembled site to the chosen developer. However, a hostile local authority, or one which simply cannot cope is a different matter.

In 1975, the government placed a statutory duty on local government to undertake responsibility for site assembly and development, through the Community Land Act in the belief that development value would be returned to the community at large. This placed local government in the developer's role, through the use of compulsory powers and by empowering it to remove landowners' ability to exploit the use of land. The measure was doomed from the start. Not only were skills and resources sorely lacking, the incentives enshrined in its purpose had more than a hollow ring. Consequently, local government failed to deliver even when the measure was joined by the Development Land Tax Act 1976. In the event, developers emerging from the dust and ashes of the property crash at the time soon became adept at avoiding the tax, without the threat of their role being removed from them.

Since then, other experiments have been tried, including enterprise zones which, through tax incentives and ring-fencing of local authority influence in the planning process, have provided developers with incentives. The enterprise zone is not yet dead, but while some have only recently been created, it has been argued that statutory tinkering with the market has not proved itself to be overwhelmingly successful. One can only observe, from the sidelines, that enterprise zones have not been without their critics.

Again, development corporations have express statutory powers designed to facilitate development in the face of objection or resistance from local authorities or private landowners. It is to the relevant development corporation to whose door the developer will probably beat a path in areas where a development corporation is still operating. However, where the developer is out on his own and, particularly, if the prospective development site is in England, a further line of approach is now available to him.

English partnerships

Selective attention is given in this book to the role of English Partnerships. Its statutory base and a wider description of its powers and function are set out in some detail in Chapter 12 of *Property Development Partnerships*. Just how effective a force it may become on the development scene has yet, even now, to emerge. Nevertheless, the assistance which it is capable of providing to any development project in England is substantial and significant, and cannot be ignored in any discussion on site assembly. The prospects of assistance will clearly be enhanced if the project is within its own published guidance notes for the time being in force.

The objects of the Agency (as its statutory creators describe it) are to be achieved, among other things, by securing that land and buildings are brought into effective use and by developing, or encouraging the development of, existing and new industry and commerce; by creating an attractive and safe environment; and by facilitating the provision of housing and providing, or facilitating the provision of, social and recreational facilities. These criteria are clearly stated in Pt III of the Leasehold Reform, Housing and Urban Development Act 1993. As mentioned in Chapter 1, the Agency is not a provider of housing as such. In adopting, in effect, any one or more of the roles normally associated with development, the Agency can be called upon, that is to say requested not required (except by the Secretary of State), to assist in site assembly and associated matters, if not development itself.

Because of its unique position in being able to override local authorities and even development corporations as well as private sector operators, the Agency can sensibly be considered as a prospective tool in site assembly, particularly where a private sector developer would have no other incentive to develop in an area requiring regeneration. The Agency has power to acquire land by agreement but, in addition, upon authorisation by the Secretary of State it may acquire land, or indeed new rights, compulsorily under s 162 of the 1993 Act. These provisions effectively bolt onto the existing law of compulsory purchase and all the implications that this has as regards valuation, etc.

In the case of land owned by a local authority, or any other public body, the Secretary of State may authorise its vesting. There is expressly excluded land held by 'statutory undertakers' (which for the purpose of the Act is given a special meaning to refer to certain statutorily authorised functions such as provision of railways, canals and certain transport related media, British Coal and in particular 'any other authority, body or undertakers specified in an order by the Secretary of State'). Where rights over land are to be extinguished, easements overridden, telegraphic lines to be removed and other obstacles to the development process, Sched 20 to the Act goes into considerable detail, and deserves careful study.

An inevitable problem for the Agency is one of financial resources. Therefore, just as one may expect to recompense a local authority for exercise of its compulsory powers in aid of a project, it is reasonable to assume that so also will assistance by the Agency be made more attractive to it by recompense in some way for its outlay.

In the case of major development involving regeneration or where the Secretary of State is persuaded land should be developed in pursuance of the objects of the Agency, it may be seen as a valuable tool in the process. Moreover, in relation to any area designated by the Secretary of State as an urban area or an area which in his opinion is suitable for urban development, the Agency may itself become the local planning authority. (See ss 170 and 171). Obviously, the exercise of such draconian powers carries with it the prospect of being politically charged, particularly if a designation order contains provisions, as prescribed by s 171(2), whereby 'any enactment relating to local planning authorities shall not apply to the Agency; and...that any such enactment which applies to the Agency shall apply to it subject to such modifications as may be specified in the order'. In short, there exists the power to take a sledgehammer to relevant planning legislation which is perceived as inconvenient.

The Agency operates under the guidance and/or direction of the Secretary of State under s 167 of the Act. Present experience suggests that despite its statutory independence of the Crown, the Agency works closely under the supervision of Whitehall and, for this book to stand the test of time, close regard should always be had to the guidance notes issued from time to time, which should at least indicate the kinds of circumstances in which a request for intervention may have some prospect of success.

Finally, it is worth mentioning that the Act contains a modified s 157 of the Highways Act 1980 relating to requirements that a private street be adopted by the highways authority, the connection of private streets to the highway and traffic regulation orders for private streets.

Third party rights

Intervention by the Agency and other public sector entities apart, every development site carries with it the prospect that development may infringe rights of third parties. Obvious examples are existing easements which may require to be modified and this is as much a part of the site assembly process as acquisition of the land itself. If no less convenient rights can be afforded (and accepted) in substitution, or substituted rights which can effectively work for the interests of third parties, these are an obvious subject for negotiation.

What developers sometimes forget is that although documented rights can be assessed and negotiated, there may be in addition numerous rights, easements, and so on which are only implied by law (until established by agreement or by the courts) and which may give an aggrieved adjoining owner or other third party a remedy in law. Surveyors and solicitors engaged in the site assembly process are on enquiry as to such matters, but the extent and scope of that enquiry may not always be apparent unless the development proposal is suitably aired at the outset. The fact that a proposal is favourably received by the local planning authority is not a reliable guide. Still less does planning permission constitute any kind of licence to override the interests of others. It does nothing of the kind.

The problem with rights acquired 'by prescription' is that, until they are tested in court or acknowledged by the owner of the land over, or in respect of, which a right is exercised (the 'servient tenement'), they are not precisely measured. Nevertheless, a developer ignores them at his peril. In acquiring a site he must look around for any sign that what he proposes to do may interfere with some state or condition enjoyed by an adjoining or neighbouring property. He then has to form a view whether that state or condition is enjoyed as of right, even though not incorporated in legal documentation. In particular, he must look for factors which go to show that the use and enjoyment of a state or condition is not as of right including, not least, limited duration. If a right is apparently exercised, but the evidence is that it cannot have been exercised for more than 20 years, curtailment of exercise can prevent the right from being acquired in law.

An obvious case in point is rights of light. A building having acquired rights by prescription over an uninterrupted period of not less than 20 years, under-pinned by the Prescription Act 1832, may leave a particular development dead in the water. If any question of light reduction is likely to arise, it is better to instruct a specialist rights of light surveyor to assess the impact and then to consider negotiation of an appropriate accommodation with the adjoining owner. This may result in a surrender of rights at a price, or the grant of a licence confined to the particular buildings or structures proposed. (Where it is desirable to inhibit a right of light for prescription purposes, a light restriction notice can be secured through the Lands Tribunal and will in turn be revealed by a search of the local land charges register following registration as a local land charge. It is not a substitute for common law rights but is a useful mechanism for putting rights beyond doubt. There are procedures for the giving of notices, and the raising of objections. Once the entry is registered, there can be no doubt that any period for acquisition of a right has been interrupted.)

Equally, development may imply removal of support from adjoining land. These are essentially structural issues in respect of which, if appropriate supportive measures are taken, the adjoining owner may have no ultimate cause for complaint even though he may be justified in having cause for concern. Similar principles apply to structures as to excavation. Sometimes, buildings are constructed in a manner which does not create party walls as such but the removal of a wall or the foundations beneath it may expose an adjoining building to risk of damage. Questions arise not just of legal rights of support, expressed or implied, but also of one's duty of care in respect of adjoining or neighbouring properties.

These issues are particularly acute in relation to true party walls. In the London area, the London Buildings Acts apply and so it may be expected that surveyors may require to be appointed to examine the issues, and to determine between them with the aid of a third surveyor, the steps to be taken to protect the retained building and for the construction of the new adjoining building. Elsewhere, it is likely that a similar procedure will be applied in practice reflected ultimately in a party wall agreement. The difference is that co-operation has its price. If there is no agreement, and if an aggrieved adjoining owner is concerned about damage to his property he may well be minded to take proceedings supported by an injunction, and the ensuing delay, perhaps the giving of appropriate undertakings to the court, etc may be less than helpful.

Proceedings should not be instituted by any landowner unless those proceedings have a reasonable prospect of success. This is the golden rule of all litigation, 'negotiation' (and acceptance of resultant costs) apart. The securing of an injunction carries with it the prospect of substantial damages in favour of a defendant developer if the proceedings are shown to have been unjustified upon eventual analysis of the circumstances by the court. If a development is going to proceed, it ought to be possible for a developer, properly advised, to place himself in a relationship with his neighbours which will allow his development to proceed unimpeded, so as to be placed comfortably within the immediate surrounds, and so that the finished results sit happily within a framework, perhaps literally, reflecting surrounding interests on a long term basis. Otherwise, again, it may be unfundable.

Nuisance

The construction process, which is considered at Chapter 5, may produce problems of a different kind for neighbouring or adjoining premises. In anticipation of that process, it is as well to consider in the context of site assembly, and the satisfaction of third party rights, the impact of development while it is in the course of construction. Special needs may have to be met and safeguards taken. Once the development is conceived, it is as well to deal with these matters at the same time. More particularly, meeting those needs may have to be reflected as a special condition of the construction contract and other commitments. Again, it is a matter of negotiation to the point where the adjoining owner is satisfied that, first, his needs are accommodated and, secondly, that appropriate redress will be available to him in case of default.

Inevitably, patience will be tried as some adjoining owners seek to exploit their bargaining positions. A responsible developer must tread carefully, however. In due course, he will have contractual commitments to his funders, pre-let tenants, joint venture partners and so on. Delays in the construction process may leave him wide open to claims by the contractor about delays, and lead to financial ruin, or at least the evaporation of development profit. To ride roughshod over adjoining owners is to court disaster. More particularly, warning bells may sound for the other principal players and this may, in turn, reflect adversely on negotiations with them. If an adjoining owner behaves unreasonably, and places himself in a position where his objections cannot be legally sustained, that is in one sense all to the good. However, if this is so, the developer must be able to demonstrate clearly to his partners precisely where the risks (if any) may lie, how they may be dealt with and the prospective time frame.

Particularly, development finance, whether provided by banks or investing institutions, is highly sensitive. Funders will need to be satisfied that the time scales envisaged for the development can be adhered to, and they are likely to reserve their positions while any such question remains outstanding. While there is any perceived threat from an adjoining or neighbouring owner, a project will very likely be unfundable.

Restrictive covenants

A chapter on site assembly is incomplete without some comment about restrictive covenants. Although they are often misunderstood their nature is quite straightforward. As with 'receivership', the term 'restrictive covenant' is often used loosely but, in a land context, it has a very specific meaning. A restrictive covenant is a covenant of an essentially negative nature. Thus, a covenant which is couched in positive terms, eg to do such and such, but which has negative overtones, eg 'only if' etc, can still be a negative covenant. It is not saying that one must do something in any event but that, if one does something at all, one must do it in a certain way. Thus a covenant to use land 'only', say, for agricultural purposes, is another way of saying one must not use it other than for agricultural purposes. It is not saying, in any shape or form, that if one fails to use it at all, even for agricultural purposes, a breach arises.

However, the negative nature of a restrictive covenant is not its only distinguishing feature. Where the covenant is either expressed to benefit, or is clearly shown as intending to benefit, other land, a restrictive covenant is characterised by being enforceable against successive owners who, therefore, assume involuntary liability merely by reason and in consequence of acquiring the land in question.

Restrictive covenants are a creature of equity, and for long relied on for their effect on case law precedent. However, in recognition of the fact that the existence, or at least precise details of, such covenants could on the one hand be lost from view but, on the other, remain enforceable, the property legislation of 1925 ensured that all new restrictive covenants could not be enforceable, as such, without registration in the case of unregistered land as a land charge class D(II) at the land charges registry, or by registration in the charges register of the relevant title in the case of registered land. A purchaser of unregistered land makes land charges searches, against all proprietors from 1925 for the period of their ownership (and once ended, the results of a search so obtained can be retained for future reference, and one can obtain particulars of the entry from the registry accordingly and compare it with the title deeds), an essential part of the conveyancing process.

Restrictive covenants should be considered with care. Their impact on development, in individual cases, may be considerable. Moreover, the beneficiary of the covenant may be entitled to damages for breach as well as an injunction prohibiting further breach. Of course, the usefulness of a particular covenant or the underlying interests which it was designed to protect, may change or evaporate. Mechanisms exist for application to the Lands Tribunal to discharge or modify restrictive covenants under s 84 of the Law of Property Act 1925, and an owner of land which is encumbered may wish to consider the benefit of making application to the Lands Tribunal to remove anomalous encumbrances.

Finally, what of land which benefits from covenants? While a covenant has meaning and relevance, and remains enforceable, it is helpful for a landowner to be at least aware of it. The fact remains that, in the case of registered land, nowhere in any register is the *benefit* of covenants to be found. Although one can readily see who has the burden (if it is to remain a burden) the identification of the land which benefits (the 'dominant tenement') may be problematical. The point having been flagged, the rest is best left to legal advisers. Fragmentation of the dominant tenement frequently leads to a view having to be taken, eg the enforcement of a covenant by a householder on a council estate who has exercised his right to buy.

The environment

Ever since God created the earth, we have had an 'environment'.

Environmental law and related issues have been with us in one form or another for a very long time. As one has become used to giving things labels, such as 'environmental law', all of a sudden the subject has been thrust into a new perspective. In an industrialised society the production of chemical products and by-products which are capable of escaping into the soil, and perhaps into our natural water supplies, have had increasing attention from our legislators. Ever since the beginnings of industry, there have been problems with land and water contamination and the common law, particularly on nuisance, has been reinforced with statutory measures as sources of pollution have increased. As the law has fought to control this burgeoning problem, so also have difficulties arisen for the developer.

Perhaps understandably, in the wake of the recession, a host of environmental experts has now sprung up. Following the failure of the government to provide a meaningful contaminated land register particulars of which, in relation to individual sites, were intended to appear in response to standard enquiries of the local authority conducted by conveyancers, developers have, as a matter of course, taken steps to conduct their own enquiries, surveys and tests as appropriate. Part of this due diligence has been adopted by private sector organisations. One such example is 'SiteCheck', now made available through a private sector initiative, which draws on numerous records of otherwise publicly available material, stored in a database and accessible on a site basis by reference to Ordnance Survey maps.

In any development, issues to be considered include, depending on what if any contamination is found, what development may be permitted at all, how contamination may be contained (or removed) in order to permit that development, and also responsibility for dealing with contaminated land. Causing contamination, allowing contamination to affect land, perhaps adjoining land, particularly water-born contamination may give rise to substantial criminal penalties. Moreover, criminal penalties may attach to persons deemed to have control, whether as directors of a company, people in turn controlling those directors, and thus even a bank or debenture holder.

A player in the development process, having secured a contractual benefit, may unwittingly acquire a statutory liability, even though he has contractually placed all development obligations on the developer instead. It suffices only for the purpose of this book that, where contamination is found, its immediate impact and prospective impact on the development should be carefully ascertained. Those involved with the ownership or development of the land, including financiers, should then consider their own positions with the utmost care and the prospects of their becoming additionally personally responsible, and perhaps criminally liable.

To put these difficulties in their proper perspective, there has been, in recent years, a raft of legislation, the most recent of which is the Environment Act 1995 and thereby the creation of a new government agency (which among other things will absorb the National Rivers Authority). Assuming recognition of environmental factors in the development process, apart from those which may arise in the course of construction, it is hardly surprising that the cautious developer will wish to buy land subject to appropriate tests being carried out. A prudent vendor will wish to avoid such measures being carried into a contract for sale to avoid uncertainty, and will wish to encourage a purchaser to have all necessary tests carried out before legal relations are entered into. However, the carrying out of tests should itself by done under controlled conditions and a properly advised vendor may wish to allow access only upon the terms of a negotiated licence.

Where environmental considerations are likely to be pivotal to successful development, a prudent vendor will have caused all appropriate enquiry to be made in anticipation, and for the results to be made readily available to a developer, his financiers and tenants. This implies that he will have appointed credible and respected consultants to report, and upon terms which may include the giving of effective collateral warranties in favour of third parties. If not, the developer cannot afford the risk to the viability of the project, and he must take it on himself to commission tests, obtain reports and ensure that all of those with whom he must deal in the development process can be properly satisfied that they will not themselves incur liability as a result. He omits any such measure at his peril.

Checklist

1. How many and what interests are required in order to assemble the site?
2. Can they be acquired simultaneously?
3. Upon what factors does acquisition rely? Is it necessary to accomplish certain steps before there is a finally binding commitment?
4. What conditions should, accordingly, be imposed in any contract for acquisition?
5. Would an option be a better route and, if so, how may a prospective vendor be persuaded to commit his property to an option with or without conditions?
6. What alternatives are open to a vendor in the face of a developer's approaches? Will he be minded to grant no more than a right of pre-emption?

7. In so far as land, rights and other matters cannot be secured by mutual agreement, how may the public sector help?
8. Does the local authority own any of the land?
9. To what extent is the co-operation of the highway authority required?
10. How much will it cost to provide the local authority with the means to purchase compulsorily? What else can be offered to the local authority by way of value?
11. If the local authority is minded not to co-operate, what other public sector body may assist?
12. Does the development proposed conform with the guidance notes issued from time to time by English Partnerships?
13. To what extent would the co-operation of English Partnerships require to be sanctioned by the Secretary of State?
14. How much would it cost to recompense English Partnerships for exercise of their compulsory powers?
15. Would the circumstances sensibly permit or require the participation of English Partnerships as a player?
16. What express legal third party rights affect the site? How can these be accommodated?
17. What third party entitlements exist as of right? Would any third party, for example an adjoining owner, or the owner of a major easement, have grounds to hinder or even halt entirely the proposed development?
18. Does any third party enjoy rights by way of prescription? How may these be assessed?
19. In relation to adjoining owners in particular, and whether as part of their accommodation in the scheme, what special needs will they have during the course of construction? What issues will, in turn, be required to be reflected in any construction contract?
20. Are there any restrictive covenants? What land has the benefit? Has ownership become fragmented? Who could sue?
21. If there are restrictive covenants, would breach today be any longer of practical benefit to anyone? If proceedings to enforce would be no more than capricious, what prospects are there of having the covenants removed? How long would it take?
22. Does the site have any history of use suggesting contamination of land? What are the implications of this for the use of the site?
23. Whether the site is developed, what further environmental consequences may arise?
24. In so far as any penalties may be exacted in relation to any environmental issue, precisely who may in the event suffer a penalty?

3 The Professional Team and Contractors

'What trade, thou nave? Thou naughty nave, what trade?'
Marullus, Julius Caesar: Act I, Scene I

As students of Shakespeare will know, the answer to that question might nearly have been 'Cobblers!', or, as the second commoner answered cheekily, 'Why Sir, cobble you'. Today's traders, and particularly professionals, are vital components in the development process. Moreover, their respective roles are by no means focused upon the developer alone. At an early stage, however, in conjunction with acquisition of the site, the developer will have begun to gather about him a number of professionals who will in due course be directly associated with the construction process.

For example, an architect will have been engaged on preliminary drawings in support of the planning application. Depending upon the kinds of players involved in the project, whether landowners, joint venture partners, sleeping partners, banks, institutions, tenants, and now professional indemnity insurers too, the relationship between the developer and his professional team can take a variety of forms. Further, the engagement of the contractor in a design and build contract or some form of managed building contract, with the contractor adopting much of the role of the developer by co-ordinating the activities of the professional team and accepting responsibility for them, will almost certainly have effect to redefine that relationship or replace it entirely.

Accordingly, as the developer goes about the business of bringing together those professional, technical and practical skills which are necessary to underpin the construction process, he must consider the contractual requirements of any such relationship and the prospective impact upon the performance of his own role as developer at the earliest opportunity. This wider dimension brings into focus the need to consider all appointments with other interests in mind, and the process of interaction between them.

In simpler (if not always happier) times, developers would frequently make their appointments on an informal basis, sometimes accompanied by a fairly perfunctory acknowledgement in writing. In the years following the 1970s crash, such arrangements often served their purposes as any additional burdens on professionals, particularly of the kind mentioned below, usually met with co-operation, if only for the preservation of fees! The world was nonetheless changing rapidly and, as the new property cycle gathered momentum, so also did the re-definition of responsibilities. Over the ensuing years, a number of cases have defined and re-defined various functions and responsibilities, showing up shortcomings in legal documentation and exposing various people, not least principals, to kinds of liability, or alternatively a lack of remedy, which they had not previously contemplated.

The basic idea of a developer owing a construction responsibility to, for example, a local authority or other principal landowner under a development agreement, or to a bank or institution under a development loan agreement or forward finance agreement, or again to an institution under a forward purchase agreement, or to a prospective tenant under an agreement for lease was already well understood. However, that obligation itself was, and is, fraught with difficulty depending upon the skills of the developer and the extent in turn to which performance of his duties is reliant upon assistance from others.

There are developers and developers and never the twain shall mix! Some will adopt a highly professional role in co-ordinating and policing the roles and functions of the professionals and contractors whose skills are combined to produce the finished product. Others will adopt less of a co-ordinating role, delegating responsibility, and others again will rely wholly upon professional support in order to function at all. The actual skills of the developer are, therefore, pivotal not just to the combination of relationships with the principal players, but also to the content of each of the contractual relationships with the principal players, between joint venture partners, and also with professional consultants.

It is therefore wrong, in principle, to assume that the simple fact of appointment of skilled professionals and reputable contractors can, on its own, satisfy the needs of the other principal players. Each of them is concerned from different viewpoints with the delivery of results. This raises questions of accountability, the extent to which reliance can, or should be, placed on the developer as well, where there is failure to perform an appropriate degree of direct access (with particular emphasis on what exactly is appropriate) and, above all, how the unhappy process of calling to account may thereby introduce conflict into parallel, but perhaps not directly related, or other contractual relationships.

All properly drawn development agreements contain provisions regulating the appointment of professionals and contractors and the conduct of ensuing contractual relationships. Mechanisms for institutional development finance were well used during the 1960s and patterns were set for many of the development and financing instruments with which we are largely still familiar today, but relationships between the wider range of players and professionals and consultants have been an evolutionary process which continues to develop.

The appointment of professionals carries with it more than contractual obligations. Contract apart, the law of negligence is also well hedged by questions of remoteness of damage, (particularly today by inhibitions on remedies concerning economic loss), and so it gradually emerged that those who depended upon the developer delivering a completed development to the desired standard, and on time, had essentially only the developer's development obligations to rely upon and to turn to contractually, but only in the first instance. Negligence is a difficult area and always has been. Harnessing responsibility contractually is more certain (depending on the quality of legal advice) so, it gradually impinged itself upon the minds of banks and institutions that their security lay not only in the site, and in the bricks and mortar so far constructed, but also prospectively in the variety and multiplicity of skills being deployed so long as such matters could be properly documented.

An initial answer to this was to require developers to hold all their respective rights of whatever kind against professionals and contractors on trust, for the benefit of the funder or whoever, and this would be underpinned by a covenant on the part of the developer to enforce those rights. However, one does not need to be too much of a student of law to realise that, upon analysis, such advantages were themselves circumscribed. The benefits were, in any case, circumscribed still further unless the original terms of engagement were in a satisfactory form. It became essential in time, for developers to define, or at least be required to define, carefully the terms of engagement of professionals and others and to rely less upon what might be regarded as a reasonable standard of conduct for the delivery of the anticipated result.

Here again, however, there was difficulty. The professional bodies have long had standard terms of engagement, which have, from time to time, been revised. They tend to be drafted with some protection for the professional in mind, hence the burgeoning practice of tailor-made appointments drafted and negotiated by lawyers.

Parallel with this hardening of attitudes has been a corresponding tendency on the part of insurers to redefine the extent of their own exposure. When a professional assumes responsibility, he also assumes risk. Part of his fee reflects that risk which in turn, he passes on to his professional indemnity (PI) insurers. This, again, presents a dilemma for the insurers. In theory, any risk ought to be insurable but, necessarily, only at a price. As contractual relationships have become more complex, insurers have themselves required to become far more circumspect. At what point does failure to perform become professional negligence? Contract and tort are inextricably interwoven.

These ideas are well worn in principle. Nevertheless, the times in which we live have brought them into sharper focus than ever before. These days, insurers are very particular about the commitments into which professionals may enter and the circumstances in which a claim may lie. For example, amongst others the Wren, who insure architects, are notably cautious as to the commitments which can properly be given by their insured particularly in relation, for example, to the matter of collateral agreements (warranties), which are discussed further below.

We are, therefore, now at the point where professional appointments (let alone warranties) are commonly negotiated between solicitors. Would that this were not necessary, but it is symptomatic of the times and in particular of the pressures brought about by the recession to squeeze the undertaking of responsibilities to the last drop. Thus, it is in the nature of professional relationships that the interests of various players also require to be accommodated and, in so far as they have not yet been contracted, anticipated. There may be, in any case, particular features of the site, third party interests and so on, and the development itself which also bear upon the exercise, and a 'standard' appointment may thus fall short of accommodating the needs of some or all of them.

Duplication of roles

So far, we have made an assumption that, in some way, a principal player in the piece will want to have access to professionals or contractors and hold them responsible. For the moment, this discussion continues on the basis that any such recourse is not necessarily as a result of developer failure. Questions of assignment (transfer) or novation (reconstitution of the appointment with a new employer under a new contract) have, as yet, not arisen.

In the whole development scenario, other principals need to be properly advised. The question arises to what extent, if at all, they should seek advice which mirrors that given, or which ought to be given, to the developer or other relevant players. A landowner, funder or tenant may reasonably expect to appoint surveyors to monitor conduct of the development, at the very least to ensure that contractual development obligations in their own favour are being met under their own particular agreements and, quite possibly, as part of the surveyors' function, to test or to arrange the testing of materials and structural integrity, to approve plans and modifications, to issue certificates, to authorise expenditure, etc. These are very much functions of the respective roles of the individual players, but viewed in each case from their personal standpoints and agendas alone.

However, like any other profession, surveyors have their limitations. They are not, and neither are they shadows of, architects, quantity surveyors, structural engineers, mechanical and electrical engineers or any others of the increasingly specialised performers who are to be found in the development and construction process. The judgment to be exercised is to what extent a player should appoint his own specialist consultants and what will be the justification for it, or how far he may or should rely upon other professionals who are willing, or who have been contracted, to provide collateral warranties.

It is to be assumed that the developer will either directly, or through his contractor, appoint or arrange for the appointment of the full range of professionals to be engaged in the development. The appointments themselves will need to be on terms which satisfy the requirements of the other players (see **Appointment** below). Further analysis is required to see whether those appointments will actually meet the proper needs of the other players. The question must then be asked by each of the players to what extent, depending upon both the nature of the role and access to it, another player may or should also rely on a particular professional. Who is checking up on whom? What additional controls are required? Do any of the players have special needs? Can a conflict of interests arise?

An obvious example is where a bank or financial institution advancing development finance will only do so under controlled conditions. Consultant surveyors may be appointed to perform that specific role, to check claims for advances, to ensure that payments have become properly due, that the amounts are consistent with relevant contracts, that there has been no default or misconduct. It is essentially a supervisory or policing role but precisely where it lies, and how deep it drives, depends also upon the relationship which is struck with the developer and others. That, in turn, depends directly upon the skill of the developer and the particular expectations of him. In this respect, nothing is merely implicit: it must be prescribed by contract to the extent necessary to bring about the desired result.

In addition to controlling mechanisms, eg issuing approvals, etc there are other functions which professionals appointed by principal players may perform. A local authority landowner, for example, may not necessarily have the skills to police the performance of a developer's obligations in a development agreement. It is likely that a firm of surveyors will be also appointed to perform that role. However carefully drawn the development agreement, and however precisely defined the role of the developer and the expectations of him, there has to be a mechanism—some practical means—for measuring performance, the results of the developer's endeavours themselves. The supervising surveyor's role is an obvious one.

However, supervision and policing are to be distinguished carefully from the professional functions which are required to produce the development at all. How far should any professional role be duplicated? Is it really necessary for each fund, tenant or landowner, for example, to appoint an engineer to check the calculations of the developer's engineer, or a quantity surveyor to check that the developer's quantity surveyor has accurately prescribed the basis upon which the building contract will be entered into? Again, is it necessary to duplicate the roles of other technical consultants, not least mechanical and electrical engineers, to make quite sure that what has been done is properly done by those whose skills are tested and known, that they meet all statutory requirements and that the resultant development fulfils the needs of its users and occupiers?

The necessity for so doing may arise through the limitations of the developer, the inadequacy of the terms of appointment of the developer's consultants or of the appointed consultants themselves, an unwillingness to give collateral warranties (see **Collateral warranties** below), inadequacy of the warranties, lack of professional indemnity insurance, even an insurer's unwillingness to allow consultants to give warranties except on certain terms. There may be any number of reasons for duplication of roles apart from the long-running debate on warranties. It is essential for a developer to recognise potential difficulty and to address it at an early stage, for fear that it will be recognised for him. Judgment must be exercised, and what is right for one project, and one set of players, may be wholly inappropriate for another.

Further, for every role which is duplicated, there is an added cost. That cost impacts, in turn, directly on the profitability of the venture. Not only the developer but those involved in financing the development ignore it at their peril. It is not helpful for a player to insist on appointing his own consultants simply because he feels more comfortable with his own team. The issue is whether it is necessary and proper, and whether this is so depends upon the adequacy of the original appointment, the accountability to him of the developer and the accountability of the professional concerned and whether, when all is said and done, what he actually needs is a warranty.

There is one simple question underlying all of this. Is there a conflict of interests? The corollary to this is whether that professional has a role which, upon analysis, is actually inimical to the player's interests. In most cases it will not be so, particularly if the consequences of failure on the part of the developer to deliver, whether in turn consequent upon failure of a consultant or a contractor, will devolve responsibility for resuming the development upon that player himself, eg a bank or funding institution, and if the services of that professional are accordingly required.

Appointment

It is always as well to look to the forms of appointment which the various professional bodies offer. They contain expectations both of duties and of professional fees and rates. For many tasks such forms may well suffice. They will no doubt also be in the minds of professional indemnity insurers.

Any such contract, sensibly drawn, will usually endeavour to be as defensive as possible on the part of its originator. From the point of view of the employer, given that as a developer he in turn will have a variety of contractual responsibilities to others, he must ask himself whether what is on offer actually meets, if not the needs of others, then his own responsibilities to (and commitments from) others and, if not, how those needs and his responsibilities may be met. The prospect is that he will need to add in a number of protective provisions to ensure that the interests of other players in the piece are fully met. Whereas he may, for example, have a development agreement in place supported by a loan agreement under a bank facility, he may not at the particular time have an agreement for lease with an occupier or an end purchaser in sight. Again, he may have perceived that the development will go forward on the basis of a standard JCT contract only to find, later, for some reason, that it is in his interests to delegate much of his role to a contractor and for the relationship with his consultants to be redefined accordingly.

Unless the way ahead is clearly marked, the employer must cater for a wide variety of possibilities and ensure that the appointment of each of his professional consultants can meet the tests which these prospects suggest.

Neither is the developer entirely free to devise his own form. Every development agreement, whether with a landowner, funder, tenant, or end purchaser, is likely to contain provisions governing approval both of the consultants themselves and of their terms of engagement. If the site has already been acquired, the bedrock is likely to be the development loan agreement with the bank, but the principles set out below apply as much to a landowner conferring a major interest upon completion of the development and/or to an institution providing finance under a forward funding agreement. Where there is a development agreement with a landowner, the interests of the intended purchasing institution are secondary, as also, in the alternative, those of a bank funder, but these must still be met.

Accordingly, following the theme of 'interaction', how free is the developer to negotiate his own terms with his consultants? The answer is, probably, not at all. Any one of the development agreements suggested above is likely to contain provisions along the lines of appointment of consultants upon terms first approved by the particular player, with consent usually not to be unreasonably withheld. Where there are appointments already in place, the player entering the scene must accept what he finds, or he negotiates a modified arrangement, or does not enter the deal.

The prospect for the developer is that he may have to satisfy a number of interests along similar lines. He must think about the interests he may have to satisfy in the future, and engineer fail-safe devices accordingly. If he relies on his lawyers to provide that protection, he must be sure that they understand (and are thus properly instructed as to) the parameters of what is being asked of them. Usually, negotiation of appointments will have preceded, or been conducted hand in hand with, major contractual engagements, with the consequence that all of these issues should have been covered.

Consequence of termination

Sometimes, appointments must be terminated, and other consultants appointed. Most players, properly advised, will sanction the appointment of additional consultants as appropriate, as and when the need arises. There will perhaps be greater sensitivity towards appointment of replacements, depending always upon the underlying cause. Funders in particular will be minded not to permit appointments to be terminated except with consent and upon good cause being shown (and will in turn place constraints upon the appointees' ability to determine through the medium of their particularly warranties).

But what if it is the employer whose interest as employer is being terminated by a professional or, worse, whose role as developer is being terminated by a major player? In this day and age, all major players will expect collateral warranties to be given by consultants to secure their respective interests. In so far as the player in question may wish or need to continue with the development upon failure by the developer, it is desirable that a collateral warranty should contain additional provisions (unless the original appointment so provides) permitting or effectively delivering either assignment or novation of the appointment in the hands of the player, such as a new developer procured by a bank.

Accordingly, where appointments are negotiated prior to a player entering the stage, such requirements must be anticipated so far as possible. Additionly, if the employer's interest in the development is to be curtailed, the appointee may be equally concerned that his position remains secure if the fault (if that is what it is) does not lie with him. In that event, he should probably also be looking not just for a novation with his new master, but also security for fees. His negotiation is potentially precarious if he has accepted an appointment which requires him to give commitments to third parties which do not cover prospective fees, let alone those already incurred.

Collateral warranties

Collateral warranties have generated a great deal of interest in recent years, with the various professional bodies and, indeed also, the British Property Federation, taking particular interest in their form and content. Professional indemnity insurers have taken a close interest also, in order to limit their own exposure as a result of commitments given by their insured. The result of all this debate has been the production of a number of standard forms in an endeavour to curtail the plethora of forms issuing from every law firm which imagines it has some skill in property development. The effect of these combined endeavours has not always been happy because, in practice, almost every development exercise of any substance now involves legally negotiated appointments and warranties.

In an endeavour to contain this burgeoning industry, quantity surveyors sometimes engage in a co-ordinating role, and the relevant professionals themselves are sometimes tempted to avoid legal representation, which in turn leads to misunderstanding, confusion and sometimes total incomprehension. This is a role which quantity surveyors, however well meaning, should perhaps avoid, and becoming a clearing house where lawyers are already involved is prospectively counter-productive. The prospective legal pitfalls are enormous and, if they are doing this because of shortcomings in the lawyers, the answer is to change the lawyers! It is not enough that they are working with draft documents originating from the requirements of development agreements.

Where consultants are legally represented, however, their protectors have acquired zealous habits and, either way, the process of negotiating appointments and warranties is sometimes a longer process than the principal development documents themselves, however much longer and more complex the latter may be. The central issue is usually one of consequential loss.

It is supremely important for a developer to be alive to the frustrations and delays which this process continues to present. It is important that he instructs his solicitors very clearly, and at an early stage, as to his long term intentions so far as they can be seen ahead, and that all of these negotiations are contained. This requires clarity of thought and intention, and sensible views need to be taken of what the relationships should contain. When he enters into a contractual commitment which binds him in any way as to the basis upon which he may appoint (and thus also seek warranties), the developer must look to all other relevant interests and ensure that compliance with one does not place him in breach of another or lead to expectations being unfulfilled including, not least, in relation to his funders as to draw down of sums for professional fees. (See also **Commitments to third parties** below.)

Building contract

This book does not seek to instruct in the detail of JCT contracts, ICE conditions, design and build, management contracting, etc although certain aspects of building contracts are covered in Chapters 5 and 6. The creation of a development usually assumes the delegation of the building function in some form or other. As with appointments, indeed as with any other function in the development process, how the developer goes about this will also be dictated by the needs of other principal players.

A landowner, public or otherwise, for example, ought not properly to require close control over appointments, whether of professional consultants or contractors in particular, except to the extent of its actual interests in, for example, the resultant investment or the accommodation works, etc. Its principal security may meanwhile comprise the site in any case. If there are buildings to be handed back, anticipation of a share in income or the expectation of overage payments, then of course such matters are pivotal in that context.

A banker providing finance is also acutely concerned because non-delivery of the building may result in forfeiture of the development agreement with the landowner and loss of his security in consequence. He, in particular, is directly concerned with such matters and will usually wish to take steps to intervene in any matter where the developer is failing to honour his contractual obligations to the landowner, thus putting his security at risk. Bank loan agreements so provide accordingly through identification of extensive events of default.

The building contract is (or, at least, should be) the heaviest item of expenditure. Therefore, the very identity of the contractor, let alone the terms of his contract, will be considered as enormously if not supremely important. A development agreement with a landowner must, therefore, be drawn with financing consequences in mind. For example, there may be requirements to short-list contractors, to prescribe in advance forms of contract, and for the detailed terms and pricing of the contract to be approved, all on terms. The developer must question the powers proposed to be taken by the landowner, what interests are being served by certain requirements, how this may conflict with the interests of those providing finance, which should generally be more stringent, etc.

In resolving the conflict between the interests of the various players, the developer must remember that those interests are not equal, because they are essentially different. A landowner laying down absolute terms may frustrate the development which may, in turn, make it unfundable. This applies to all aspects of the development agreement. A banker, by contrast, may lay down absolute terms but inflexibility may place the developer in breach of the principal development agreement, and thus impair the security. A bank may yet do precisely this to protect its own interests but, in so doing, it must accept the resultant responsibility for taking this line.

If the developer is lacking in development skills and is relying on his professionals and contractors, it may actually be wholly appropriate for the bank to take absolute powers. In so doing, it shifts the responsibility to itself for ensuring that the development agreement with the landowner is performed. The lesson, quite simply, is the more power you arrogate to yourself, the more responsibility you incur, and the more the blame for failure lies with you.

From the point of the view of the player with whom you are dealing, say you are the developer, in answer to any requirement of control over appointments or indeed any other function the question must always be 'Why?' Developers fail to ask it at their peril. A banker's interests lie in protecting his security and, therefore, it is not just a matter of what he prescribes in the loan agreement but, equally, how he approaches it. His role as financier is pivotal, but it is also, usually, transient, and the developer must negotiate at all times with the longer term in focus, consistent with his commercial aims and those of the other players. The developer's dilemma is always that he must negotiate terms with each of the players which he can implement without endangering his contractual relationships with others.

It may be in the nature of the building contract ultimately entered into that it will be so structured as to absorb existing appointments of professional consultants. It would be foolish to set up a series of appointments consistent with a development agreement, to secure a raft of collateral agreements in favour of funders and other principal players, only to have to seek the consent both of those funders and others, and particularly the consultants themselves, to reconstitute the appointment in another form entirely and in circumstances where one or more of those players is afforded a complete discretion. Accidents do happen, however, and new circumstances will require negotiation. Where there is a permitted assignment or novation of an appointment, in either case without alteration to its terms, such problems can be contained.

Sub-contracts

However, whatever the form of the building contract, it is likely that the contractor himself will wish to delegate a variety of functions, particularly specialist roles. It is possible that one or more of the players, particularly the bank funder, will wish to lay down precise rules as to the responsibilities of sub-contractors.

There is nothing unusual in having nominated sub-contractors and the standard JCT forms cater for them. As with professional appointments, if the building contract is being negotiated in advance of other interests being in place, the developer must anticipate the negotiation so far as possible.

At the very least in larger developments, it is likely that the identity of sub-contractors (particularly those relating to design functions) will require to be approved and warranties given in support to interested players. The building contractor may, therefore, be required to give such a commitment but it depends also upon the calibre of the contractor. It is also important to remember that, given that the effect of the warranty is effectively circumscribed by the limitations of the appointment/contract in respect of which it is given, it is of precious little value if the appointment/contract is itself defective, and so the letting of sub-contracts is an important consideration as well.

Warranties are not, and can never be, an end in themselves: they must be seen in the context in which they are given, ie the underlying appointment. If the appointment is not right, a warranty made by reference to it can be no better.

Commitments to third parties

Much has been said about warranties. It has been assumed that they are in support of comprehensive appointments or contracts which meet the needs of the developer and of the principal players whose approval is also needed. There is a golden rule in development that, where there is conflict, an exit route must be clearly shown, or if it is not, the ensuing deadlock is conscious and deliberate. If the developer himself is not in immediate breach of one or other of his contractual obligations to the principal players, placing himself in breach of subsidiary relationships may still bring about that result, eg non-payment of fees.

As will be seen in Chapter 8, a provider of funds has a dilemma as to whether to pay contractors and professionals direct or to route payment through the developer in the first instance. This is a matter of judgment for the funder. However, whether it is the developer or the consultant/contractor who is at fault, what is the impact upon those who are relying upon performance? Most warranties now avoid the mistake of making the warrantor responsible only to the extent of his liability to his employer. It is, prospectively, a mistake because if the employer has parted with his interest, perhaps it is the developer who has sold on the completed development to the fund and received value for it, that developer can hardly be perceived as having suffered a 'loss'. A little sensible drafting can avoid this obvious mistake of law. (Contrast this with making the warrantor liable as if the third party had been the original employer—there is thus an ongoing live interest.)

The greater difficulty, particularly in negotiation, is (always assuming that the warranty is intended to be fully effective) what the consequences may be of serving another master. The landowner or the bank, using our earlier examples, will clearly have an interest in prospective assignment or novation during the course of the development. An institutional purchaser, whose agreement with the developer is conditional upon the development being completed, will want neither until the completed development is actually delivered to him (unless he has instead funded the development himself under a forward funding agreement). If it is not delivered to him, he walks away and leaves all behind him, but may still have suffered some financial loss.

Assignment and novation of appointments

Appointments are essentially personal in nature and need to be expressly assignable or subject to novation. This can be done in the body of the appointment, but can be achieved for convenience by inserting appropriate provisions in a collateral warranty, backed by arrangements in the relevant development agreement between the developer/appointor and the player in question.

A lead tenant, or indeed any tenant, taking a collateral warranty should not properly be permitted to prescribe for the benefit of an appointment/contract to be assigned to or novated with him, unless of course the lease he is taking, instead of being rack rented, is effectively a headlease to which the whole of the capital value of the development attaches, and again he should not be able to require assignment or novation until his lease is granted in order to access directly any outstanding obligations or ones which materialise during a period of limitation.

(The fact that a lead tenant is taking a full repairing lease of the whole of the development is *not* usually a good reason for assignment or novation of the full benefit of a contract or appointment even at the end of the development period. If the entire capital interest is moving to him, perhaps because he pays only a nominal rent and the reversioner has a nominal interest as well, that may be a justification. If he pays a full rack rent, his full repairing obligations may not extend to putting back something which was never there to start with. More to the point, in case of forfeiture and surrender the benefit of the appointment does not revert automatically: further contractual machinery is inevitably required.) The reality is that assignment or novation of contracts and appointments should be available only to those with a residual need to carry out and complete the development in place of the developer or, when once completed, acquiring the capital asset comprised in the completed development.

Provisions nevertheless for assignment or novation require great care. Although an end user may be justified in seeking to mitigate his loss by acquiring as many contractual benefits as possible, the effect of so doing may also be to pull the feet of the developer out from under him in case of outstanding contractual obligation. If the developer is relying on an appointment to deliver a result, and he fails to deliver, and if the relationship with the appointee is taken away from him, he cannot perform. If he still has a contractual obligation to the purchaser, tenant or indeed someone else, he may incur liabilities which, in the event, he has little or no hope of performing himself.

Accordingly, before entering into commitments with principal players which will require that terms of appointments allow the giving away of assignment/novation rights, and that he step aside to permit another player to pick up the baton, a developer must be completely clear in his mind as to the potential effect upon him.

Care is thus required: assignment or novation in favour of a tenant of only part of the development is wholly inappropriate, in any case. Accordingly, depending on the nature of the interest of the particular player, a warranty may merely give the recipient a handle on the appointment or contract, and so provide a remedy in damages. Alternatively, if the continuation of the development is at stake, or the interested party will own the whole and every part of the completed development and stand to lose, eg through loss of rental income unless he can enforce the appointment or contract, he will naturally seek a warranty in his favour to include provisions permitting assignment or novation backed by appropriate co-relative provisions in the development agreement.

In any event, there are numerous instances of careless mis-use of common clauses to be found in warranties which are applied in inappropriate circumstances and which may, because of misapplication, actually damage the value of the resultant investment, because, for example, an onward purchaser cannot effectively benefit. The context and prospective application of the warranty must be fully understood from the outset, and it should be drafted accordingly.

Finally, where developer default, post-practical completion, points to default on the part of any of his contractors or consultants a prudent developer should seek to negotiate his original development obligations, if he can, so that remedies under warranties, and indeed any defects liability insurance, are first exhausted, and also seek to curtail his exposure to the extent that any appointments or contracts have been assigned or novated.

Defects liability insurance

Defects liability insurance essentially comes into effect when construction is completed. Such insurances have gained in popularity because, to some considerable extent, they obviate the need for the players to take a raft of protective measures in order to benefit from the variety of appointments and contracts which are a necessary part of the development process. The developer himself will have given contractual commitments to, say, a purchasing institution and any dilution of the benefit of such contractual obligations is similarly covered. During the worst of the recession years, the maintenance of defects liability insurance has proved beneficial if only because of the insolvency of so many of the firms and companies concerned, and upon whose skills and resources reliance was being placed.

Just as many contractors and professionals will themselves seek to contain their liability contractually by limiting it to a period of so many years, defects liability insurances habitually do so. The ten-year period commonly applied to such policies of insurance has thus given rise to the term 'decennial' insurance, by which defects liability insurance policies are frequently known.

There is still a fairly limited market, but such insurance presents the means of tidying up and packaging the responsibilities of numerous people. Such insurance can deliver protection in a variety of ways. For example, some such insurances assume subrogation rights against consultants and contractors. Others do precisely the opposite, providing protection for them as well as for the principal(s) insured. (Expect to see exceptions and exclusions however.) Such insurance is seen as a means of avoiding the quagmire of enforcement of collateral warranties, as well as claims against contractors. Neither should it be forgotten that, in the first instance, it was the developer's responsibility to deliver (subject always to his contractual development obligations), and the taking of collateral warranties is now, and has always been, an additional protective measure against the developer's failure so to do. Defects liability insurance is an expensive, but effective, protection which is becoming increasingly attractive.

Precisely what protective measures should be taken in the development process are a matter of judgment including, not least again, the matter of cost. Costs reduce profits and the size, nature and cost of the development will dictate precisely what protective measures can sensibly be taken. A defects liability insurance which is contracted at the outset of the development process will allow monitoring by the insurers' own advisers (usually engineers) so that, upon payment of a fee when the development is completed, the insurance will come into force immediately. Post-completion insurances are also available but there are cost implications consequent upon the absence of monitoring during the development process.

Overview

By now, the developer will have secured his professional appointments and his construction contract. The requirements of all the principal players in the piece will have been met. Their individual requirements will have been so framed in each of the development documents relating to their particular interests that no one requirement can or at least should effectively frustrate the requirement of another. Either there is a remedy contractually available or, albeit less satisfactory, the inappropriate exercise of discretion will work against the person exercising it. Banks in particular have learned to be more flexible in their approach albeit that development loan agreements, secured on the site or in turn on a development agreement, are usually very tightly drawn. Nevertheless, even where some flexibility is written into the documentation, it remains as true as ever before that, in all probability, the developer is in breach of some term or other simply because of what such agreements contain, and the way they are usually expressed.

Meanwhile, as other players have joined the piece, their requirements should have been correctly anticipated by the developer. Failure to do so can only be inimical to the project. Although, in one sense, a purchasing institution is only interested in the outcome, throughout it is concerned whether that outcome has a reasonable prospect of being fulfilled. Thus, although it may not be providing interim finance, it is still concerned with the development process but, until the development is delivered the interest will not usually lie in wanting to take over the development as such, unlike that of a banker or a landowner with a major reversionary interest, but it is certainly concerned about the application of the funds which have been reserved for the event, whether they should be deployed elsewhere and what loss may be accrued as a result.

In the light of the various interests in the development, which are concerned with professionals and contractors, there will also be measures in place which cater for additions, replacements and terminations. Those immediately concerned with the course of the development, particularly those providing finance, will also have prescribed that the developer shall not dismiss a consultant or a contractor, nor engage others in their place, without prior approval, usually, on terms not to be unreasonably withheld. Finally, it should not be thought that all initial appointments or engagements will be in any shape or form contemporaneous. An architect is likely to be the first appointee, if only for the purpose of planning permission and feasibility. That particular appointment is thus likely to be a two-tier arrangement with a full appointment being put into place, once the development is formally conceived.

Provisions for appointment, termination, assignment and novation should always be negotiated to meet the circumstances, not just the interests of the player who requires it, for fear that performance of outstanding obligations may be impaired.

Checklist

1. Who are the developer's consultants?
2. Have they been appointed yet?
3. What are the terms of their appointment?
4. Would their terms be acceptable to third parties, particularly financiers? Would they give commitments to third parties?
5. Will they accept new masters? If so, upon what terms?
6. If required to give collateral agreements, will those agreements be inimical to the requirements of their professional indemnity insurers?
7. Can the consultants be replaced? If so, what are the criteria for replacement?
8. How much control will a third party, eg a bank or fund, have over appointments, terms of appointment, replacement, etc?
9. Who may legitimately seek novation or assignment of an appointment or contract? Does some other player have a greater need?
10. Who are the proposed contractors? In so far as contractors are not yet appointed, what should the selection process be?
11. What will be the terms of the building contract particularly as to price, timing, etc (see Chapter 5)?
12. What form of building contract should be used?
13. Again, what commitments to third parties can be prescribed and

upon what terms? Will they accept new masters and upon what terms? From whom will committments be required in the light of CDM (see also Chapter 5)?
14. If contractors give commitments to third parties what will the attitude of their own insurers be?
15. Consider again issues of assignment and novation in the context of contractors.
16. What interests do the players have in the roles of sub-contractors? Should these also give warranties and what will such warranties provide?
17. What professional advisers should be involved separately, on behalf of third parties, and how much supervision/duplication is appropriate?
18. Who pays the fees of such further advisers?
19. What is the covenant strength of all or any of the contractors, sub-contractors, professional consultants and so on? How much insurance should be maintained?
20. Should defects liability insurance be employed? If so, to what extent should it also cover contractors and professionals?
21. Who can benefit from such insurance and what bearing will this have on negotiation of terms of engagement, collateral agreements, etc?

4 Development Cost

> 'Loss of virginity is rational increase, and there was never virgin got 'til virginity was first lost. That you were made of is metal to make virgins. Virginity, by being once lost, may be ten times found: by being ever kept, it is ever lost. 'Tis too cold a companion: away with't!'
>
> Parolles, *All's Well That Ends Well: Act I, Scene I*

It is not often that a man enters a room and surprises those present by asking one of the ladies 'Are you meditating on virginity?' Helena, a gentlewoman protected by the Countess of Rousillon, was fairly robust in her response. However, this exchange demonstrates, if crudely, that something must be given up or sacrificed for a benefit to accrue. The principles of book keeping were even thus. So it is, with development cost, not just in the simple sense of inevitable expenditure, but because it is a component both in the measure and gaining of profit. Moreover, it is not necessarily measured in terms of cash outlay. It may be incurred, expended, or deemed expended without being spent, or even spent without being deemed expended depending upon the nature of the transaction, the purpose for which it is being assessed, the calculations to be made, the impact upon contractual obligations and so on.

Depending upon the nature of the transaction, the way it is being funded, the relationships between major players or joint venture partners, development cost is reflected in so many different ways that the developer will not be permitted to maintain a single development account for the entirety of the project. The interests of others are as diverse as the nature of the cost and expenditure.

However, the developer will be incurring cost in one form or another from the outset of the project. As soon as he contemplates site acquisition, his expenditure on the development process will be earmarked for that development scheme. So begins a process that will develop a life and momentum of its own. Development cost touches every player in some way: it means different things to the players, different responsibilities, different amounts and different outcomes.

True development cost

The 'developer' is an entity which may exist in very different forms. Those players holding an interest in the developing entity, whatever it may be, will all see their commitments, and their respective benefits, in terms of profit and loss. As players in the piece, their perception of what is development cost may be very different from development cost in the eyes of the developer as such.

For simplicity, however, let us assume that the developer is a single entity, however contrived, and that it is the development cost in the hands of that developer, and expended by him, which is now in focus.

Unless expenditure on the development is incidental to, or parallel with, some other kind of activity, it is essential from the outset that development cost, in all its respects, is isolated and dealt with separately. The developer's accountant will see it entirely in terms of profit and loss, and so also is it with any development company which is undertaking just one or a number of projects under the umbrella of perhaps no more than one entity, say its principal development subsidiary.

However, the practicality is that, with the needs of others to accommodate, particularly those of a bank providing finance pursuant to a development loan agreement, the cost of the development will attach to a single entity, because of the need for a bank to be able—through the appointment of an administrative receiver—to ring-fence the company. Again, one is on familiar territory for an accountant who is thinking in terms of profit and loss. The books of the developer will show every income and capital receipt and also every expense or liability, current or otherwise.

Within the possibilities of *sine qua non*, all of this must rank as obvious. However, the developer must, in addition, use all of this material for different purposes and in different ways. Whether his sources of finance come from a bank, an investor, his own resources or wherever, the self same expenditure will be reflected over and over again in different ways.

Landowners and institutional purchasers

A landowner may be employing a developer who, while meeting his own costs and expenses, may be rewarded by the grant of a major interest in due course. What is the consideration for that major interest? It may simply be the provision of buildings or facilities, it may be that the landowner is seeking some kind of overage payment based upon a profit formula relying upon factors such as development cost and rental income received or (more usually) receivable, it may be a capital sum on completion of the development (or even 'up front'), or a combination of any of these.

The landowner is thus prospectively interested in the development cost expended or incurred by the developer. Take, for example, a development agreement entered into between a major landowner and a developer under which, upon completion of the development, a headlease will be granted. Upon lettings being achieved an overage payment may be made to the landowner. For the purposes of this agreement, therefore, a development cost schedule will be incorporated and, whatever provisions there may be for the practicalities of development, and whatever controls the landowner may wish to employ to ensure that the development is completed on time and in an appropriate manner, there will be an associated cost implication, but *not* necessarily a mirror image of actual expenditure. There will be constraints, not in terms of what the developer may actually expend, but in terms of what may be brought into account.

If overage payments are to be based upon a cost driven formula, there must by implication be some supervision of the cost of the development itself. At one level, the landowner may be said to have no interest whatsoever in what the developer spends, so long as the results are achieved. However, unless particular items of expenditure are capped, for the purposes of his agreement, the prospects of overage payments are diminished.

Thus, unless the development is carried out in a certain way, contracts and appointments approved, pricing controlled, etc the developer can deprive the landowner of his payment in due course. Suppose, for example, the developer is a subsidiary of a major contractor which is awarded the contract. If the building contract price is enhanced because the developer has freedom in his choice of building contractor or the contract itself, it is the contractor's profit which takes the top slice. It is, therefore, necessary to consider development cost as an essential element of every kind of development agreement with a financial outcome. One cannot prescribe development obligations unless the reasons are known and understood. Therefore, the actual cost to the developer must be distinguished carefully, from the authorised cost under a development agreement whose sole purpose is a factor in a calculation.

Accordingly, imagine a development agreement under which every item of expenditure on the project is monitored. The incurring of that expenditure will be approved under operative provisions in that behalf. The landowner is not concerned, at least at this level, about where the money is coming from, only that it is properly expended on the project. Moreover, as part of the development costs, it may be that the landowner is itself incurring certain expenditure. It may, for example, have appointed consultant surveyors in a supervisory role both of the development and its completion, and also of expenditure by the developer for the purposes of the development agreement. Quite possibly, it may require the developer to meet that expenditure which, in turn, will become part of the development cost.

Just as there are limits on expenditure both in terms of what is properly approved by the landowner under the development agreement and also for the purpose of any necessary calculations, the expenditure incurred by the landowner may be similarly inhibited in terms of what the developer may be required to pay and what is actually to be debited to development cost. As with the developer, the actual cost expended by the landowner may be greater. Some expenditure may, for example, be confined within what is properly and reasonably to be incurred in the circumstances. Other expenditure may be confined more closely, whether within rates or categories or subject even to a cap. In complex development agreements, where there are substantial costs involving checks and balances of different kinds, the landowner fails at his peril to isolate those costs to which he himself is entitled within the relevant categories, for fear that he may not be able to recover the whole or part from the developer. It is not entirely uncommon for development cost definitions to cap expenditure throughout on an item by item basis: there will need to be good reason for this but, usually, a more flexible approach is adopted.

There may be other kinds of expenditure which the landowner requires the developer to meet, but which are expressly *not* required to be brought into account under the development agreement. However, expenditure incurred by the developer on the development, including reimbursement of the landowner will always be development cost in his own books in terms of profit and loss. Similarly, just as the developer has succeeded in excluding certain payments to the landowner because they did not fall within the criteria set down by the development agreement, so also may he in turn, having undertaken expenditure of one kind or another, including that of the landowner, be unable to justify it for the purposes of other parts of the agreement or in related transactions.

Funder's view

Funding mechanisms apart, the sources of cash coming from a bank or fund into the credit side of the developer's books of account may not cover the entirety of expenditure. First, who is providing? The developer may be an entity deriving cash from a variety of sources, eg loans from members, initial capital, etc. It is always a matter of the terms upon which that cash is advanced. So is it also with any other funding source, but what does this mean?

Imagine a development which is intended to be funded entirely by bank finance. The loan is only of so much, it can be drawn down in tranches and the criteria for draw down will introduce a pattern of expenditure (see Chapter 8). Whatever the pattern, the tranches, the applicable interest and so on, precisely what is it that is being drawn down? The answer is, of course, development cost, but a banker's idea of development cost is likely to be quite different from that of the developer.

The loan agreement will contain its own list, and its own criteria for determining what constitutes legitimate development cost within that list. It may, for example, include whatever sums were in the event payable to the landowner (see **Landowners and institutional purchasers** above). Very likely, it will state that it will include sums which were 'properly' payable, eg that the landowner could legitimately claim under the principal development agreement. If the developer made a mistake, or gave the landowner an over generous benefit of the doubt, it is his loss: the bank will not pay for it. (There are implications here if the landowner and the developer determine between them a particular amount by reference to an alternative dispute resolution (ADR) mechanism: see Chapter 9.) Every other item of expenditure is likely to be that which was properly incurred in any event and, otherwise, reasonably incurred.

A loan agreement should not be entirely discretionary (save beyond the confines of agreed heads of expenditure), otherwise the developer cannot be secure in the knowledge that the expenditure which he needs to incur will in fact be met. As has been seen, the greater the discretion, the greater the responsibility in exercising it.

Every player concerned with development cost is concerned with minimising it. The landowner will want to minimise it in order to secure an enhanced overage payment (but he will be not concerned at all if his interests are unconnected and no overage will ensure, if it is simply buildings which are delivered or he takes a share in the rental income alone). The banker is obviously concerned with minimising development cost because his loan is essentially finite. (The same applies to an institution advancing money under a forward funding agreement.) The scheme will have been costed and there must be financial controls throughout. More particularly, the bank will wish to be sure that the developer can meet his development commitments, however well the security is hedged with guarantees, further security, etc.

It follows that the bank will, in turn, be employing a monitoring process. The landowner and the bank will both very likely have been employing surveyors, both of them concerned with progress of the development but from different standpoints, the latter (banker) in any case being concerned that its cash advances are being appropriately used. Almost certainly, incidentally, these professional appointments cannot be considered as duplication of roles because the roles, although similar in nature, serve different interests and aims. (Moreover, it would be highly unusual, rather than merely coincidental, for one firm of surveyors to be appointed to both roles. In any event, the roles must be seen as mutually exclusive particularly if, for example, the developer is in default of its relationship with the landowner and is in danger of forfeiting the agreement whereas the banker, on the other hand, will either be supporting the developer or, ultimately, stepping in to rescue the package. A conflict of interests would arise.)

The upshot, however, is that development cost under a loan agreement or a forward funding agreement may, in terms of the kind of expenditure, be rather less than the expenditure actually incurred for the purposes of the agreement with the landowner, and the developer may have to fall back on own resources (see also Chapter 8 'Funding'). The differing contractual mechanisms, based upon the different needs of the players, point to the underlying need for interaction (as discussed more fully in Chapters 5, 6 and 7).

Purchasers and tenants

Both purchasers and tenants are distinguished by their ongoing interests in the completed development, the tenant as occupier and the purchaser as an investor or personal occupier.

The cost of works carried out specially for a tenant may be rentalised. They, therefore, form part of the wider development cost incurred by the developer. In so far as not contemplated by the funding package enjoyed by the developer, whether through forward funding or bank loan, these simply fall into his general costs of the development reflected by profit and loss, or they may be the subject of a re-negotiation with the funder. (Development is a flexible process and the largest and most complex schemes can be subject to modifications along the way necessitating re-alignment of contractual relationships at all levels. Where changes are made, the exercise requires careful analysis to ensure that other interests are accommodated and that contracts are not breached.) Alternatively, in so far as met by the tenant instead, the profit and loss account is not impaired because of balancing receipts.

Principal players generally

All development costs, however originated, may have relevance for other purposes beyond principal agreements, eg a project manager's fee based upon construction cost, etc even a developer's project management fee based upon overall development cost and calculated as a first charge on profits within a joint venture.

A developer's project management fee may also be an element of development cost in a forward funding agreement and thus also be a reward to him in advance of overage. In this case, far from being a mirror of the developer's costs, it is a prior credit item to him whereas other expenditure is pure debit for which he obtains only corresponding credit from his funders (see again Chapter 8). The figures, therefore, have to be worked and re-worked, according to the nature and variety of relationships, and recorded with each such relationship in mind.

Again, the landowner who was entitled to receive (but failed to categorise and identify) certain expenditure, failed in turn to recover it from the developer, but in so doing perhaps marginally decreased the anticipated development cost for overage purposes. Almost certainly, these two will not have balanced themselves out: it depends entirely on the particular calculation required to be made.

For an end purchaser, development cost can be looked at in a variety of different ways. For a purchaser of a completed development, in simple terms, there is usually only one criterion which is market value, the price he pays. However, in the case of new development supported by the prior commitment of a purchaser, there is a rather different scenario. In the case of new development, which is essentially conditional upon, first, the carrying out of the development and, secondly, letting, a number of factors are brought into play.

First, in the case of forward purchase, such a transaction is based upon an agreement. It is in all respects a development agreement. When the buildings are completed and so long as such and such rents are achieved, and the tenants are approved by the purchaser, (presumably with consent not to be unreasonably withheld) or the developer can give an income commitment perhaps backed by guarantees from a joint venture partner, a number of different negotiating positions are available. It is to be assumed that there will be a base purchase price, which, in such circumstances, is unlikely to be based upon development cost as such. (It is sometimes difficult to convince investors from other parts of Europe that a building in the UK is not necessarily valued by what it costs to build.) Assuming that base purchase price, the success of letting may then produce an overage payment in addition for the developer. The prospect is that if a base cost for the building has already been established and, given that letting will assist in establishing the market value, an overage calculation can be devised based upon such factors. Combine this with a commitment to purchase in any event, so long as the building is completed (as to which see Chapters 5 and 8), and so long as an income is forthcoming, in the absence of tenants then supported by the covenant of the developer and/or its backers, the scene is set for a development scenario which is naturally attractive to bankers providing interim finance for the development, ie so long as the project is completed, there will be a purchase, and the loan will be repaid.

Forward funding

Development cost will also be relevant to a purchasing institution which itself is providing finance. This is the basis of the classic forward funding agreement. Instead of taking security, the purchaser acquires the site at the outset. In selling the site to the purchaser (fund) the developer is possibly making a profit. However, the price paid by the fund is part of the development cost, but whose? In the case of purchase by the fund, as with the project management fee, it is development cost for the fund. Nevertheless, at the same time, the developer is itself incurring costs, a profit and loss item, and to the extent that monies advanced by the fund mirror those expended by the developer, the profit and loss account balances.

Forward funding is not in any sense a lending transaction. Some developers like to think that they are dealing, notionally, with a loan. It is nothing of the kind. The property belongs to the purchaser, the purchaser is advancing cash to the developer against expenditure, always under controlled conditions (see Chapter 8) and it is those controlled conditions which determine precisely what can be advanced to the developer, whatever is actually expended. Moreover, it is not just a matter of expenditure but also timing. A developer who pays out on a certificate issued by a building contractor may find that, under the regime imposed by the forward funding agreement, the particular item of expenditure was not for some reason approved (by the purchaser's surveyors) and therefore the developer remains out of pocket.

Construction costs are particularly problematical, especially in cases where there is defective work. Nothing can interfere with the building contract or indeed any other contractual relationship between the developer and its suppliers/professionals/contractors (except if it is assigned or novated). Under the funding agreement the propriety of making payment to meet committments under any of those contracts is another matter, and the position of the purchaser (fund) is not that of an arbiter.

In forward funding agreements, purchasing institutions habitually impose controls not only over expenditure but also, in certain cases, over the ability to utilise funds advanced to pay contractors and others directly. From a developer's point of view this should be resisted wherever possible but it rather depends upon the status of the developer as to whether this can be negotiated. An experienced developer whose judgment can be trusted may be allowed to control the purse strings of each drawdown, once drawn. There may be good reason for letting him do so, for example where the architect has already issued a certificate under the building contract but the developer is slightly less than satisfied and is seeking to bargain his way through to other concessions.

Notional interest

Under a forward funding agreement, as with a back loan, there may be expected to be a maximum commitment on the part of the purchasing institution (fund). During the currency of such an agreement, given that the fund already has the land and, therefore, has the security of that land and the construction works upon it, the only way of enhancing the initial outlay is by some sort of interest charge. However, interest, *per se*, is not charged by an owner upon expenditure on his own property. It is not a loan. Instead, the fund debits notional interest, for want of a better description, which is sometimes given the label 'account charge', or some other designation. The effect of this is to accelerate the apparent outlay of development cost, as perceived by the forward funding agreement, towards the maximum commitment.

In the books of the developer, there has been expenditure on development cost, perhaps including items not advanced by the purchaser (fund), and, in turn, the purchaser has been advancing items of development cost, at least as perceived by the funding agreement, to the developer. Because of notional interest, the maximum commitment, afforded by the purchaser, is reached before true expenditure in the hands of the developer reaches the contractual maximum commitment. The fund's books are thus not a mirror image of the developer's expenditure. What happens next?

The fund has perhaps paid out to the developer as much as it is ever going to, at least as development cost under the forward funding agreement. It has watched the building grow because, under that agreement, it has taken powers (see Chapter 8) to monitor and control the conduct of the development by the developer. (It may be that lettings have been negotiated meanwhile into which the fund, as owner of the property, will enter in due course. Every contracted letting of the development provides security of a certain kind to the developer because in the fullness of time, it will relieve him of the burden of providing an income to the fund (but see Chapter 7). This will impact directly on what happens

Development Cost 61

in financial terms once practical completion has taken place.)

During this interim period, the development cost incurred under the development finance agreement takes on a significant dimension, whatever the actual cost to the developer, for fear of a cut off of funds once the maximum commitment has been reached. It must be kept down.

Once the maximum commitment has been reached, the developer is faced with the prospect of a real charge on the purchaser's outlay. It may take a variety of forms, whether by way of interest actually paid on the outlay to date, or later upon completion of the development by assuming a notional lease or, indeed, actually taking a lease subject to a right of determination when lettings are achieved. It may be a combination of such ideas. (Further outlay on interest, subject to lettings achieved, is sometimes absorbed by an institution as a factor against prospective development profit. This is known as 'profit erosion', and so a 'profit erosion deal' can be attractive to a developer in times of uncertainty, and disastrous to the institution which has entered into it. The recession has wrought heavy losses for institutions in deals of this kind.) There will otherwise usually be an interest charge imposed until the development is complete.

Meanwhile, the developer must meet the continuing cost of the development out of his own resources. The need for careful feasibility calculations is obvious. If the developer survives, then under the terms of the forward funding agreement he may still be entitled to an overage payment of some kind in due course. Unless profit erosion based, this will derive from a formula (see Chapter 8). If the building remains unlet following completion of the development, the developer may also—and probably will—be required to maintain it fully until lettings are achieved. His interest payments may translate into, in effect, an equivalent to the market rent of the property and, by default, he may find himself as a tenant. Sometimes this is expressed in simpler terms by imposing on the developer all the obligations of a tenant as to rent, insurance premiums, outgoings, repair and so on, (the notional lease, mentioned above).

In due course, the developer hopes he will have his reward in an overage payment based upon development cost and lettings actually achieved. There will be at least two sets of development cost figures, ie including those of the purchaser, running in parallel (but by no means similar) for the purpose of such a transaction although only one set of figures is relevant for the developer's profit and loss.

Other interested parties

As already discussed, the interest of a landowner, public or private, in anticipation of grant of a major interest may give rise to the need for definition of development cost of one kind or another. A bank's perception of development cost, circumscribed by limitations on advances both in total amount and as to what is approved, is another. If there is an end purchaser with a purchase price based upon a formula (based upon development cost, maximum commitment, etc) there is yet another perception of development cost in play. If there is a combination of the three, with the end purchaser buying under a forward purchasing agreement only, the developer is faced with a number of different regimes. If the scheme is forward funded, ie with the end purchaser taking either the property (or the agreement for a major interest) at the outset, there are still two main streams of expenditure to be contended with, whatever the actual expenditure incurred by the developer.

It is therefore essential that, in keeping his own books of the development, the developer keeps separate records to reflect each of the various contractual commitments into which he has entered so far as development cost is a factor in them. It also follows that he must not frame his contractual relationships in such a way that the incurring of expenditure, or failure to incur expenditure, is so inimical to one of his relationships as to impair another. If the transaction is forward funded, so that in effect there is no other source of finance except that from the fund or from the developer's limited resources, failure to meet expenditure of a certain kind should not be allowed to become a breach of the development agreement with the landowner who will grant a major interest in due course. Indeed, an institutional purchaser, properly advised, will in any case have carefully scrutinised the principal development agreement to ensure that this does not happen.

Fund costs

Where either the purchaser under a forward funding agreement or the banker under a loan agreement is itself incurring expenditure which may be debited to the development cost, the developer should be particularly advised to insist on a provision that all deemed advances, for that is what they are, should be notified to him and debited to development cost only upon such notice being given. Otherwise, he has no means of checking such cost until much later which could give the illusion of working within budget when in fact he was not within budget at all. Such omission discloses poor fund management and, once again, experience dictates the need to bring to attention.

Again, a bank providing finance of the development does itself no favours by withholding an advance, or part of an advance, if to do so would impair the security on which it relies. The principles of interaction therefore permeate all these transactions and the way that they interlock. Very similar considerations apply as, for example, to the various contractual relationships into which the developer will enter with his contractors, professionals and others. Everything must interlock, and no contractual relationship should be impaired by another except with good cause and against measured risk.

Other relationships

Standing back from all of this, one then has to consider the impact of development cost upon subsidiary relationships, perhaps within a joint venture. As has been seen, a joint venture may comprise the simplest arrangement, for example a profit share agreement with the vendor of land who has been happy to release his land outright at a certain price with the promise of an overage payment (if any arising) in due course. Once again, development cost is a factor in the calculation. A developer sensibly advised will ensure that all of his true costs incurred in the development are taken into account. However, as always, it is a matter of the strength of one's bargaining position and so, for the purposes of his overage calculation, a vendor may wish to exercise control over expenditure *in this context* whether or not actually expended. This may be done in a number of ways.

Given that the property will have changed hands and that, in all probability, a profit share agreement is relying upon contract only, it is not a matter of prohibiting the developer from incurring expense as such. It is his money wherever it came from. The issue is whether the expense was justified. Thus, there may need to be some kind of mechanism to ensure that the development cost for the purpose of the profit share agreement is kept within bounds. Again, taking the example of a developer subsidiary of a construction group who relies upon its parent to provide the building contract, the vendor is hardly likely to allow the developer to enter into a building contract at any price, particularly if it is the parent contractor who eventually takes the contract. In one sense he has no power to stop him save in contract, if to place the building contract except on an agreed basis would be a breach, but, on the other hand, for the purposes of calculation a more realistic figure has to be worked out. Otherwise (in parallel with the similar dilemma in a full development agreement—see above), the contractor's price will amount to no more than a first charge on profits thus depriving the vendor of his overage and making a mockery of the whole arrangement. This is simple common sense.

Similar considerations apply within other kinds of joint venture depending upon the relationship between the participators. A project management fee may be based upon development cost: again, depending upon who is incurring the development cost, and how it is

64   *Practical Property Development and Finance*

calculated, this may signal the need for some discipline as to calculation of that cost, if not the incurring itself, then for the purpose of calculating that fee. The extent of the input of the developer into the process, its relationship with those with whom it contracts, etc all bear heavily on the thinking behind the derivation of profit and how it is to be calculated. A developer's reward based upon a percentage of development cost alone does not provide any incentive to maximise profit, and vendors of property looking to benefit from development should look to building in an incentive, such as sharing the development profit itself.

Overview

The most that can be done, in a book of this kind, is to point to the need to be aware of the many forms which development cost can take, quite apart from the actual expenditure on the project, and how it manifests itself. Development cost is a measure for a variety of purposes. Particular functions of the various players will dictate whether, and how far, expenditure can actually be incurred, if it is simply a device for the purpose of a particular calculation, or if it will impact on the incurring of further cost, eg drawing down of a bank loan, advance of finance under a forward funding agreement.

Whenever a contract is entered into, under which somebody is entitled to be paid for some service or another, the question arises as to what obstacle (or obstacles) there will, or should be, placed in the path of that payment being made. Even if there is no obstacle, what are the consequences of that payment being made and, in particular, what sanctions can be exercised against the person making the payment or incurring the cost as a direct result?

Where expenditure is incurred before all contractual relationships are necessarily in place, how will that be viewed, can it be recouped and will like expenditure be similarly recouped? Cost, in all its many forms, has one underlying characteristic: it hits someone's bottom line, and so we are back to the accountant and his profit and loss account.

Checklist

1. Has the feasibility been fully worked out?
2. What contingencies are there?
3. Who is providing the finance?
4. Upon what contractual relationships does the transaction rely in order to be achieved? Precisely what financial commitments do

these entertain and how do they impact upon feasibility?
5. As negotiations progress, how will expectations and feasibility change?
6. If funding is confined within a certain source, will that funding at least meet the requirements of the feasibility? To what extent, if at all, does the financial commitment fall short of any expectations of any other player who may require to be paid or that expenditure be incurred?
7. Is the developer resourced to deal with contingencies, eg cost overruns, failure to let, etc if expectations are not met? What are the downside risks?
8. Do the financial provisions of any loan or other funding package cater adequately for other contractual commitments? Can the developer be sure that his funding source will pay?
9. Consider the interests of joint venture partners, and how their interests may be calculated.
10. Has the developer put in place sufficient internal mechanisms to ensure that every contractual commitment can be reflected by such calculations as are required to be made under the agreement in question? Where there are other players with financial interests, what procedures have they set up to enable them to claim, as well as police, expenditure?
11. If funding dries up, for whatever reason, does the developer have an escape route? (NB: Chapter 8). What other resources are available to him?

5 The Construction Process

> 'We first survey the plot, then draw the model;
> And when we see the figure of the house,
> Then must we rate the cost of erection;
> Which if we find outweighs ability,
> What do we do then but draw a new model
> In fewer offices, or at last desist to build at all?'
> Lord Bardolph, *Second Part of King Henry the Fourth: Act I, Scene III*

In the eyes of construction professionals, construction itself is sometimes perceived as development. The reality is that, far from being development, it is but an element in the process—a natural consequence of the bringing together of players and resources, and a variety of commitments enshrined in contract. Neither is construction of any intrinsic value unless it can be used for a purpose and there is actually a demand for it. Bricks and mortar cost money and, therefore, present a liability before they become an asset. The construction process is thus no more than an intermediate stage in development and, while those involved in construction have a contribution which is pivotal, as before, equally so is their co-operation.

Our developer is still contemplating his prospective contractual arrangements with the respective principal players. Having identified if not assembled his site, conceived the development, obtained planning and other consents and brought together his prospective professional team, financiers and others, he must now consider how all of their respective roles will impact upon the construction elements of the development process, and indeed *vice versa*.

He is at the point where, having negotiated in principle with numerous players, he is faced with a variety of detailed contractual commitments. In any event, upon signing the development agreement (if there is one) he may have had to pay a premium, or he has already bought the site outright. He has thus paid substantially for the privilege, if that is what it is, of carrying out construction at all, let alone incurring the building costs. Further, perhaps the scheme is not forward funded, but is debt financed by a consortium of banks working under a lead bank who will enter into a loan agreement with the developer. The (lead) bank has made quite clear in its offer of finance the extent of its financial commitment based upon feasibility of the scheme.

The feasibility has included particular items of expenditure which, under the principal development agreement, the landowner will require to see covered, and to this extent the parallel negotiations are beginning to interact. Particularly, not only the professional fees of the landowner's surveyors must be met, the developer must carry out certain accommodation works for the landowner in relation to neighbouring property. This work has also been costed and is in the eyes of the landowner as much part of the development as the development which will be carried out by the developer upon the subject site. In the eyes of the developer, however, the accommodation works are essentially another expense the incurring of which will justify that part of the development with which he is primarily concerned, ie the part from which, despite the overall cost, he hopes to make a profit.

The upshot, in construction terms, is that the developer has a significant cash commitment even before construction starts. Add to this the cost of construction itself (including the accommodation works) and, more closely than ever before, he realises the need to ensure that nothing can be left to chance. If he suffers cost overruns, or the project is delayed, or if he is in dispute with other players, the prospects of letting—even if there are committed pre-lets—all point to prospective additional expense and the diminution or erasure of profit. His initial costs, as outlined above, are essentially fixed. His construction costs, even under a fixed price building contract, can still escalate unless the construction process is managed and controlled, and unless all principal and ancillary players conform to a co-ordinated pattern of activity. The intervening interests of other players are all potentially hazardous. Events must be anticipated.

Consents and approvals in the construction context

Co-operation of third parties such as adjoining or neighbouring landowners will have been assessed. Planning permission will have been obtained for the development including any necessary listed building consent, where demolition or modification of existing buildings is required, and the buildings are either listed or in a conservation area. Inevitably, so much of this ground work will have been done beforehand that individual requirements in the developer's respective contractual commitments should have been substantially met before the deal is signed. They must be carefully catered for.

However, other kinds of approvals must necessarily be obtained along the way, in turn governed by the interests of the respective players and approvals of the players themselves. For every one of these, the process of interaction is relevant. What interest is being served by one player requiring its consent either in such form or subject to such conditions which, in its absolute discretion, it may approve or not as the case may be? The apparent intransigence may be justified, but that justification must be identified and understood. A player should not enter a commitment which can be defeated at the whim of a third party player, unless his own commitment is in some way ring-fenced. (Hope that another player will 'do the decent thing' is no way to proceed and will *never* be acceptable to a bank or funding institution because it creates something over which there can be no control (a purchasing institution is a little different: it can lay down a time scale (see Chapter 6), and will take a view on commitment of funds, based upon a balance between its faith in the developer and the needs of the bank providing interim finance to keep a tight control over draw downs and, in particular, the satisfaction of appropriate tests to justify them (not to speak of letting prospects)).) As has been seen, however, the bank (or fund) which may need to wrest control from the developer in case of breach or non-performance, may need to take a more robust view, and afford for itself discretion beyond the reasonable.

Beyond all of this must always be that a development cannot proceed, be completed or occupied, unless all proper statutory requirements are also met. To this end, all such consents must be applied for, the other players notified, and the results must similarly be notified. All of these matters require contractual commitment. There is no general understanding, as such, in development, albeit that there are expectations (such as those set down in this chapter). For those expectations to be realised, they must be encapsulated in contract, and the construction contract is but one of many.

It is often provided in draft development documentation that all necessary consents and approvals must be obtained before construction is commenced. In practice, this is often unrealistic. First, the development may be being carried out in phases, or at least in steps one or more of which do not require a particular consent to be obtained before work is commenced. Obviously, if one stage is dependent upon another, there may be a justification for the requirement.

Particularly, care is required both as to the substance of the consent being sought and also the need for it. Take, for example, building regulations. Essentially, construction must be carried out in accordance with building regulations. It is helpful if plans and specifications can be shown at the outset to meet these requirements so far as they go, standards of implementation and practical requirements of building inspectors apart. The reality is that, so often, the workings of local government are such that the obtaining of any such consent will not have been achieved by commencement of the project, and may indeed not be achieved until after. In some cases, local authorities will refuse to issue a building regulations consent at all or, if they do, they will in any event wait until after the development is commenced or even completed. In which case, it is necessary for the players to rely upon their appropriate professionals and the contractors to ensure that all construction is designed, planned and implemented in accordance with all relevant regulations for the time being. All of the kinds of inhibitions suggested above will accordingly form a backdrop to a building contract being entered into.

The construction programme

It is inherent in the development process, and not just the building contract, that some programme should be devised. Each of the players is relying upon this programme for delivery of the completed development within a designated time frame, itself placed in the context of a development period. It is only when the development is completed, or a phase or phases of the development are completed, that certain events can follow; overage payments to the landowner under a development agreement, or to the developer under a forward funding agreement, or to the developer again under a forward purchase agreement, repayment to the bank upon the completion of an onward sale under a forward purchase agreement, income coming on stream following first letting and, last but not least, the developer being relieved of his interest burden. The implications are formidable.

Every principal development agreement should, therefore, address the need for a construction programme within the context of a wider development period. The developer may have devised a programme already: but for some reason, in the course of the development, it may need to be re-appraised, particularly if the scheme itself is changed (see below) but more likely because of some external factor which has set back the programme (see Chapter 6). Within that programme again sits the programme to be prescribed by the building contract.

In one sense it does not matter to the landowner that the bank's requirements are more stringent although, if the bank exercises it rights as mortgagee (as we shall see under the sub-heading of Alienation in Chapter 9) breach of a development loan agreement may deliver a new developer to the landowner. (If the bank's short-sightedness in relation to any of the developer's obligations places the developer in breach of his obligations to the landowner, then both suffer, the bank perhaps most of all because it endangers its security, and impairs the developer's ability to repay.)

In another sense neither does it matter to the onward purchaser, who will simply walk away if the development is not completed on time (an unhappy event in legal terms if committed funds must thus be diverted). However, in a forward sale agreement, it will be prescribed in what events the purchaser can walk away. Unnecessary delay will be one of them. The same applies to an agreement for lease with a tenant. In either case, the developer should be under no illusion that he may also face a claim for damages for non-performance.

(A worrying thought—as between himself and other players the developer is charged with providing a building. Contractors are always extremely sensitive to the possibilities of being held liable for consequential loss, for example an occupier's loss of trade from being unable to occupy. See for example the standard JCT forms. An investor's needs are at least in part covered by loss of rent insurance consequent upon delay. It is not often, if at all, that a developer expressly excludes such liability in his development obligations, usually because it is simply not permitted. By covenanting simply to provide a building in accordance with plans, specifications, etc prepared by others, he probably escapes liability for the wrong-doing of others but if, despite this, he fails to deliver anyway he may still incur a liability for delay, albeit that insurance will probably suffice for most practical purposes. A developer's building covenants require great care, and attention must focus upon the true burden which the developer is shouldering.)

The construction programme is therefore a vital component of the development process. In so far, for whatever reason, it cannot be fully developed and fixed in advance of contractual commitments, the implication is that there will need to be machinery in every relevant agreement for provision and approval of the programme. This is prospectively hazardous, even where a degree of reasonableness is injected, depending on the expectations first suggested by the developer. If, for example, it is made clear by a player that he is effectively relying on certain expectations being reached, as a backdrop to entering into legal relations and particularly if it is made clear in the documentation (if there is any such issue to be put subsequently to proof in the absence of an express indication in the development agreement, it will make for difficult litigation), it may even be reasonable for him to refuse consent to an extension of the period, on any grounds let alone otherwise reasonable ones. Usually, matters entirely beyond the developer's control will be permitted as grounds for extension (see Chapter 6).

Other factors may be in play. For example, for the landowner, the timetable for seeing his accommodation works completed may seem too long. For financial partners, the commitment of funds may be impaired. From a banker's point of view, it will usually be found, in a development loan agreement, that if funds are not committed by such and such a time, the difference between the interest payable by the developer under the loan agreement and what the same money would otherwise earn on a deposit account may have to be met. The bank must see its funds being put to work and cannot simply let them lie fallow.

The banker's expectations of timing of repayment of the loan may also be relevant (although given the experience of recent years, this may give rise to a hollow laugh). Again, a purchasing institution under a forward purchase agreement may accept that, while it is not committed to complete the purchase until the development is completed, and until other criteria have been met, undue delay means that there is uncertainty as to whether funds that it has earmarked can be tied up within a certain time frame and whether, after all, it might have been better if its funds had been tied up elsewhere.

Inevitably, the construction programme will be set against the background of discussions and negotiations with contractors, and also the tendering process. The construction programme in the development context is a statement of intention against the background of what is perceived as both practical and feasible translated into a contractual commitment. It may be broken, for example, because of the failure of the contractor and the need to employ a new contractor (and thus modifications to the construction programme in this context are to be seen differently from extension provisions in the building contract): in that case it will need to be modified and every development agreement, whatever the expectations of the players, has to recognise that there may be circumstances which halt the development, albeit only temporarily. Again, some physical characteristic or some external matter affecting the contractor's ability to deliver will give rise to the construction programme being modified.

Building contracts—the tendering process

Just how far the process of regulating the appointment of contractors, indeed the appointments of professionals, should be catered for in a development agreement, depends among other things on the size and complexity of the development and in particular upon the interests of the players. In the case of major development, the performance of the development agreement will rely heavily upon the ability of the contractor to deliver, perhaps through the medium of numerous specialist sub-contractors. Great care will have to be taken in the case of the initial appointment. Moreover, the principal players, because of the size and importance of the development, may also have marked preferences for particular contractors (and indeed their sub-contractors in turn).

Accordingly, the prospect is that in any development agreement, not only the terms of the building contract, but also the identity of the contractor(s) will first need to be approved, upon terms, no doubt with approval not to be unreasonably withheld. Again, the precise form of the building contract will also be in issue, the chosen form of the building contract being, *inter alia*, related to the developer's ability to manage the scheme, as well as what is convenient and appropriate to the circumstances. The relationships between the developer and the players are therefore a vital factor.

As always, any inhibition proposed by a player must be matched with a cause. For example, whatever the landowner lays down, every other agreement is affected by what he prescribes. As with any development proposals, one has to ask is it bankable, will it be acceptable to the end purchaser, can a tenant realistically expect the development to be got under way and completed within the time-scale envisaged?

The practicality is that the developer will have broadly shortlisted his contractors at an early stage, there will have been consultations with his quantity surveyors and with prospective contractors, and all of the players will have been able to see some of the way ahead.

Accordingly, a shortlisting mechanism must be devised for the documentation, to enable prospective contractors to be brought forward in a manner with which the players can feel comfortable. Those with an interest in possibly having to complete the development in the absence of the developer will be concerned with the identity of contractors and the form of contract, while those with a financial interest (who by definition have the same interest also) will also be concerned with the building price, as also anyone interested in sharing in development profit.

While ensuring that the relevant agreement will not allow imposition of a choice of contractor or contract, in face of the terms of another agreement so as to place him in breach, the developer must ensure that the mechanism is workable in practice, and that the contractor is identified, and may be expected to sign a building contract and enter into appropriate collateral agreements without delay.

Players place themselves at risk if collateral agreements (warranties) are signed up late. It is only slightly less of a problem when the contractor's tender documents (or a professional's appointment) expressly prescribe for it, and the collateral agreement prescribes for the whole of the contractor's function from inception, however late it is entered into.

Perhaps more seriously, it is often the case that the building contract is itself signed up late and this can be equally worrying for financiers and others holding development agreements of their various kinds with the developer. Although some may consider it even amusing to hear of a building contract not being signed until after practical completion, it is a bad practice and, in any case, can be easily avoided by the imposition of a little discipline (a funder paying out on a certificate meanwhile has only itself to blame). Development should always be seen as a disciplined process. Lack of discipline unfortunately goes hand in hand with omission of all kinds, and trusting to luck was never a basis of sound business.

Licence to go on site

Where the developer owns the site outright, and whether he has entered into loan finance commitments under which the site is secured, he is on site as of right in any event.

However, if he is performing development obligations on land which does not belong him, eg under a development agreement with a landowner, or under a forward funding agreement where the institution will hold the land (or the entitlement to it pursuant to a principal development agreement), there are other issues to be considered. First, it is implicit that the developer's natural right to enter the land will only arise as and when he has actually acquired the relevant major interest.

It is therefore necessary, in any such agreement, for express licence to be given to go on site meanwhile. The licence will itself only be granted upon terms. Those terms will essentially ensure that the licence is confined to the carrying out of the construction elements of the development. In turn, carrying out that process can only be done so long as it is in accordance with all the terms of the development agreement.

It is to be assumed, therefore, that the licence will be made conditional throughout upon such compliance, the corollary to this being that non-compliance may in due course lead to curtailment of the licence. That is the landowner's/institution's security, and it is also the developer's loss if the building contract is in turn inconsistent with, and in turn inimical to, the licence provisions of the development agreement, ie, loss of licence consequently places the developer in breach of the building contract.

In any event, if the developer is carrying out work on land which will never form part of his major interest in due course, for example for the purpose of constructing a public library, or other accommodation works on the nearby highway mentioned earlier, he must in any case ensure he has licence and comply with such conditions as may be imposed by the development agreement in that regard. They must be tested at the outset as being practical and feasible for fear that either inability to perform, or breach, may invalidate licence to go on the wider development site, quite apart from any damages ensuing in favour of the contractor.

Thus, where a developer is in breach, the implication is that licence to enter will be withdrawn, which again can only impact adversely on the other players quite apart from the developer's relationship with the contractor. (see Chapter 9). In anticipation of that chapter it is as well now to look further at the rights of a developer going onto a site, afforded to him by a landowner who will in due course grant him (or a fund) a major interest, and also the rights of a developer going on site which is now owned by an institutional purchaser under a forward funding agreement, under which the developer expects no major interest at the end, but may earn an overage payment and/or some other reward for his pains, eg a project management fee. (In respect of the latter, time was when overage upon delivery of a building could be zero rated for VAT. No more, so that the fee will be standard rated, as with other elements of the development cost.)

Those advising landowners on conditions for licence to enter will wish, in addition, to consider those matters which are ancillary to the construction process. The construction process itself should also embrace all the relevant interests of third parties (as distinct from the players in the development), particularly adjoining owners, eg diversion of pipes and other conducting media, support of walls, land, etc and the building contract may need additional special provisions and/or be hedged around by a method statement.

The need to comply with statutory requirements, or an express obligation not to cause nuisance or interference with others may not on its own suffice. For example, traffic movements, even on the open road, may need to be regulated. Vehicles departing may leave a trail of debris which needs to be cleaned away, protective site hoardings may be required to be erected around the site, security measures taken to prevent members of the public entering and being injured, the highways authority may need to give express consent for the erection of scaffolding or safety barriers in the street, and other particular requirements may need to be met for the purpose of the particular development.

These issues may be critical for a local authority landowner, for example, and because its functions as local authority is its highest priority, it will therefore be appropriate to make these contractual matters in addition to any powers it may have as a local authority. Many of such issues, having originated both within a principal development agreement, and also outside it, may also have to be reflected as appropriate in the building contract. Standard forms contemplate many of such issues (for example damage to highways under cl 30, ICE Conditions, 6 ed) but there is no excuse for drawing a building or engineering contract in complete isolation, and without thinking of the relationship between that contract and any relevant development agreement. Such matters must be drawn to the attention of the person preparing the contract, and catered for accordingly.

Again, there may be environmental issues which require the work not just to be done, but to be done in a certain way, and so it is not just the 'what' but the 'how to' factors which will first need to be built into the development agreement, and in particular to the terms for licence to enter (and also, by implication, so far as necessary into any relevant building contract).

Finally, where the developer is in breach of his obligations to his bank providing finance for the development, he may yet be precluded from proceeding further and the bank may be seeking a fresh developer, with all the implications this may have for the relationship with the landowner, the status of the building contract apart. (See above and as to alienation in Chapter 9).

Procuration of construction versus implementation *per se*

It is to be assumed that every player will prescribe in so many words that the developer will carry out the project in a good and workmanlike manner and so on, all of which is expanded upon below. As between the developer and each of the major players, and according to each of their respective development agreements, the developer is apparently standing in the shoes of the contractor, the professionals and everyone else whom the developer appoints to assist him in the development process. Therefore, in one real sense, the developer is himself perceived as a contractor. The primary building obligation in the eyes of each of the players rests upon him according to the development agreement in question. When those obligations are breached, perhaps irretrievably, the player in question also looks to such collateral agreements or warranties that he has with subsidiary players, the contractors and professionals, as well as to the contractual commitments of the developer and the security he has given. But how deeply do the developer's responsibilities reach?

The developer may have ring-fenced his commitments to ensure he is being required only to produce what his contractor and professionals have been required to produce. But failure to produce at least this much, or in any case breach of a commitment to provide something more, may raise questions of consequential loss, and the developer must tread warily. The building obligation is an almost unique function in that, while a primary obligation is imposed on the developer, almost certainly, unless the developer is a contractor, there will be subsidiary relationships with contractors and others whereby the obligations are actually performed. Accordingly, the judgment to be exercised and the distinction to be made lies in the choice of obligation, ie is the developer's skill in providing the development itself to be relied on, or should his obligation essentially lie in procuring the development in accordance with plans, specifications, etc and particularly procuring the commitment of others? Once the obligations themselves are prescribed, precisely what can be expected of this developer entering into these obligations at this precise moment? Is it possible that, notwithstanding the contractual obligations, there may be some mitigating factor which dilutes the personal obligations of the developer in some way? It is questions such as these which have led, in turn, to developers' warranties to third parties as well, and so questions of consequential loss arising through all such contractual commitments should be considered seriously.

For example, a developer may be required to warrant that he has the necessary skill and care to carry out the development in all respects and that he will use that skill to the best effect throughout the course of the development. In so doing, he is maximising the prospective claims against him in the event of failure by assuming the mantle not just of responsibility, but also of the skills he must hire in order to carry out the development. For that reason, alone, a developer may be discouraged from giving any such warranty, and having first considered the prospective impact of his principal obligations he must think, very carefully, of the consequences of so doing. If the developer is asked to give warranties to those benefiting from the development, perhaps a tenant taking a lease from an investing institution, he should seek there also to avoid a commitment reflecting skills which he himself does not actually have.

In any event he must always seek to avoid entering into a contractual commitment which may give rise to claims for consequential loss, and in particular he should be discouraged from warranting a building's suitability for a particular purpose. Blandly drawn building covenants may be adorned with a velvet glove which hides an iron fist. Careful drafting can confine exposure to the proper level of expectation, but so often the true nature of development obligations imposed is not fully addressed.

On the other hand, there may be some other weakness in the project which makes it appropriate that the developer should notwithstanding shoulder this burden. If the developer really does have this skill, if it has a track record and, by any objective standard it is likely to perform, a player in a contractual relationship with the developer is likely to look more to the developer's judgment than to the availability of other safeguards. That is not to say that those safeguards are not taken: rather, it is a matter of concentrating reliance upon the developer.

A contractual commitment, however, can crystallise these sentiments and, in turn, the developer may find that the door is open to a more relaxed attitude on the part of the other players in relation to those matters which the developer is undertaking to procure. The taking of collateral protection from others to provide additional protection is in any case only a recent phenomenon in the overall scale of things.

General building obligations

The building obligations in a development agreement will usually commence with a general clause that not only will the developer build in a good and workmanlike manner but also, in so many words, that he will do so with good quality materials of their several kinds. It is likely that the developer will have little option to do anything else having been required to have the bills of quantities and specifications duly scrutinised, and not least also having had prescribed for him his construction obligations in terms of what will satisfy competent authorities, and everything is circumscribed by the kinds of considerations mentioned above.

Depending upon the nature of the exercise, the question of materials is not just a matter for prescription by quantity surveyors and incorporation into the building contract. Funders, investors and end users are particularly concerned that appropriate standards are maintained and can be expected to prescribe for these in considerable detail in every relevant development agreement. Such provisions are usually not inherently controversial but may represent an area in which, in procuring the development in accordance with the building contract, the developer may be undertaking a particular responsibility to ensure not just that the building contract so prescribes but that that is what happens, thus placing an additional burden on him. No matter, for example, that the fund's surveyor did not check the specifications fully and compare with the work in hand if the funding agreement expressly places the onus on the developer despite such an omission. (See also Chapter 6.)

The obligation will then extend to carrying out the project in accordance with all approved plans, specifications, relevant consents, etc. Apart from relevant consents and approvals, it will be provided that the development be carried out in accordance with certain plans which have first been approved by the relevant player. These will have usually been approved in advance and, as the development progresses, further plans may require to be approved particularly if there are modifications to be made. The extent of approval and the need for it will be expressly determined according to the interests of the player in question. Perhaps the landowner has particular requirements which must be met, the banker wants to ensure that they are so met and a contracted purchaser and tenant respectively, as end users, each have specific expectations related to their individual interests. All such matters are relevant to timing and questions of delay.

Development periods

Delays caused *by* the contractor are one thing, delays caused *to* the contractor are another and may impact directly on price. Quantity surveyors, in negotiating the building contract, should be made fully aware of the developer's contractual commitments, the nature of them and the impact upon feasibility and timing. One wonders how often this is done in this context, although special construction requirements of a development agreement are themselves usually imported successfully into the building contract. Determination of the construction period is essentially left to the advice of quantity surveyors in consultation with tendering contractors, notwithstanding that all other interests revolve around what they have prescribed. A construction programme is usually devised under the provisions of a development agreement so that compliance then becomes part of it. It would be a bizarre approvals process which allowed insistence upon a construction period to which no contractor could sensibly subscribe in his tender.

It is, therefore, as well that consideration be given to the opposite side of the coin and, in particular, how many and to what extent additional plans or specifications may need to be approved by other players, what other approvals may be required from whom, and the impact on timing accordingly. The knack, in development agreements, is to consider not just the programme but also what other mishaps and pitfalls one can reasonably expect, how much time the approvals process may take, and any other relevant factors. A development period will emerge from this within the framework of which the construction programme will sit, a sort of construction programme plus a bit more for luck! The development period is a vital component in a development agreement. If the developer exceeds it, then sanctions may be applied (see Chapters 6 and 9).

So far as concerns those actually giving approval are concerned, it may seem a little trite to suggest that they ought to know why. However, by way of anecdote, personal experience of one public sector body in particular showed that, for example, testing of materials by one of its subsidiary elements in one capacity was taken by a developer as being an approval for the purpose of another element representing the landowner role of the authority in question, which, in the event, it was not; nor was it intended to be. The body in question was not a local authority, as it happens, and neither was it a mistake of statutory authority, but it simply goes to show that in a large organisation with many departments, it is particularly important that there is clear internal communication and even clearer external presentation.

Management contracting

Any building contract which devolves a management responsibility onto the contractor (of course, all building contracts do to some extent, that is to say, in that sub-contractors of one kind or another are likely to be appointed) must be drawn in such a way as to reflect the developer's commitments.

This is not to say that the two cannot be made to align: the issue is how it can be done, in the subject case, and how effectively the developer's respective obligations elsewhere can be covered. The notion is simple, if not simplistic, but the pursuit of apparent convenience by a developer, while appropriate in one case, may be disastrous in another. In any event, where such management functions are devolved, the player who stands to lose the most in consequence of default may be advised to take stronger powers to avoid that default.

Nevertheless, assuming the form of the building contract has been appropriately approved under the relevant documents, it is not surprising that the developer's obligations will, notwithstanding, also include that the developer will carry out the development in accordance with the terms of the building contract, all relevant codes of practice, British Standards and so on, which is better for the developer if his responsibilities are confined in this way. If he does all of that, to the letter, he has perhaps not, therefore, failed.

A managed contract effectively devolves implementation of responsibilities without the contractor necessarily performing them himself. Professional appointments, even some contracting functions may be engaged directly by the employer and responsibility may seem to be diffused. Contrast a design and build contract which is essentially a package deal which may suit a developer admirably, and more particularly so the other players, if the developer has limited resources or capabilities or is simply a conduit for a joint venture of wider ranging, perhaps non-specialist, interests.

CDM

A new layer of regulations, the Construction (Design and Management) Regulations 1994 (SI No 3140), came into force on 31 March 1995, CDM, 'Condam' as it has been dubbed by some, requiring the appointment of a 'planning supervisor' to supervise health and safety aspects of design and construction, and as to the preparation of a health and safety plan for the project. There must usually be a principal contractor as well, who will undertake a primary role in implementation of safety measures. Developers now need to consider the impact of these regulations, what additional appointments need to be made, which of the professional team if any will most effectively perform the role in the subject case, whether the appointment will satisfy the bank, and so on. Landowners, institutions and other principal players may be expected to prescribe for such appointments, or at least require that their prior approval be sought. Collateral agreements may, therefore, be required from such persons to reflect these additional duties.

Approval of works

Finally, there is the matter of satisfaction with work done and not necessarily in terms of certification and related events. A bold declaration that the developer will do this in accordance with that creates uncertainty, not least for the developer. He will, therefore, usually comply with his several obligations 'to the reasonable satisfaction' of the player in question. What is reasonable is always a matter of degree. If the obligation is to carry out, say, in all respects to the satisfaction of the player, the test is entirely subjective: the obligation may never be or be deemed complied with and the developer can be seen potentially as permanently in breach even though his architect has issued a certificate under the building contract (see Chapter 6). At the hands of a landowner, whose subjective satisfaction alone would lead to grant of the major interest, pursuit of the objective may be fruitless or, at least, delayed through capriciousness. For the bank wanting to realise its security in due course, for the purchaser and also the tenant, this can never be wholly satisfactory. Absolute obligations should always be resisted and, where possible, some objective test interposed between the parties. Not that this, on its own, will suffice (see also Chapters 6 and 9).

Supervision—defective works

Every well drawn development agreement prescribes for supervision and monitoring. Construction is a lengthy process and the adoption of fast track methods in particular, while speeding the overall process, carries with it the need to ensure that not only is the project kept on track in terms of timing but that all works are carried out properly.

Both the developer's and the contractor's worst nightmare is the discovery of a defect which requires the undoing of otherwise perfectly good work. Neither is it just a matter of the relationship between the developer and the contractor, even in the case of the developer as personified either by his supervising architect or employer's representative depending upon the form of the building contract.

It is unhappily the case that other checks and balances are required. The principal players will themselves wish to see that standards are being maintained. It reflects not only the requirements of the building contract but also the performance, or perhaps the non-performance, of the developer's obligations as developer. To this end, therefore, the principal players, usually through their own representatives such as supervising surveyors, will seek to afford themselves the right (as always, in contract, in the relevant development agreement) to enter upon the site to inspect, take tests and so on. There are clear implications here for obstruction or delay to the construction process.

In any case, the mechanisms for the carrying out of supervision must, in turn, be suitably reflected by the terms of the building contract. This is primarily achieved *via* the interface between the terms of the building contract itself and the powers of the architect or employer's representative on the one hand, and the duties of the architect or employer's representative as reflected in his terms of engagement, on the other. In this way, if the developer is properly called to account by one of the other principal players under a development agreement, the concerns of the particular principal player can for the most part be satisfied.

A properly advised developer will ensure that any such rights afforded to a principal player will be circumscribed by inhibitions in the development agreement so as not to impede the construction process, nor to cause damage (preferably common law damage as opposed to damage to the structure) and, where tests are taken, and to the extent that they show that the work was not defective, there should also be provision for the cost of making good including, if possible, consequential loss items as well. This is a difficult area, but in general terms, while supervision is essential, the taking of tests upon the structure by the players is perhaps less than routine and used as a fallback measure only where there is genuine concern that there may be some fault in the construction process, unless the process itself demands that such steps be taken in order to prove fitness for the next stage in the process.

Routine testing of materials, prior to use in the construction, is another matter entirely. The prescribing of materials is in any case carried out initially and provided for in the specification. Testing of samples of the materials actually supplied is another matter and, ideally, is best done before they are *in situ*. A developer ultimately has to accept that a development agreement of whatever kind may contain safeguards, albeit that in most cases this will be achieved by relation back to the building contract. As to delay in consequence of testing, see Chapter 6.

Finally, any construction requirements which are not reflected in the building contract imply a commitment on the part of the developer which reposes with him alone, questions of certification apart (again see Chapter 6).

Supervision—generally

Defective works are but one facet of the supervision process. As between the developer and the principal players, it is essential that there is an on-going dialogue. Again, this can only be provided for contractually. In order to minimise the possibilities of dissatisfaction with work, it is essential that there be agreed mechanisms for liaison. This may take the form of affording the right for supervising surveyors to attend site meetings. Depending upon the size and scope of the development, it may be appropriate for permitted attendance to be limited only to formal site meetings. In any case, a supervising surveyor should usually be supplied with working drawings, specifications, bills of quantities and so on. The supervising surveyor, of say the bank or landowner, will also be charged with the task of giving consents and approvals. In addition, it will be provided that he is to receive requests for consent to appoint professionals and contractors, to approve plans and specifications, to receive copies of valuations given by quantity surveyors and certificates issued by architects and so on. For much of the time he will be happy to rely on the flow of information which will demonstrate to him that the professional team are doing their job effectively.

This flow of information will also indicate not only whether the development is being carried out in a proper manner but also whether there are difficulties, prospective if not actual delays, etc. When it becomes necessary for him to become more pro-active, he must be given the facility to inspect for himself, and to attend meetings and to receive information at first hand. It may not always be necessary for him to do so, and as a protection against any misjudgement, a player will prescribe that approvals given, attendances and so on, and very particularly non-attendances and other omissions shall *not* relieve the developer of any of his duties. Such a provision may not relieve the player in question of the consequences of pure negligence, but it should serve to maintain a balance of duty. One can neither generalise nor speculate, but the omission of such a clause will undoubtedly offer at least the possibility of an escape route for a developer in default.

There is a dilemma for those in a supervising role as to the steps that may be taken in the event that fault is actually found. First, a developer should discourage the assumption of a right by a player through his supervising surveyor to instruct professionals or the contractor. (It is another matter if an appointment has been assigned or novated.)

Meanwhile, an appointee has, or should have, only one master and should not be required to accept contrary instructions. A warranty, on the other hand, may often prescribe that the appointee will do precisely that. However, in such circumstances, if not in consequence of assignment by the employer or novation of the appointment in question, the reason may be that a bank or fund has assumed the right to do so on taking over the development upon notifying an event of default. The professional concerned will want to provide that this may be permitted only upon all outstanding fees being paid, and upon a commitment to perform all the employer's obligations in the future. The developer, on the other hand, thus deprived of his authority, must look to his relationship with the bank or fund. The relevant development (loan/finance) agreement must make clear the circumstances in which exercise of the power arises (usually a notified event of default which the developer has not effectively remedied within the prescribed period contained in a notice in that behalf).

In some development agreements, the draftsman sometimes slips in a bland proviso, on the one hand prescribing that the supervising surveyor shall not have power to give instructions directly but, on the other, adding such words as 'except in emergency' (whatever that may mean). In practice, it is better to be entirely clear as to the line of command and responsibility.

Finally, every intervention is, prospectively, a source of delay. If there is a delay, there is an implication of fault and it is then a question of defining precisely where the fault (if any) lies. The fault itself must be precisely identified because it may impact on each of the players in different ways. If the contractor is blameless and the fault lies with a poorly regulated, or over-regulated, supervisory process in a development agreement, it may result in the developer being severely out of pocket through his own default as employer under the building contract, apart from being in breach of contractual obligations to other principal players who, in the particular circumstances, are not tainted with the delay in question. (Another example of when is a development cost not a development cost? Answer: because the bank took powers in the loan agreement affording its overbearing surveyor to hold up the development unnecessarily, with consequential cost implications for the developer under the building contract.)

It is so much easier to draft, or approve, documents at the outset with possible consequences in mind. A developer may be said always to be in breach of some kind of contractual obligation. If the bank are being unreasonable but are entitled to exercise a discretion, there may be little he can do except capitulate, or go out on a limb and thus challenge the bank. This book cannot encourage any player to place himself in breach but must encourage every player to consider the consequences of his actions as far down the line as possible, and the extent of his own accountability.

Insurance and indemnity

Every player has a prospective insurable interest. It consists in two principal elements of his involvement. First, there is the matter of his own responsibilities and the consequences of his failure to perform. Secondly, perceiving the outcome of the development and the benefits to be derived from it, he may wish to insure against the failure of others, ie to protect his potential benefit. For example, if income fails to come on stream in time, because construction has been delayed and, in turn, contracted tenants cannot occupy, loss of rent insurance will obviously ameliorate the immediate consequences of that delay.

It is necessary to identify as far as possible the risks naturally attendant upon each part of the development process and its outcome. Well drawn development agreements prescribe for insurances to be effected in order to hedge against the consequences of a number of perils which may arise in the course of the development (as well as the construction) process.

Buildings insurance

Every well drawn development agreement will require the developer to insure the works. This insurance should also be required to cover any attendant professional fees and VAT. Thus, if the premises are destroyed, there should be sufficient cover without further funding to complete the development. (If the damage causes delay to completion of the development, the benefits of loss of rent insurance will become only too clear.) If, under the relevant development agreement the insurance monies must be paid to the bank or fund, then they must be credited to development cost so as to ameliorate actual or notional interest, and the agreement must not therefore inhibit double draw down, as it were, to cover the same ground as earlier draw downs. (This is to be distinguished from provisions in loan agreements which state that where any capital is actually repaid it cannot be drawn down a second time.) Otherwise, insurance monies may be paid directly to the developer who will thus not be able to draw down any more development finance as such in respect of that particular damage.

Shortfalls in insurance proceeds are another matter and, usually, the developer must make them good himself. Arguably, if the insurance is to be as prescribed or permitted by the bank/fund in an arbitrary manner (extremely unlikely) a developer could prescribe in the agreement (even more unlikely) that the bank/fund should meet the excess out of its own monies. There is, nevertheless, nothing to prevent the developer from effecting such further insurance as he considers necessary, at his own cost, if he finds himself in such a dilemma.

Buildings insurance, covering fire, etc will also be required by a landowner under a development agreement because it is only completion of the development, and the delivery of certain benefits to the landowner, which will result in a major interest being granted to the developer. Again, a bank or forward purchasing institution will require insurance to be effected, in the case of the former so as to recoup the outlay upon advances so far made and, in the case of both to ensure that the product is delivered. An institutional purchaser under a forward funding agreement, tenants, joint venture partners with various financial interests, etc all have a concern to see that buildings insurance is put in place. There should be consistency between agreements to avoid overlap of cover, or breach of insurance obligation.

Building contracts in any case require contractors themselves to effect appropriate insurances. The requirements will also go as far as public liability and, indeed, developers and others who may suffer like claims, should themselves also always carry public liability cover.

Period of insurance and contractor's insurances

A development agreement will normally require the developer to insure while the project is being carried out. Once completed, it depends thereafter upon who actually owns the insured property and the nature of the interests of various players, where the need for insurance specifically lies. However, before examining this principle, it is important to reflect on the various insurable interests which subsist *during* the development, and within that the construction process. The practicality is that, during construction, the principal insurance relating to the development will be effected by the contractor. It is logical, therefore, in imposing an insurance obligation on the developer to allow a proviso that, while the contractor's insurances are in force in respect of the project, then so far as they go, ie towards meeting the particular obligations of the developer, the effecting of such insurances will suffice for the purpose of the development agreement. Where possible, interested parties should become joint insured or at the very least have a noted interest in the policy even though the latter does not afford them the ability to adopt a pro-active role in the making of a claim. Any obligation to insure jointly with the contractor is obviously effected only by agreement with the contractor.

So long as the contractor is obliged to insure, or can have insurance effected for him if he fails, such a process ought to suffice. It should be remembered at all times that, if there is a duplication of insurance, there is the prospect that, once one claim is met, another insurer will look to the principle of 'other indemnity' with the consequence that ultimate division of the one and only cake has been achieved consequent upon payment of unnecessary premiums.

(Insurance has been unkindly described as a contract of indemnity under which, in consideration of a sum called a premium, the insurer agrees to indemnify the insured against certain risks, subject to conditions which, upon application in case of damage by an insured risk, so distinguish the insured that the insurer is not obliged to meet the claim!—the subject deserves the most careful attention!)

However, under most building contracts, once practical completion has been reached the contractor's liability to insure falls away. This may, in turn, expose the developer to an intermediate responsibility to insure, for example pending sale, or because his forward purchaser has rejected practical completion in terms of the forward purchase agreement, has refused to complete the purchase and a dispute is in full swing.

If the developer fails to insure or procure insurance, his lending banker may do so in his stead and add the cost to the advance. While the developer maintains an interest in the development, he must insure in any event, or see to it that others do, in order to be able notwithstanding fire or other peril to make good the damage and to realise the development as an asset, whether by way of onward sale, or by letting, or simply as an asset on his balance sheet. As a prospective landlord he probably has a commitment to insure in any case.

Once the development is sold on, risk for buildings clearly passes to the purchaser, but precisely how far? As at completion of the development, the purchaser under a forward purchase agreement, for example, will complete his purchase and be in the same position as an investor under a forward funding agreement who had acquired the major interest (or was entitled to it) at the outset. The buildings are clearly at his full risk. What then is the outstanding interest of the developer?

Insuring the overage

Until the premises are let, the prospect is that the fund or institution will in any case require the developer to stand in the tenant's shoes to the extent of unlet portions. Prospectively, if not through an actual lease containing provisions for surrender on letting to an occupation tenant in due course, the developer will meanwhile probably have to meet at least the cost of buildings insurance. The practicality is that the purchaser, as owner, will insure the buildings and pass the whole or part, as the case may be, of the cost back to the developer in the same way he would a tenant. Most leases of institutional quality place an obligation upon the landlord to insure the buildings (and to lay out the proceeds in reinstatement) and the tenant, in turn, undertakes to pay the premium, or at least the relevant proportion of the premium attributable to the premises to be demised to him.

It does not necessarily follow that the developer will have to pay for insurance: he may have to, as in the example above. However, much like a tenant in occupation, until he derives a benefit from the development—overage, the developer must ensure that the building remains insured. It is important in development agreements, therefore, that where a developer's overage is at stake, the developer sees to it that there is some commitment on the part of the fund, post practical completion, to effect such insurance or, at the very least, to reinstate the premises in the case of damage by insured risks. Once all prospects of overage have evaporated, for whatever reason, the developer's insurable interest dies with it.

Reinstatement in course of works

If damage is caused by insured risks during the course of construction, then the developer will probably be required under the development agreement to ensure that all damage caused is reinstated without delay. This assumes a continuing obligation on the part of the developer to carry out the development and there may be consequential set-backs for the construction programme in consequence of the delay (See Chapter 6.) This clearly triggers the corresponding contractor's obligations, and if the contractor has failed to insure (unlikely in practice) and the developer in turn has failed to insure, a severe breach will have occurred. In practice, his bank or fund will have monitored the obligations and required evidence that all appropriate insurances are in force. (See also as to draw down under **Buildings insurance** above).

Some forward funding agreements go so far as to relieve the developer from his development obligations where the damage is so severe that there is little prospect of the development being completed (on time). Such instances must be rare: however, occasionally circumstances may arise in which, perhaps for example because of the dependence of the development upon other premises which are similarly destroyed, the practicalities evaporate into impossibility. Any such release should only be contemplated where there is no reasonable prospect of the project being resumed, and thus no prospect of overage for the developer.

The insurers

Contractors' insurance apart, the principal players will usually require the developer to effect insurance, if not in a named office, then in an office or offices (reasonably) acceptable to the player in question and against such risks, upon such terms and in such amount as may be prescribed, reserving the right to effect insurance and to debit the developer and/or development cost accordingly. Prospective insureds should always ensure that their interests are protected at all times and, particularly, care must be taken to ensure full cover from the point at which the contractors' insurance falls away. Care is nonetheless required to ensure that insurance provisions do not conflict, ie development agreements *inter se* and the building contract.

Indemnity clauses in development agreements

Insurance is a contract of indemnity. Accordingly, a full indemnity purported to be given by the developer for all default under the development agreement may, unless qualified in some way, have effect to avoid an insurance policy: the 'other indemnity' principle again. All development agreements should contain general indemnity clauses in order to sweep up any outstanding obligations and particularly breaches. However, it is ultimately in the interests of all concerned to provide expressly that the indemnity is effective to the extent only of sums not actually recoverable/recovered from insurers.

In circumstances where insurance is not effected by the developer, the indemnity requires closer analysis. For example, the development may be complete, the contractor's insurance may have fallen away, the development is unlet and the developer is awaiting lettings before recovering his overage. On the basic principle that a plaintiff must mitigate his loss, it goes without saying that he can reasonably look to the fund, by then owning the property, not only to insure but to make good damage for failure to insure. Again, such obligations require express provision.

Particular care is required as to the period during which any indemnity should be required to be given. There may be a point in a development agreement, of whatever kind, when there is no reasonable prospect of the developer deriving any further benefit, even perhaps when the building is complete and, in any event, when the developer has derived such benefit as he may.

One has become used to seeing development agreements in which there is a completion date, a settlement date, etc all signifying events in the process, without clear thought to the other side of the coin, the respective insurance obligations, when they arise, when they end, when one responsibility takes over from another, and so also the mobility of insurable interests. Often it is clear from the circumstances, but it is so much easier to make it entirely clear from the documents.

PI cover

Professional indemnity insurance is usually carried by developers. A clear need to do so is signalled by the variety of commitments into which a developer enters. PI cover for professional advisers as such, is well advanced, hence earlier comments about insurers' reluctance to sanction professionals entering into contractual commitments which may impact directly on liabilities which professionals may incur and, in turn, claims made upon insurance policies. This is a natural consequence of the deployment of all skills, of whatever kind. As with any policy of insurance, the insured must look closely at the terms of the insurance to consider the parameters of the cover which the policy provides. Likely as not, there will be limitations on the professional commitments which can be given by him or at least, if they are given, then upon the nature and level of indemnity which the insurer will assume or cease to assume. Sometimes this will be implicit because the insured had voluntarily undertaken a responsibility beyond the scope of his professional duties contemplated by the policy.

It is beyond the scope of this book to look in depth at the role of an insurance broker and, in any case, the relationship between client and broker will itself be circumscribed by any express terms of engagement between them. However, when brokers are engaged to arrange suitable cover, it is perhaps an over simplification (but nonetheless a general principle) that the broker is being engaged by the client to procure insurance which is suitable for him. Turning to the person whose complaint may lead to an insurance claim being made at all, it is incumbent on the developer, any assignee of an appointment or one who novates an appointment, or who takes the benefit of a warranty, to be satisfied that the developer or professional in question is resourced to meet his obligations. In turn, this suggests that one should be looking closely to the PI cover available to the developer or professional in question. One wonders how often this is done once the project is under way. Suffice it to say here that legal complexity abounds, but as with much else in this life, clarity of thought and purpose is helpful.

A well drawn appointment, upon which the full benefit of a warranty relies, and indeed a well drawn warranty also, will lay down express requirements as to professional indemnity insurance. Failure to maintain that insurance may place the professional in breach of his contractual obligations. Not that such measures are fool-proof: the professional may let cover lapse at a critical time in the performance of his duties and before the lapse has been noted. The track record of the professional, and a great deal of common sense, will determine the importance of PI cover in context.

As the development industry begins to pick up, it will be interesting to see how the conflicting interests in the insurance debate will further develop their thinking, given the dramatic change in culture over the last 15 years or so. An added dimension today is defects liability insurance incorporating protection for contractors and professionals. Possibly, the time has yet to come when such insurance will be seen as an answer to so many (if not all) of the problems which have arisen in practice and which have served to add so much complexity to the development process. In an ideal world, perhaps a cradle to the grave insurance will some day become commonplace in which professionals, contractors and all relevant players, will be covered from inception of their involvement in the project, and the cover will merge in defects liability insurance on completion. Professional fees could perhaps reduce against truly comprehensive cover initiated by the developer which would remain in place until statutory limitation served to evaporate liability both in contract and tort.

Overview

The whole of the construction process is a balancing act between the respective players, underpinned by a building contract or contracts. Just as the players will have laid down requirements as to appointment of professionals, the consequences of a developer's need to replace them, additional appointees and so on, they will be particularly concerned about the identity of the building contractor, the form of the contract, and the essential commercial terms including price. Price will be of varying relevance depending upon the interest of the player in question. Even without an immediate financial interest in the consequences of the development, every player will have some interest in pricing, if only in terms of viability and feasibility and the actual prospects of successful outcome.

Means must be found to ensure that all consents and approvals which impact on the construction process itself are duly obtained and that such which are obtained conform to the expectations of the players, that machinery exists for ensuring that they are obtained at all, and that omissions are made good. The approvals process should be sufficiently flexible to allow for any necessary consents to be applied for at appropriate times during the development process.

In turn, however carefully contrived a construction programme, not only the needs of the contractor but the conduct of any other ancillary processes beyond the immediate confines of the building contract, should be considered and accommodated as necessary. In practice, these processes will be largely anticipated by the building contract but, in the case of a particularly complex transaction, it is helpful to negotiate into the package the knock on effect of the needs of interested parties and related events, including price implications.

The tendering of building contracts, unless the contractor has been identified at the outset (in which case one is catering in effect for the outside chance of a replacement) must be subjected to a satisfactory mechanism. In very large projects, the identity of the contractor, as well as the terms and the price, will come under intense scrutiny. Not only the building contract itself but sub-contracts also will be similarly scrutinised including, not least, the need to sub-contract. Where specialist works are inevitably involved, approvals of sub-contractors and sub-contracts will assume particular importance. It also goes without saying that the principal players will be concerned to receive warranties in a suitable form from contractors and sub-contractors, always remembering that however well drafted such warranties, the benefit to be derived will be circumscribed by the underlying contract to which the warranty in question relates.

Licence to go on site to carry out works is only required where the developer does not have such a right as of right. He clearly has such a right if he owns the site albeit supported by bank finance, and the giving of security. He does not have such a right, say under a development agreement or a forward funding agreement, under which he does not own land as such, unless it is expressly conferred upon him. The prospect is that licence will be granted upon terms reflecting the interests of the landowner in question and, if necessary, any possible inconvenience to adjoining or neighbouring properties. However cautious the developer, a landowner will wish to ensure that the developer takes suitable precautions so that the landowner may not be held liable for permitting activity which causes damage, in the common law sense, of one kind or another.

A developer's building obligations can often be blandly drawn with apparently marginal shades of emphasis having nonetheless dramatically different effects. If the developer is being cast in the role of builder, is it his skills, or his skill in procuring the contractor's skills such as they are, which are being looked for? Is the developer being required to procure the development in accordance with the terms of the building contract, however poorly designed or specified or however poor the techniques to be applied, or is it his own skill which is being relied upon to procure the construction? If the latter, depending upon how the provisions are worded, it may be that the developer will also acquire consequential loss liabilities and his solicitor should amend the development documentation to mitigate this prospect. The enormity of the responsibility can be ameliorated by limiting the responsibility to procurement in terms of delivering what his contractors and professionals are required to deliver, in clear terms of bringing about that result alone, whether or not the result itself is desirable although he can, in turn, (as also the other players through the medium of warranties) call the contractor and professionals to account for their own shortcomings so far as they go in contex.

General buildings obligations should, therefore, be regarded in that light and building contracts and appointments should be drawn to reflect any particular characteristics of the site, relevant consents and the development agreement.

Finally, never underestimate the need to insure against all necessary risks and in appropriate amounts, and to ensure that there is no unnecessary overlap of insurable interests. There should be an accommodation of such matters during the construction period but, equally, where interests begin to diverge, for example upon practical completion of the works, there should be a consequential realignment of interests for insurance purposes, and again at the end of the development period. Accordingly, who requires to be insured, against what and for how long?

The following checklist should help to crystallise the above thoughts.

Checklist

1. As contractual commitments of all kinds are undertaken consider what consents are required.
   1.1 From whom?
   1.2 When?
   1.3 How?
2. How may the obtaining of consents impact upon timing?
3. If one player is entitled to refuse consent which ought not properly to bewithheld, how may this impact upon other contractual commitments? Can one afford to yield to such a requirement? If so, what is the consequence? Who has the most to lose?
4. How has the construction programme been compiled? Does it depend upon purely construction related considerations? Are there other factors to be taken into account; if so what factors and do they include the interests of whatever kind of parties other than the employer and the contractor? How do the provisions of the building contract sit within it?
5. If licence to go on site is required, what special features should govern conduct of the activity on site? Will it suffice that the contractor is there merely to carry out construction?
6. What interests other than those of the developer (employer) and the contractor will or may be affected by licence to go on site?

Are any additional consents, for example affecting the rights of third parties or the requirements of the local authority, required? If the landowner lays down particular requirements, will they, upon analysis, be practical and feasible in terms of what may reasonably be expected of the contractor? Will it impact on cost, or timing or both?

7. What is the developer's role in construction? Is he being treated as a builder or a procurer of the services of others? To what extent is he associated with the skills of others? Is he assumed to have skills which make up for the shortcomings in the skills of others or the results which they were engaged to deliver?
8. In undertaking construction obligations, of whatever kind, will the developer, wittingly or unwittingly, assume some liability for consequential loss?
9. What insurances are required and by whom? What are the insurable interests? At what point may circumstances diverge, necessitating a realignment of insurable interests? Who may stand to lose in consequence?
10. What insurance obligations should be imposed both upon and by the developer?
11. What is the duration of the developer's insurable interest and, in turn, at what point do all interests become those of the purchaser, his tenants and occupiers?

6 Timing and Completion of the Development

'We fortify in paper, and in figures
Using the names of men instead of men:
Like one that draws the model of a house
Beyond his power to build it; who, half through
Gives o'er and leaves his part-created cost
A naked subject to the weeping clouds
And waste for churlish winter's tyranny.'
Lord Bardolph, Second part of King Henry the Fourth: Act I, Scene III

Of course, Lord Bardolph can only have been referring to the folly of getting only so far with a project, to the point where it becomes clear that the remainder cannot be carried out. Completion of the project itself is, accordingly, by no means the yardstick by which performance is judged. If so much (or so little) has been achieved today, what are the prospects for tomorrow?

Fulfilment of the construction programme, anticipated delivery date of the building, occupation by tenants, the prospect of an income stream, the realisation of development profit, all depend on timely and satisfactory implementation as well as completion of the development. From the very inception of, and indeed throughout, the project, time is a critical factor. It impacts on cost, and above all on commitment and the nature of the commitment of every one of the players. Both timing and performance are thus in issue from the start. The sooner evidence of failure to perform can be identified, the sooner the project can be restored to schedule, or if necessary the building period extended. Questions of timing and delay are potentially also matters of default and dispute, which are dealt with in Chapter 9.

Preliminary stages

Development is essentially about forward planning. In earlier chapters we have underlined and recalled again the need for consents, both in the context of those which are required from public authorities and also in the sense of satisfying the interests of the respective players. Every kind of development agreement, comprised in the project, will seek to control in some way a particular part of the process. We have also seen that conflicting interests of different players may, in imposing an obligation in one agreement, create a difficulty under another and that in the course of original negotiation such a result should be avoided.

Accordingly, the entire approvals process is at all times time sensitive and impacts directly on all stages of the development through to completion, and even upon completion itself. Every delay in such a process suggests the possibility of dispute. Where there is dispute there is again delay. The construction process is perhaps the most vulnerable because delay, of whatever kind, tests the resilience of the building contract as well as principal development agreements.

Certificates and draw downs

Once essential approvals are obtained and construction is under way, the process of supervision may give rise to delay while one party or another is satisfied, on-site tests are taken or, perhaps, remedial works are carried out. There may be a cost implication where delays are unnecessary, and the contractor is put to expense. It must be seen as entirely the developer's fault if he arrives in a situation where on the one hand the contractor has been unnecessarily delayed, and additional expense is caused yet, on the other, the player who caused the delay in the first place was quite legitimately able to cause it under the terms of his particular development agreement. That is why it is essential for a developer always to seek a proviso that any such intervention must not, in so many words, unnecessarily delay the development and in particular the conduct of the building contract.

However, at various stages along the way the developer's contractors and professionals will, in any case also, require to be paid for their services. The question is when and, not entirely foolishly, why. Usually, every appointment or contract will have some mechanism for stage payments and, in the case of professional appointments, the delivery of certain services will, without too much difficulty, determine when a payment should be made. Under the building contract, it is a rather more complex matter, and here starts a process of further interaction between the various players according to a variety of agreements, all designed to meet different needs.

Under the building contract as it stands, and in whatever form, the time will come when, say, the architect will issue a certificate that a certain stage has been reached. The work will have been valued by the quantity surveyor, according to the bills of quantities and the provisions of the building contract and, assuming the work has been satisfactorily carried out according to the requirements of the particular stage as prescribed, the architect (or employer's representative according to the type of contract) will issue a certificate. As between employer and contractor, payment accordingly becomes due, but it does not necessarily follow that, on this account alone, the developer will in turn have funds advanced by his bank or funding institution. One must look instead to the relevant development (loan/finance) agreement for the answer.

We have also seen how the role of a supervising surveyor operates, and in particular in relation to monitoring of construction generally and in ensuring that development obligations have been met. That role may be performed not only by surveyors for a landowner, but also by the respective surveyors for the bank or funding institution. It is when the developer requires a contribution from his bank or fund to meet the cost of development expenditure that the role of the supervising surveyor comes into its own.

A supervising surveyor, in turn, must now issue a certificate of his own in some form or at least signify his approval. It will not necessarily cover merely construction cost but perhaps also other development costs for the time being, such as professional fees, statutory fees, considerations for a variety of third party interests and so on. The relevant development agreement should lay down precisely his authority on behalf of his principals in relation to the development and it is to him that the developer will usually make the formal application for a draw down of funds.

The agreement should again show clearly how draw downs may be justified and the circumstances in which they can be applied for. For example, there may be invoices, receipts, etc. For the most part, assuming that the developer is careful and scrupulous, and has had regard to the relevant terms of the development agreement, the cost will be shown as justified and can be drawn down. However, the developer still has to meet the construction and other criteria of the agreement and it is not necessarily the architect's opinion for the purposes of the building contract which will justify payment out of an amount equivalent or at least related to his certificate. It may have been prescribed that the supervising surveyor must be reasonably satisfied that the terms of the building contract have been complied with, that the architect's certificate was justified, and that payment is in turn permissible. This is not to say that, in some instances, the bank or fund is not prepared to fall back upon the judgment of the appointed professionals on the basis of warranties supplied and the architect's certificate is often acceptable in practice. It is always a matter of original negotiation and documentation, but the trigger for sanctioning the draw down will usually be pulled by the supervising surveyor on behalf of his principal.

Even though the cost itself may be justified under the building contract or appointment, the amount may be beyond the expectations of the development agreement. It will be recalled that in some instances, items of development cost are capped on an item by item basis, and so (retentions under the building contract apart) the developer will only be able to draw down a limited amount. When the maximum commitment is reached, however, the implications are obvious: he must look to his own resources. Apart from all of this, development agreements usually prescribe for draw downs to be on a coherent and co-ordinated basis. (Incidentally, retentions can usually be expected under development finance agreements and the developer should seek to ensure that these mirror so far as possible the like in the building contract both as to amount and also entitlement.)

It is not a matter of allowing a stream of invoices to flow through: rather, it is likely that draw downs will be permitted on a systemic basis, say monthly, and usually for a minimum amount (save, obviously, the last). If the minimum cannot be accounted for in a particular month, it will have to be carried on to the next, and so on as necessary. Therefore, it may be that certification of a stage for payment purposes will be left until the architect has certified that a further stage payment is due under the building contract.

This presents a dilemma for the developer who must balance his financial commitments against the incurring of interest charges, whether actual or notional, and consider whether it is worthwhile holding back certain invoices for inclusion in a draw down request so as to ensure that when a major invoice comes in next month, the combined amounts will satisfy the minimum requirements for a draw down. Maintenance of cash flow is a hazardous business.

Completion of the building contract

The building contract stands as a contract independent of all other agreements comprised in the development. Depending upon the form of the building contract, every stage in the construction process will be monitored either by the architect as under the JCT standard form (1980 edition as amended) or by an employer's representative, as under a wider-ranging agreement embracing professional skills as well, such as design and build. The responsibility for issuing certificates lies with that person.

Interim certificates

As between employer and contractor there will usually be a series of stage payments. Because the building contract absorbs the greatest amount of expenditure upon the development, the developer will usually time his application for draw down of funds from his financiers around certificates under the building contract but by no means necessarily (see **Certificates and draw downs** above). It really depends upon what development agreements he has entered into, the financial commitments therein contained and the manner in which they are incurred and become payable. The last certificate, signalling practical completion, is not the final certificate. That follows the defects liability period(s) and the making good of defects (see **Defects liability** below).

Partial possession by the employer

Clause 18.1 of the JCT standard form states:

> 'If at any time or times before the date of issue by the Architect/the Contract Administrator of the Certificate of Practical Completion the Employer wishes to take possession of any part or parts of the Works and the consent of the Contractor (which consent shall not be unreasonably withheld) has been obtained, then notwithstanding anything expressed or implied elsewhere in this Contract, the Employer may take possession thereof. The Architect/the Contract Administrator shall thereupon issue to the Contractor on behalf of the Employer a written statement identifying the part or parts of the Works taken in possession and giving the date when the Employer took possession...'

Construction professionals will consider carefully not only to what extent that this clause may apply but also (if appropriate) to what extent it should be permitted to apply. Nevertheless, in general terms the more complex the development and where, in practical terms, it is feasible and reasonable for the employer to have possession of part, then such a certificate ought properly to be given.

In the case, for example, of a shopping centre where a mall of shops is ready for fitting out, is fully accessible and all parking and other facilities are in place it is hardly surprising that the employer will be eager to permit tenants access for fitting out works under the terms of their respective agreements for lease. Every agreement for lease, in a development scenario, is likely to be in part a development agreement. This will be so if only because completion of the lease is directly related to completion of the development, and that agreement will have been drawn expressly with time and delivery of the unit in mind. As with every other development agreement it will also be concerned with performance during the development period. Thus, tenants properly advised will ensure that they too are afforded appropriate contractual protection during the course of the development and indeed after (see below generally). However, in the case of major development, phasing will be organised under strictly controlled conditions reflected by the building contract and by every relevant development agreement.

Practical completion

When are the works practically complete? Answer: when the architect says so. There is no definition as such of practical completion; it is in all cases a matter of judgment. Clause 17.1 of the JCT standard form states simply:

> 'When in the opinion of the Architect/the Contract Administrator Practical Completion of the Works is achieved, he shall forthwith issue a certificate to that effect and Practical Completion of the Works shall be deemed for all the purposes of this Contract to have taken place on the day named in such Certificate'.

It follows that the architect bears a heavy responsibility in determining whether works are sufficiently complete for him to issue his certificate. There is a general principle of law applying to the entirety of the architect's duties, ie that he must act fairly and in an unbiased manner. This principle permeates the building contract and is not confined merely, for example, to issue of certificates. The position of the architect under the building contract is a complex area. Suffice it to say, for the purpose of this book, he is not to be perceived as the agent of the employer except if he is authorised to do so. Indeed cl 4.1 of the JCT standard form states:

> 'The Contractor shall forthwith comply with all instructions issued to him by the Architect/the Contract Administrator in regard to any matter in respect of which the Architect/the Contract Administrator is expressly empowered *by* [my emphasis] the Conditions to issue instructions…'.

Thus, he may be empowered to issue variations of the works (for which the standard conditions also make provision) but he cannot vary the conditions themselves.

Defects liability

However, once a certificate of practical completion has been issued by the architect, what happens then? First, it is to be expected that there will have been retentions from the building contract price of so many per cent which will be made good to the contractor in part upon practical completion with the balance to be paid upon issue of the final certificate under the building contract, that is to say the certificate to be issued when certain notified defects have been made good.

Meeting liability for defects can be approached in a number of ways, and not merely through the defects liability provisions of the building contract. First, there is an informal practice of issuing certificates of practical completion subject to a 'snagging list', being those items which in the perception of the architect need to be carried out but which, in themselves, are so minor that they will not inhibit occupation and use of the building and it would be unfair not to issue a certificate. Such items will be swept up in course of defects liability duties. Snagging is not a subject much beloved of lawyers not least because, in theory, it does not exist. It is, nonetheless, a practice and one which at the same time should be avoided. On experience, one has come across developers, in collusion with their architects and contractors, advancing issue of the certificate of practical completion well ahead of the point when the works could, by objective standards, be regarded as practically complete. This practice may have been motivated for any number of reasons, whether for tax or other financial benefit, and it also implies that there may be some corresponding disadvantage for another player. Worse, there comes a point where the benefit of any doubt must give way to the possibility of fraud in context.

Whatever the reason, however, the advice must be to avoid such practices entirely if possible. There can be no good reason for unjustified issue of certificates, but there can be any number of bad ones. It is trite to say that architects and other property professionals should strive hard at all times to uphold professional standards. If they fail, there may be dire legal consequences both for themselves and also between the players under their respective development agreements, particularly for conspirators. Although major players will frequently accept a professional responsibility from the developer's team through warranties, so as to avoid unnecessary duplication of roles, the area which carries with it the greatest sensitivity is probably that of certification, particularly of practical completion. A whole variety of events depends upon this single event, depending upon the development agreement in question (see below).

Snagging apart, liability for defects needs to be distinguished in two further ways at least. A building is a complex entity, and even more so in this day and age when occupation and utilisation depend on complex mechanical and electrical functions. The building will therefore require a bedding-in process which is fully recognised by the JCT standard form which prescribes, at cl 17, very precisely for a defects liability period and, in particular, for defects which 'are due to materials or workmanship not in accordance with this Contract or to frost occurring before Practical Completion of the Works'. Reference here is very specifically to defects arising during the defects liability period and which must be notified not later than 14 days after the expiry of the defects liability period. Thereupon, the contractor must make good those defects within a reasonable time. Note also that reference to frost damage is expressly to such damage occurring prior to practical completion, and not after. Depending upon the nature of the damage and when it was discovered, it suffices only to say that there are prospectively interesting points for lawyers to debate!

Final certificate

The making good of defects arising under the defects liability procedures in the building contract will give rise, in due course, to the issue of a final certificate. Once that is issued, the balance of the retention under the building contract can then be released to the contractor. Quite often, one may expect to see different defects liability periods for different processes. Mechanical and electrical engineering aspects, for example, are frequently distinguished.

Certification under development agreements

The building contract is the developer's front line response to the construction obligations placed upon him by the other players. This underlines again that construction and development must at all times be distinguished. Each of the players having an interest in the outcome of the development will wish to look to separate development obligations, outside of the context of the building contract, to protect its own position.

The landowner/local authority

The construction programme and the attainment of stages in the development/construction process will assist in determining not just when the development is likely to be complete but, indeed, if it will be completed at all. If there is a delay, is the developer at fault or is there some matter beyond his control? If it is a question of default, then this reflects upon other interests as well. (See Chapter 9.)

The landowner also has to decide at the outset what are to be his own particular criteria for satisfaction with each stage of the works. Will he rely upon the developer's professionals, through the medium of warranties? In the event of default, are his interests such as to justify bringing the agreement to an end or requiring the developer to assign the construction contract and various appointments to him (perhaps not, but again see Chapter 9)? However, the landowner cannot be pessimistic unless such concerns as he may have are identifiable (in our example of the local authority landowner who required the developer to carry out additional work specifically for the public benefit—that is one legitimate concern).

Again, if the landowner will derive some financial benefit, for example a share in rents derived from the development, that is another concern. Perhaps the landowner will be taking a leaseback of part of the premises, say for additional local government offices. In that case, the council as landowner has the same concerns as any occupation tenant to see that everything is done properly and on time. The landowner will, therefore, be monitoring the development but, during its course, may not issue interim certificates as such.

When practical completion takes place, however, it is a very different matter indeed. The landowner has a contractual commitment to the developer, in our example, to grant a headlease. The developer, in his negotiations, will have wanted to encourage the landowner to rely upon the developer's architect's certificate of practical completion under the building contract. The developer will similarly wish to argue the same point in all of his contractual relationships with the other players. After all, once the developer has his lease he has something far more marketable than the development agreement: the final doubt on that point has been removed. The development agreement was only bankable because it would lead to grant of the lease in due course so long as the development was completed.

It is also not difficult to see that the more optimistic a view taken of practical completion, the sooner the major interest can be secured. Without impugning the integrity of the architects' profession, it is nevertheless a normal and natural function of a major player to take its own view as to whether practical completion has taken place. Nothing can alter the terms of the building contract as between developer and contractor. If practical completion is certified under the building contract, it crystallises the relationship between developer and contractor in a certain way by deeming that the works are complete, but under that contract alone.

What happens meanwhile if the landowner is not satisfied? As always, it is a matter of contract. The landowner, not being a party to the building contract, can, therefore, work to his own agenda as set down in the development agreement. It is, therefore, in the developer's interests to ensure so far as may be that practical completion both under the building contract and under every relevant development agreement should coincide as far as possible. To that end, it is often arranged that the architect be instructed to indicate, so many weeks before issue of his certificate of practical completion, his intention to do so. The relevant players are then given an opportunity of making an inspection. They may do so in his company but not necessarily. They will themselves then be given the opportunity to express a view. Depending upon what and who is involved, it may be better if the developer himself becomes the clearing house for any representations which can then be put to the architect. Essentially, the architect has only one master, ie the developer.

The architect's judgment, however, as to whether practical completion has taken place under the building contract, is his alone. There is, therefore, no reason why, on this issue, he should actually accept representations from anyone including his employer. It may be that the terms of his appointment will require him to liaise or at least to receive representations. To receive instruction, on the other hand, would almost certainly be inappropriate as representing a clear conflict both with his duties to the employer and, in any event, with the independence on matters of professional opinion with which his role is imbued.

Nevertheless, this bringing together of minds, however organised, provides the opportunity for thoughts to be exchanged and, at least, for expectations to be identified. In practical terms, an opportunity is afforded for the players to consider their respective positions and to reflect. It permits a better prospect of a meeting of minds than if the architect merely issues his certificate and other players are simply left to react. At all events, however, given the architect's clear professional position, he cannot be inhibited from issuing a certificate if he considers it appropriate and, if he does so, and the landowner remains dissatisfied, it is no problem of his. If the dissatisfaction was justified, however, it may result in a dilemma for the developer, and the possibility of negligence proceedings being instituted against the architect in the wake of the breach of the developer's development obligations implied by the architect's failure. It may also signal a breach of warranty.

Questions of default and disputes apart, the dilemma for the developer is potentially compound. If he sides with the landowner, the inference is that there was something wrong in the construction process thus implicating the architect or the contractor or both in prospective legal process. Alternatively, if he is satisfied that issue of a certificate of practical completion was justified, it implies the prospect of a dispute with the landowner in order to secure grant of his headlease.

What happens if the landowner is right? Let us say that the landowner's surveyor has reasonably refused to issue a certificate under the principal development agreement. If he reasonably refuses (particularly if his argument is that the certificate of practical completion under the building contract was not properly issued) the developer's first remedy may lie against the architect/contractor. In the case of the former there may be issues of negligence in particular, and in the case of the latter issues of contract as well. This is worse than an oversimplification, however, and legal advice should be taken.

Perhaps the worst possible scenario is where, under implementation of separate disputes procedures, performance of the building contract is upheld but performance of the development agreement is not (see below also). The practicality is that rarely will any of this happen if the respective required standards equate (particularly if the building contract is allowed to take precedence) and, if they do, the developer has the further dilemma of choosing the horses to back. If they do not, the developer was at known risk from the outset.

Moreover, if the landowner had a discretion whether to grant the headlease, or if a tenant has a discretion whether to accept the building and thus take up the lease, the developer has made a clear error of judgment in negotiating his agreements if the prospective consequences are not perceived. In the case of the tenant, the agreement for lease will be effectively an option but in the case of a landowner, happily in one bizarre sense, the development agreement may have been essentially unbankable. In that event, the developer would have been likely to find out his error as soon as he tried to raise development finance, and hopefully before he signed.

Subjective criteria for determining events are always to be avoided. The point is underscored so heavily here because, on experience, one has seen investment purchase deals where precisely such criteria have been employed and, bankability apart, a developer needs to weigh carefully the practicality of dealing elsewhere or simply holding the investment if such criteria are not satisfied.

The danger for the developer, therefore, is in actually trying to reach a view or a compromise. Particularly, if he sees appeasement of the landowner by carrying out certain remedial work himself, the net effect may be in turn to relieve the contractor of the burden of carrying out those or other remedial works, the need for which arose during the defects liability period, because the works carried out by the developer, at the behest of the landowner, constituted an interference. Before contemplating any such work, accordingly, the developer should take careful advice from his construction professionals and his lawyers and identify as closely as possible the nature and extent of the risks which attention to remedial works, outside of the building contract, prospectively imposes.

The bank

The bank will have been considering the stages of construction in terms of compliance with the conditions of the loan agreement as well as with the principal development agreement. It will have had its own systems of certification for draw down purposes and also of approval for monitoring progress of the development. In the case of a major interest already held by the developer, eg a freehold or a subsisting lease, the bank's dissatisfaction with progress may simply be signified by withholding a draw down because the developer is in breach. Accordingly, unless the developer has other cash resources, this may in turn place the developer in breach of his contractual commitments to his professionals and the building contractor. *In extremis*, this may have effect to collapse those relationships and the bank will then need to look to its security if it has not done so already.

In practice, of course, given the need for the development to be completed, the bank will have organised its relationship with the developer and its attitude to the development by preparing for the consequences of default so that, not only are the terms of appointment and the building contract suitably framed, but the warranties extracted will recognise or permit assignment or novation of those contracts with the bank or rather its appointed nominee, ie a new developer. Put simply, it will be possible for the bank, perhaps through its appointed receiver, to reconstitute all the relationships concerned with construction in order to complete the job.

If default under one or more of those relationships has itself led to the default of the developer, and the developer has not acted properly or has in consequence been unable to do so, it would in such circumstances be open to the bank, having otherwise no contractual commitment to the professional team or the contractor, to reconstitute its team.

From a bank's point of view, and in relying upon the appropriate professional warranty, a certificate of practical completion issued by the architect may well suffice. However, let us say that the bank only funded this particular development because the developer had also secured a forward sale to an institution. In such circumstances the bank, in considering the security to be taken, will have had careful regard to the terms of the forward sale agreement (and, hopefully, taken careful legal advice accordingly). If the bank is to be repaid from the proceeds of that forward sale, its corporate mind will be focused upon the criteria by which the fund or institution judges that practical completion has taken place together with such other events if any as may trigger completion of the purchase under that agreement. If the fund is satisfied and will pay the price and thus deliver repayment of the loan to the bank, there is little for the bank to complain about.

The bank is at the same time concerned that, if there is one, a development agreement with a landowner has triggered the grant of a major interest. It is also concerned that the terms of a pre-let, upon which the forward sale is itself also expressly conditional, have been sufficiently complied with to trigger grant of the occupation lease. It is then concerned whether there is any other factor which may inhibit completion of the purchase by the fund or institution, or of the lease by the tenant.

If there was no forward purchase, but the bank had funded on the basis of a pre-let it will be concerned with sufficient completion of the works to trigger completion of the occupation lease and also that the development becomes a marketable security whereby the property can in due course be disposed of in the open market. In so far as the development has not been pre-let, the bank will still be concerned to ensure that the works are completed to a satisfactory standard and that they will be lettable to their maximum potential sensibly available and that the resultant investment may be as marketable as possible. (The loan agreement should at the very least require the developer to observe and perform all its obligations in each of these agreements.) (As to letting, see Chapter 7.)

The bank may wish to impose its own criteria. In this sort of negotiation, the developer is prospectively vulnerable to a bank requiring to exercise a degree of choice. The bank, properly advised, will have ensured that, if its security is a development agreement with a landowner, it can deal with that agreement in such a way as to meet its own requirements. Thus, in the event of default by the developer, it may be possible for the bank as mortgagee to assign the development agreement to another developer and the prospect is that, under the terms of the principal development agreement, there will be clear criteria for acceptability of such a new developer. Indeed, usually, the prospects of alienation of a development agreement will be confined to the circumstances in which a bank taking the agreement as security for development loan finance, wishes to exercise its rights. (See also under **Alienation** in Chapter 8.)

The landowner will nevertheless have been looking for a commitment from one developer in particular, and (privity of contract apart) a development agreement is not usually intended to be a readily saleable commodity. In such circumstances, the expectation is that the ability to assign will be closely defined. The agreement will be bankable, nonetheless, because from their respective viewpoints there is likely to be a meeting of minds between the bank and the landowner as to who is best suited to carry out and complete the development in order that each of them can realise the full potential of their respective agreements with the developer.

Investing institutions

Under a forward funding agreement, where the fund or institution already holds the land (or the benefit of the principal development agreement as the case may be), practical completion is no less important. If it attaches to a development agreement providing a major interest which then becomes the fund's investment, the latter's concerns as to that agreement broadly equate with those of a bank. For the developer, however, the significance is greater still. Practical completion clearly signals substantial compliance with his building obligations. Usually, also, it signals a fundamental change of relationship with the fund. Development cost roll up ceases (see Chapter 8), a new financial regime is imposed, prospects of overage appear, perhaps a project management fee is payable, etc. His active role is beginning to diminish and opportunities for reward emerge.

As with a bank, draw down of development cost will have been overseen by the fund's surveyors. If during the development process the fund's maximum commitment has been exceeded, the developer may have been paying interest as such while still meeting outstanding development cost out of his own pocket.

A developer has exactly the same concern as before if he is required to carry out work beyond that certified as completed by the architect in order to satisfy the fund. For that reason he must negotiate as far as possible towards the fund accepting the architect's interim certificates and also the architect's certificate of practical completion as being the criterion for practical completion under the forward funding agreement. He should be seeking to confine the fund's surveyor's role to seeing that precisely these events have taken place rather than the operation of a separate agenda.

Precisely the same concerns attend practical completion under a forward purchase agreement with the difference that, until that point, the agreement has constituted in one sense no more than an agreement to purchase conditional on providing the completed (and possibly let) development. Concerns of a bank providing interim finance, secured not just on the land but on the prospect of sale and realisation of its security apart, once again completion under that agreement signals important events for the developer.

In this instance the developer will, instead of gaining an interest in land which he may hold or sell on, be disposing of one. The insurable interest in the land moves away but the developer may have the same concerns as before as to maintenance of the buildings until lettings are achieved, and until he receives his final overage payment. Either he must seek to put obligations on the fund to preserve his interest (including by insuring), or the fund is treated as effectively if not actually as a landlord, and the responsibility is shared according to such relationship. Ultimately, when the building has been fully let, usually for the first time only, and the developer's overage if any has been paid, his (insurable) interest evaporates.

Meanwhile, there will still be concern as to defects liability, and the issue of the final certificate in due course. The fund (including under a forward funding agreement) may be expected to make retentions similar to those in the building contract and, in some cases, this is arbitrarily imposed as a fund's standard requirement which may not, in the event, match precisely the retentions made under the building contract. When negotiating retention clauses the developer should always seek to steer the fund towards the making of retentions which match the building contract, not just pound for pound, but also as to timing, particularly if the building contract ultimately entered into provides for multiple defects liability periods (see **Defects liability** above).

Tenants

It follows that much also depends on the reaction of tenants to completion of the development. As we shall see in Chapter 7, the process of interaction means that each of the players may have an interest in lettings, closely defined by reference to their particular interests and functions within the development. It is, therefore, to be assumed that the ability to let at all, again see Chapter 7, will be controlled. Among the many issues which this raises will be satisfaction of the tenant himself both with the progress and outcome of the development including, not least, the construction itself. As always, timing is critical.

From a tenant's point of view, it is not just his unit of accommodation which is at issue, but also other aspects of the development which will service his needs. If parking is required or any items of infrastructure should be provided to make it possible for him to trade, he may need to place a substantial burden upon the developer. The larger multiples, including not least the supermarket operators, work to sophisticated programmes and exacting specifications. Requirements of retailers such as these, when translated into legal documentation, inevitably lead to demanding contractual obligations. Again the banker and the purchasing institution in particular, in negotiating their involvement in the scheme, are perhaps as closely concerned with the negotiation as the developer himself.

They will, therefore, all be concerned that development obligations to prospective tenants are so framed that it is practical and feasible for the developer to enter into those contractual commitments, the bank perhaps the more so because without delivery of results the prospects of repayment of the development loan may be impaired.

In turn, nevertheless, when appropriate criteria for practical completion are negotiated, and the tenant ought properly to be satisfied, the developer should be afforded the ability to require that the tenant accepts his lease and the income commitment which it implies. An entirely subjective standard for practical completion under an agreement for lease, on the part of the tenant, cannot be an acceptable subject of investment. It is effectively an option only, but it is axiomatic that the tenant is perfectly entitled to demand that his agreement is expressly conditional upon grant of the major interest under the principal development agreement, as much as a bank or institution, without which he will receive no lease. If the developer cannot deliver and do so within a particular time frame, the tenant may not be able to wait even if others are prepared to do so and he may thus require to have the ultimate freedom to walk away.

Delay and delay clauses

Notwithstanding all of the foregoing, delay is a risk inherent in all development. Delay on the part of the contractor may lead to the employer/developer being entitled to damages. Under the JCT standard form, at cl 24, provision is made for liquidated and ascertained damages which, when certified by the architect, may be deducted from sums due or to become due to the contractor under the contract or may be recovered from the contractor as a debt (cl 24.2). Conversely, under cl 25, an extension of time may be available and, in particular, cl 25.4 lists such matters as *force majeure*, exceptionally adverse weather conditions, strikes, lock outs, etc. It will be for the contractor to give notice of such matters and if the architect is of the opinion that the matters contained in the notice comprise a 'relevant event', an extension of time may be allowed accordingly.

An extension of time does not, on its own, allow the contractor himself to claim damages but under cl 26, upon application made by the contractor to the architect, on specified grounds, an addition to the contract sum may become available. Suffice it to say that if the cause of delay is traced back to the developer or his own professionals, for example because the architect has failed to supply drawings on time, the failure of the developer to conduct himself properly or to police the conduct of his professionals may rebound from each of the players to whom he has a development obligation, quite apart from such recompense as he may have to provide to the contractor.

All of this leads, inevitably, to the need in every development agreement to make provision for possible delay and to track, at the very least, the permitted grounds for delay set out in the building contract, with corresponding extensions to the construction programme and in turn the development period in every relevant agreement. The developer fails to secure this provision at his peril. In this context we are considering delay to the development at large and not just construction, and thus possible extensions to the development period and not just the construction programme: there may be issues giving rise to delay beyond those concerned directly with construction.

The developer should therefore also look to other factors which may be beyond his own control and which, in some way themselves, may give rise to the delay. To omit this may also compound the difficulty created if the delay has been caused by something on the one hand outside the developer's control but which, on the other, has nonetheless entitled the contractor to recompense. (It is worth remembering, incidentally, that where any one or more of the players reserves a right, in a development agreement, to enter to test and take samples, etc and does so, the exercise of any such right requires co-operation of the contractor. Interference by an employer or representatives of the employer for the purposes of the building contract can in the extreme entitle the contractor to terminate under cl 28.)

The architect's duties must also be formulated so as to take account of the needs of third parties. Until assignment or novation of an appointment, or unless express authority is given, however, the architect will not, and indeed should not, serve more than one master and, in any case, nothing in the foregoing can compromise his professional obligations (see above).

It so often happens that delaying factors are matters of such mutual concern in any event that conflicts of loyalty and commitment will not in the event arise. When they do, it is usually because either there was an inconsistency of contractual commitment or there was a breach. The former is inherently avoidable though careful negotiation and drafting at the outset: it is part and parcel of the same principle of interaction which runs through the major contractual relationships which go to make up the development, but it does not resolve the nightmare scenario of parallel disputes on the same subject matter leading to different conclusions. Between development agreements, this must usually be seen as a rare event.

Finally, a developer negotiating a delay clause in a development agreement should also include as a factor any unreasonable or unnecessary delay on the part of the player with whom he is dealing. Moreover, where the player in question reserves to himself rights to do things which may have effect to cause delay, the developer should not shrink from negotiating the inclusion in the development agreement of provisions not only that the exercise of such rights shall not cause unnecessary delay or obstruction, but that damage to the works shall not be caused: indeed, preferably, he should be seeking to cover damage generally including on the basis that if the player concerned causes delay under the building contract entitling the contractor to damages and/or to determine, or the developer is placed in breach elsewhere, the developer should be entitled to recover in turn. (Establishing rights at common law against any player is inherently far more difficult than having a clear contractual commitment to follow, but that was always so whatever the matter in issue.)

Checklist

1. Are development covenants enough? What, if anything, needs to be certified, when and why?
2. What stages need to be contemplated? Particularly, what stages other than construction should be brought into account?
3. Distinguish certification of events in the development from applications for draw downs. Given the various contractual commitments in negotiation, how often should draw downs take place and how may the developer's application for draw downs be justified?
4. Should a bank or funding institution reserve the right to make payments direct, eg to the contractor under the building contract upon issue of an interim certificate?
5. Will the interests of the development be served by so framing the building contract and every relevant development agreement that a certificate or certificates of partial possession may be awarded? If so, to what extent may outstanding works impact upon the ability to occupy?
6. The architect's opinion alone will determine what is to be practical completion under the building contract. What other interests are concerned with this event and for what purpose?
7. What is the prospective impact of a parallel test of practical completion for the purposes of a development agreement? How may it produce conflict with the interests of other players?
8. How may the entitlement on the part of one of the players to exercise a discretion impact upon the interests of the developer and/or those of the other players? Is it bankable?
9. In the case of development loan/finance agreements, what are the criteria for payment of retentions or amounts equivalent to retentions under the building contract? Can circumstances arise where the contractor is entitled to payment of a retention but the bank/fund is not obliged to pay the like amount to the developer and at the same time?
10. What interests are the respective players seeking to serve in imposing requirements at relevant stages during construction which go beyond the co-relevant provisions of the building contract? Should the building contract itself be modified to suit or are the particular concerns matters entirely for the developer and the player in question?
11. How and in what ways can compliance with development obligations impair the relationship between developer and contractor under the building contract? Can it give rise to any liabilities on the part of the developer, for example, through unnecessary

interference, which he cannot recover from other players?
12. If there is a delay, what is the cause? Must delay be permitted by the developer to the contractor which is not permitted to the developer by other players?
13. If the delay is attributable to, say, the contractor, or indeed any other player, what is the consequence for the developer and/or the other player or players? (See also Chapter 9.)

7 Letting and Letting Policy

> 'Leave not the mansion so long tenantless,
> Lest, growing ruinous, the building fall
> And leave no memory of what it was!
> Repair me with thy presence, Silvia!
> Thou gentle nymph, cherish thy forlorn swain!'
> Valentine, *The Two Gentlemen of Verona: Act V, Scene IV*

Perhaps the relationship of client and agent is not always so close. However, the *raison d'être* of development is the creation of value. Unless the resultant building or buildings are for own use or outright sale, the need to generate an income stream lies at the heart of the matter. It is the stuff of investment. Indeed, until premises are let, the bricks and mortar from which they are made are a liability, particularly when financed by debt. Stories of spec built offices having lain fallow during the recession and being turned to other uses are now commonplace. Some have been converted for residential use, for example. More worryingly, there are also instances of buildings having no takers at all, and of being demolished without ever having been occupied.

The letting market is essentially the preserve of agents and valuers. The surveyors for each of the developers and the other major players will have advised as to the prospects of letting at a very early stage and such prospects will continue to be monitored throughout. Without at least this input, except perhaps in the headiest of booms, the project would never commence.

The objective of maximisation of income should be a *sine qua non* but, in terms of development, precisely where the initiative comes from, on whom the obligations lie, whose advisers will seek tenants, who will appoint those advisers, the terms of appointment, the criteria to be applied to choice of tenants, lease terms, etc all present areas of possible conflict between the players. The interests of the players are not identical and neither, in consequence, are their respective views on the issues to be addressed, some of which are suggested above.

It is, therefore, vital to the development process that letting criteria are identified, and that each of the relevant development agreements makes appropriate provision. Every effort must be made to avoid conflict in implementation. Conflict may itself inhibit the timely negotiation and completion of lettings, and is not wholly resolved even by the most effective of disputes procedures (see Chapter 9).

Sometimes the determination of a letting policy is considered by letting agents alone on behalf of their principals, particularly if they are the same firms as the firms of surveyors engaged by those principals in supervising or monitoring roles. In devising a letting policy, however, it is not just the letting agents who should be involved. For example, there was a shopping centre constructed pursuant to a forward funding agreement, ie a development agreement under which the purchasing institution bought the site at the outset and advanced development finance to the developer during the development period. The developer appointed agents who were particularly experienced in retail agency and were as likely as any to achieve results. The fund in turn had engaged a large firm of surveyors who were, unquestionably, also experienced letting agents as well as having a track record in institutional investment and they had, for that particular reason, been appointed as fund's surveyors in addition, to monitor the process, control draw downs, maintain the development account, etc for the purpose of the forward funding (development finance) agreement.

The tale ends thus. Both firms of agents were instructed to act jointly (as to appointment of agents see below). The development finance agreement contained detailed criteria for lettings as agreed upon between the agents at the outset. That, the principals on both sides insisted, was to be the blueprint for all lettings. They and particularly their agents were the experts and the lawyers should set down, precisely as the agents had between them agreed, the letting policy in a schedule to the agreement, pursuant to operative provisions directing the conduct of letting according to that schedule. The agents knew their business, and understood precisely, it was insisted, what was expected of them as reflected in the schedule.

Subject to this letting policy, the developer was to be obliged, through the offices of the two firms of agents, to seek tenants for the development. The agreed letting criteria would need to be followed and, subject to the fund's consent which was not to be unreasonably withheld, lettings could be negotiated and concluded. On this basis the fund also agreed in the funding agreement that it would enter into leases to tenants on the terms so approved.

Result? Disaster. Why? Philosophy, culture, call it what you will. The stated letting policy agreed between agents, when put to the practical test, actually allowed for the accommodation of widely differing views and interpretation of the nature of the tenants who might be attracted, and the respective retail businesses they would bring with them. The result was slow progress towards letting and one does not need to be an agent to appreciate that if space is not taken up rapidly, inertia tends to feed on itself. Granted that there were inhibiting features of the shopping centre which, in time, began to show through (for which the developer, the fund and their respective advisers can all be blamed) the example also goes to show a further dilemma for the developer.

As will be seen in Chapter 9, disputes are inherently unconscionable. Whether the dispute in question arises in course of construction, or at any time in relation to letting, or indeed any other aspect of the development, formal resolution (or indeed informal resolution) is prospectively damaging. Time is money: it is as simple as that, and the effect on marketability is potentially equally disastrous.

Now, given that our example concerns a shopping centre and an inadequate letting policy the possibilities of formal dispute over lettings were in that case of no comfort to the developer for whom success in letting represented the basis for deriving development profit. If the forward funding agreement had been of the variety under which not only would the developer not receive overage until requisite lettings had been achieved and at the desired level, but also had a continuing income commitment to the fund meanwhile, then the probable answer is one which would probably have been completely unpalatable. Developers are not, by nature, inclined to enter into formal disputes—at least with their financiers—and, as the property boom of the 1980s ran its course, the prospects of securing development finance at all became more difficult.

Lawyers and agents

Lawyers involved in the development process rely heavily on the input of other professionals which will in some way, or other, become part of the respective contractual commitments. Whether the resultant ancillary documentation is a method statement for construction, perhaps special conditions of work in a particular environment, for example working within and around a fully operating publicly used railway, a construction programme, modifications to the JCT standard form, even a letting policy, quite frequently the lawyer will not be entirely involved if at all, because what is being said is indecipherable without the added technical knowledge of the appropriate professional. Perhaps a building contract is a less than perfect example of the difficulty because that is a purely contractual document but, because of the use of standard forms, it is frequently negotiated by quantity surveyors whose amendments and modifications are not necessarily designed to make legal history. They may also need to incorporate technical material peculiar to their own skills and those of the construction industry. In more complex construction cases, however, lawyers will of course become involved on essentially legal aspects.

In the case of letting policy, lawyers involved in development are expected to have a clear understanding of the legal mechanisms which combine to bind landlord and tenant: they may have some difficulty, however, in identifying with, and in recognising the nature of, the market which the letting policy seeks to exploit. It is difficult to cut hot air with a knife and even more difficult to convince one's client, sometimes, that one has a point (particularly if no one else agrees with you either). The lawyer's difficulty is that in practising his profession he must always be vigilant and, whether so perceived by the client, he is at all times on enquiry; again, whether the need is so perceived by the client, he must ask what is meant and why and be prepared, if need be, to qualify his advice. It takes courage to do so in times of an ever decreasing pool of work, quite apart from the agenda of his own client which has led to his being instructed in the first place. As with everything else in the law, it is not so much sticks and carrots as sticks and backsides and the ever present danger of a claim in negligence.

In the context of this general introduction, we can thus consider letting and letting policy with a little more purpose.

The needs of the players

The landowner

Assuming that the landowner has an interest of some kind in prospective lettings, his agreement with the developer will be paramount: everything else is subject to it. Just as discretion as to acceptability of what the developer does by way of compliance with his development obligations may make the agreement unattractive to a bank, a purchaser or a tenant, because of the uncertainty which it creates, so also is it with lettings.

However, even assuming that some objective test is applied to letting in the development agreement, it is the test itself which must come under scrutiny. It also depends how and when it becomes relevant and, in addition, what distinctions there are to be drawn between the imposition of letting obligations before and after grant of the major interest. If after, it does not necessarily imply that the developer is in some way released because the interest in lettings may then continue in addition *via* the developer's obligations as tenant under the headlease granted by the landowner.

If the alienation provisions in the headlease are unduly onerous in pursuit of preserving the landowner's share of income, the development will probably not have been a fundable proposition in any case.

However, it all depends on what the deal is about and then analysing it to see if it works. In this respect, the role of the letting agent may be seen in one sense as a secondary consideration but in terms of letting policy, he clearly has an important role to play in devising and negotiating the parameters which will shape permitted letting and the definition of alienation provisions. It is the lawyer's role, nevertheless, to ensure (if he is allowed) that what is prescribed has a meaning, and that so far as possible (eg see **Lawyers and agents** above) the meaning is fully understood and, particularly, that it is correctly reflected in the legal documentation.

Rental income apart, overage for a (landlord) landowner under a development agreement can work in different ways. If the landowner is not taking an interest in rents, perhaps he will instead receive an overage payment from the developer based on (initial) lettings with the result that, if the developer is to achieve pre-lets, there will be a sum, or a further sum, to be paid upon grant of the headlease. Moreover, in order to confer a clean break as at the granting of the headlease, if that is the intention, a valuation may be taken of the unlet portions with a formula applied to them so that, in one form or another, the landowner receives the full overage benefit. Alternatively, the overage formula can be required to continue to operate and the outstanding obligations can be contractually imported into the headlease to afford overage until, for example, the whole of the premises have been let for the first time. Likely as not, the calculations will be made using development cost as a factor.

Overage may move in the opposite direction as well, but this kind of overage is usually associated with an addition to the purchase price paid to the developer by an investing institution under a forward funding or forward purchase (see more particularly **Overage provisions** below).

If the landowner has a continuing interest in income, through lettings achieved, it is not enough to say that the value of the resultant investment will be determined by that proportion of the income which the developer is entitled to retain for his own benefit. Consideration must be given to the obligations which the landowner imposes, through the medium of the development agreement, and those which he in turn imposes through the headlease. In practice, there will very likely be no difference in letting terms between these two save in one important respect, ie the obligation to seek tenants which is but one of many obligations in the development agreement, dependent upon the diligent pursuit of which is grant of the headlease in due course. The development agreement may impose an obligation to seek lettings which will be subject to such criteria but, once the lease is granted, the security of withholding grant is lost, and is thereafter represented by tenants' covenants and the ultimate sanction of forfeiture (which may include elements of outstanding obligations under the development agreement, but *only* if the latter has so expressly provided). There is a balance to be struck between maximising income and inhibition of lettings, and that is the underlying purpose of any letting policy.

A developer cannot sensibly be expected to produce what the market will not deliver, and so the developer should seek to negotiate objective standards for fulfilment of the letting dream. This principle applies to all the development agreements to which the developer is party. It is precisely such assumptions of minimum acceptable criteria, imposed by development agreements, which with the onset of recession produced letting obligations which in the event were frustrated (but that is not to say that an income cannot be secured by other means).

It is not enough to answer back in terms of 'If that is so, why are we doing the deal at all?'. The better answer should be that we are doing the deal because our expectations are along these or those lines, but if the market frustrates our expectations we should perhaps have a fall back. As between landowner and developer, it has been proved entirely unsatisfactory to refuse lettings at all because, for example, a minimum rent cannot be achieved. That is not a lawyer's point however, and principals must now learn to focus on the down sides and decide what their commercial attitudes are going to be, what safeguards and sanctions can be imposed—by whom and on whom—and so on. For example, will the chosen formula make the resultant investment unacceptable to an investor or a lending institution at *any* price?

It is not *naiveté* but folly to ignore entirely the down sides however remote. Nonetheless, acceptance of risk lies at the heart of all economic activity. It is failure to attempt to identify and articulate it which is inexcusable, the incentive to do so being measured by 'confidence', and therein lie the seeds of boom and bust.

Then comes the letting policy itself. To this extent, there may be a perceived need today which, possibly, will not necessarily stand the test of time. It is an over simplification but the needs of a landowner retaining a minor interest in income are less than those of the investor enjoying the greater proportion of the income. The interests must be weighed and the principal issues are, of course, for letting agents and valuers to consider initially. It all depends upon the purpose which the development itself is seeking to achieve. To the extent that the landowner has such an interest then some parallels can be drawn with the interests of an investor (see **The investing institution** below). Nevertheless, the alienation clause in the headlease will seek to prescribe for the manner of underletting in order to enhance the income so far as possible and also, where relevant, the manner in which the premises are let. This may cover such matters as units of accommodation, use, mix and so on. Whenever such matters are prescribed in a long lease, the question must also be asked how the lease will stand the test of time.

The more pressing debate in recent years seems to have surrounded the future of the 25-year term. When a long lease is created, however, prospective letting and alienation may indeed produce problems for today but what of tomorrow? Whatever views property professionals may express on that subject, the prospect is that, in many cases, lease terms will themselves also be an inhibition on redevelopment. The greater problem in that particular area lies in buildings either becoming out of date or that the purpose which they were originally designed to achieve has evaporated. Under a headlease reserving a rent, what may have seemed a workable alienation clause suddenly becomes the main plank of a landowner's opposition to redevelopment, or, more crudely, an instrument of blackmail. Other provisions of the headlease are significant, for example alterations and repair clauses (a rebuilding obligation can be particularly damaging) and, particularly also, insurance clauses which require reinstatement by rebuilding the self same development. A very long lease may quickly lose its attraction so soon as any question, howsoever arising, of redevelopment arises, as many long leaseholders of 1960s and 1970s shopping centres are learning.

A number of mechanisms have been devised to tackle this issue including complex criteria for redevelopment, preservation of the landowner's income during the development period and so on. The danger with such attempts to look into the future is that, in time, they may look as much out of place as the developments which themselves require replacing. There are a variety of schools of thought as to whether one leaves it to chance and negotiates at the time, on the basis that there should be something in it for everyone, or one attempts some kind of formula, or one writes a deal which avoids the problem entirely. One thing is quite certain, however, that lettings and letting policy are a long term as well as a short term consideration. For investors and occupying tenants, the issues are more immediate.

The investing institution

Before imposing its own criteria, an investing institution is clearly influenced, if its investment is to lie in a long lease, by whatever alienation provisions may be imposed in that lease as well as the initial letting criteria prescribed by the enabling agreement. If the lease is the product of a development agreement which contains controls over initial letting, it must clearly satisfy itself that the provisions so imposed are acceptable to it. The alienation provisions of the proposed headlease are intended to stand the test of time thereafter and must, therefore, be looked at critically with the long term in mind.

Initial lettings produce a further dilemma, however. In this scenario the developer has two masters to please but his decisions are clearly subordinated to those contained in the development agreement with the landowner. He must, accordingly, negotiate in his forward funding/forward purchase agreement sufficient latitude to ensure at the very least that the landowner's requirements are accommodated. It is unlikely that the institution would not be amenable to this if it is prepared to proceed on the basis of the 'head documents' as negotiated, but equally the institution will, in laying down its own criteria, require the developer to seek its consent in much the same way as for a free standing investment. Even if the developer enters into a letting agreement with a tenant, it is the institution itself which in due course will probably grant the occupational lease. (Incidentally, lawyers drafting agreements for lease will now need to take particular care, to ensure that developer obligations are not visited upon successor landlords, by virtue of the provisions of the Landlord and Tenant (Covenants) Act 1995 (effective 1 January 1996).)

However, assuming a free standing investment, ie a freehold or a long leasehold which itself does not depend upon a letting policy, what letting policy provisions are required between developer and fund? Depending upon the nature of the investment, the following may be in issue between any of the players. For example, what is the nature of the development itself? What is it to be used for, how many units are to be created, how may they be subdivided? In the case of an office development, there may be a reluctance to allow sub-division because of difficulties of management, re-letting (particularly in the wake of shrinkage of the 25-year term and the prospect of the smaller the individual premises the shorter the let). Moreover, covenant strength apart, consideration will be given to the type of tenant and business, but attitudes change. Time was when, for example, letting to a government department or even a local authority was discouraged. Such a tenant is hardly to be discouraged today. Above all, given the example of a failed shopping centre mentioned above, there must be clarity of purpose, and once a policy is agreed upon it must be tested carefully for breadth of interpretation.

Overage provisions

As part and parcel of a developer's obligations in relation to letting comprised in a development finance agreement, there will be letting obligations which provide an incentive to the developer to seek lettings on advantageous terms, but precisely to whose advantage? Where there are void portions, and depending upon the contractual relationship with the (institution) fund, it may be that the developer is required to support the fund by standing in the shoes of a (notional) tenant. In the alternative, or in addition, there may be provisions whereby the developer receives an overage payment based upon letting performance. Financial incentives will be examined more closely in Chapter 8.

During the development period, and particularly if the nature of the deal is such that the fund's purchase of the property is conditional upon completion of the development (forward purchase), the prospect is that any pre-let agreements will be entered into directly between the developer and the prospective tenant. Even if the letting criteria have been met, and the fund has approved the prospective letting, occasionally there has been an omission from the finance agreement of a positive obligation on the part of the fund to complete the lease to the tenant as a means of avoiding a commitment because, for example, the fund later perceived that there were still better lettings to be had. Accordingly, as between developer and fund, such a positive commitment on the part of the fund to complete the leases meeting the letting criteria should always be contained in the agreement.

As regards development obligations *per se* it is usual for funds to require developers to enter into agreements for lease to deliver development obligations to tenants while continuing their own obligations to grant of leases as such.

The next problem for the developer is one of achieving lettings at all. Reverting again to 'Why are we doing the deal?', it is understandable, given a fund's prospective input, eg a purchase price of such and such amount, that the fund will want to see a maximisation of income which will probably be reflected by an overage calculation clearly designed to provide an incentive to the developer. One became used to seeing over many years a minimum rental commitment based upon market expectations, ie prescribing for a scenario without regard necessarily to the prospect that the market might not deliver. With such provisions in a finance agreement, the recession undermined, in some cases completely, the operation of financial formulae. If the developer could not secure a letting which met the minimum letting criteria, in financial terms, ie a minimum rent, the fund was not obliged to proceed with the tenancy. If the tenancy was not completed, the developer had an ongoing income commitment. In such cases, in particular, there was no frustration for the fund because there was a simple contractual answer. The developer paid (until he drowned in insolvency).

However, take a similar scenario underpinned by a slightly different financial formula. Assume that the letting criteria are exactly the same as before, indeed down to the last detail including as to minimum rent. Then assume that the developer does *not* have an income commitment as such, but that the equivalent of lost income meanwhile is required to be aggregated and set against his development profit, ie a profit erosion deal. Again, the fund has a measure of built in protection but *only* until such time as the profit has eroded completely. In other words, once the value of the investment is *less* than the aggregate of the fund's maximum commitment and developer's notional income commitment, the loss is that of the fund.

In such cases, it is appropriate that stock be taken. The developer is unlikely to be successfully sued under his covenant to seek lettings at a minimum rent, because that obligation has been frustrated by the market: if he has no positive income commitment the point arises when the letting obligation ceases to have any meaning or relevance. Impossible in real life? Hardly, as once again the example is taken from experience. The question then arises as to whether, even after the developer's prospect of profit has evaporated, the developer's letting obligations should continue until market conditions are more propitious.

It is prudent for a developer, having actually met letting criteria, to ensure that letting commitments are confined to first letting only. Once a lease has been entered into, ie between fund and tenant, it is hardly the developer's fault that the tenant defaults under the lease, becomes insolvent, etc (unless it is a tenant over which the developer has control in which case, questions will have arisen as to the desirability of securing the developer's guarantee).

Mix of uses in the context of overage

A mixed use development brings with it problems of its own. First, the use of the buildings themselves will be circumscribed by permitted planning use. Letting criteria are usually based upon the intended use for the buildings, within certain parameters (and a fundamental change of use suggests a failure to let or otherwise dispose which is probably beyond the contemplation of the particular development agreement). Within a town centre, for example, there may be a purpose built mix of shopping, offices, leisure and municipal facilities. However, within those bands of use there is also the matter of mix of occupiers and trades. Shopping developments are particularly problematical and the difficulty of formulating a letting policy should not be underestimated (eg the example earlier given).

Apart from whatever may have been prescribed/encouraged by a development agreement (if any) with, say, a local authority landowner, reflected not only by that agreement but, possibly also, by the resulting alienation provisions of a headlease, the investor will have its own ideas about the mix of tenants it wishes to encourage, the market for which the development will cater and, thereby, the prospects of continued enjoyment of income through its investment in the project.

Appointment of agents, and accountability of developer's and fund's agents is dealt with more fully below but it is in that area in particular where conflict may lie. Where there is more than one agent, perhaps serving different masters or, possibly, two masters at once (as to which in particular see **Letting agents** below), there really is no practical room for allowing a polarisation of views on the suitability of a prospective tenant. It is precisely that scenario which arose in the example at the beginning of this chapter, and which may result in severe damage to actual or prospective rental value.

In addition to clear criteria, the parties must also strive if they can to agree a fall-back formula, or at least recognise very clearly the limitations of what they have prescribed. One cannot prescribe for all eventualities. The intention must be to break the log jam, to achieve lettings, minimise financial exposure and maximise profit. Thus, while it cannot be appropriate in every case, it should be prescribed that letting agents as agents be accountable in any event to the developer in the first instance but if the agent in question is also accountable in some way to the fund the matter should be capable of being so defined that the issue can be couched in terms of whether, as between developer and fund, the letting criteria will be met and, if not, whether there will be a dispute between developer and fund, *not* between agents as such who must be considered as having an essentially advisory role. Accordingly, it is not just a matter of the developer's obligations to seek tenants, and a definition of letting criteria, but also, very particularly, the terms of appointment themselves (see again **Letting agents** below).

The bank

A bank or other lending institution as a *long* term investor may align its requirements closely with those of a purchasing institution. More usually, the role of a bank is in providing interim (ie shorter term) finance circumscribed first, by a development agreement with a landowner (if any) and, secondly, by the terms of any forward purchase agreement with a funding institution the completion of which will ensure re-payment to the bank of the development loan and thirdly any constraints deriving from the title, eg restrictive covenants. These inhibitions apart, what otherwise is the relationship between the bank and the developer?

It may be that the whole project has been set up on the basis of a pre-let. Accordingly, once the deal is signed the need for a letting policy at all may be confined to secondary lettings (ie other than to the lead tenant), and the concern thereafter may be confined to the tenant failing to sign the lease. To the extent that a development is speculative, the prospects of letting are vital to the creation of an equity gap. A letting policy must be evolved.

Commercial mortgages effectively prohibit every activity with regard to the subject property. Lettings are no exception: they are usually prohibited absolutely. A commercial mortgage has aligned with it a development loan agreement and lettings will be contemplated as much as in any development agreement. Lettings are vital to the bank's security. The loan agreement will usually be expressed to prevail where there is conflict so that, as the development and letting obligations are achieved, they are gradually displaced by the underlying terms of the mortgage.

Breach of that agreement by the borrower (developer) will in turn permit the bank to exercise its rights as mortgagee, including sale. Where a developer is in breach of his building obligations, for example, the effect may be such as to repudiate the development loan agreement, thus resulting in the bank perhaps appointing a receiver either to continue the development or to sell the land with the partially completed development in order to recoup, so far as possible, its outlay in financing the development. The impact in financial terms will be dealt with in Chapter 8, but lettings also have a unique position in the development process so far as the bank is concerned.

Fundamentally, because a letting, or indeed a pre-let encapsulated in an agreement for lease, is a dealing in land, the bank has a right in priority over the agreement for lease with the tenant (unless the pre-let preceded the charge over the land and is protected by registration). In this day and age the prospects of development being off the back of unregistered land are increasingly remote, thus also the application of the unregistered rules of priority. The practicality is that one will be dealing with registered land and questions of legal priority will be considered in that light.

The tenant will want to ensure that it has an interest which is registrable and which can be enforced against successors in title of both developer and the bank exercising its rights as mortgagee. There is an interesting twist, in terms of English land law, and also the continuing debate over the 25-year term. Unless a lease is granted for at least 21 years, or has not less than 21 years to run, it is not actually registrable. A tenant of newly built development under an agreement for lease for, say, ten years, will have at best when that lease is granted only an 'overriding interest', as it is known, being one of a number of interests which are prescribed by s 70(1) of the Land Registration Act 1925 (as amended by s 4(1) of the Land Registration Act 1986). The prior agreement for lease will, however, still be capable of protection so far as it goes by registration of a caution and post 1995 the agreement for lease is likely to bind successors to the prospective landlord as well.

A receiver appointed by the bank, being an agent of the developer, may continue to honour the developer's commitments to the bank but, having no personal obligation for failure to do so, leaving the tenant to pursue the developer as he may with possibly no other asset of the developer on which to draw.

A prospective tenant, in such circumstances, is in a precarious position and may resolve his dilemma, at best, by an action for specific performance against the developer. If the developer has been entirely dependent upon bank finance, the prospects of success may, in context, be unrealistic. The developer will very likely have secured the whole or substantially the whole of its assets to the bank. Worse, if the developer subsequently goes into liquidation, the liquidator can probably avoid the developer's commitment as an onerous contract in any case. The tenant must be satisfied at the outset that the developer is resourced and can deliver, and assess his risk accordingly.

Secondly, as between tenant and bank, if the agreement for lease is registrable only in priority after the interests of the bank, it is essential that the bank's consent has been obtained for the letting (see **The bank** above). Most tenants are content with this because it signals that the bank is of a mind that its own interests are best served by ensuring that the commitment is honoured. Strictly, however, consent alone is not enough and a tenant particularly concerned with the prospects of a developer's obligations being honoured will be concerned to impress upon the bank that if the bank exercises its powers it will procure that any purchaser from the bank novates the agreement for lease with the tenant. (However, depending upon how the agreement for lease has been drafted, the provisions of the Landlord and Tenant (Covenants) Act 1995 may well have effect to pass the developer's obligations as landlord to a successor in any event.) As to other tenant's concerns, see **The tenant** below.

Finally, the relationship between bank and developer in relation to lettings and letting policy demonstrates their different agendas in stark relief. The developer is obviously seeking to maximise the letting potential in order to profit from the venture after the bank has been repaid. The bank is interested simply in being paid off (unless there is a profit sharing mechanism in play), and although it may impose stringent letting obligations on the developer, these may be deemed well satisfied so soon as the prospective capital value of the completed development is generated by lettings reaching a level sufficient to realise the bank's security. At this point a bank's attitude may change, particularly if the loan period has been extended to cover a slow take-up of lettings.

Indeed, on experience, even in the case of a sophisticated letting policy, the inclination of a bank to press the developer to conclude terms with a tenant less advantageous than the developer felt could be achieved, produced conflict and anxiety which, happily in the particular case, fell in favour of the developer who argued carefully and painstakingly, but at enormous expense of time and energy. The lesson, as always, is that while there are limits to what can be prescribed in a letting policy, it is essential for the players to understand their respective agendas and to devise a policy which comprehends this accordingly. Somewhere in all of this, that word 'interaction' emerges again.

The tenant
Assume, however, that the development does not comprise one unit of accommodation alone. The tenant's concerns may also impact upon other aspects of the letting policy with which he himself is as much concerned.

For example, in a shopping centre, depending upon the nature of the trade, the tenant will be concerned that his own trade is not undermined by an excess of competition if, indeed, competition at all. The best laid plans, in any letting policy, may require to be modified if a tenant negotiates his position by requiring an anti-competition commitment from the developer. This may require all the other principal players to reconsider their perception of tenant mix and, in turn, a fundamental re-negotiation of the overriding letting policy.

It is a characteristic of every agreement that the parties to it are free to modify it by agreement if they wish. However, modification of one development agreement may not be feasible without modification of others and the full impact on all the players should be carefully assessed and all relevant contractual commitments re-negotiated accordingly.

Moreover, a tenant is not concerned merely with tenant mix at the outset but, more particularly, the mix of tenants and uses during the term of his lease and this implies the possibility of incorporation of a landlord's covenant which will be binding on successors in title to the reversion. A properly advised tenant will, in such circumstances, also wish to consider writing into the lease appropriate sanctions upon the landlord in such areas, for example, as rent and, indeed, possibly a right to determine. Care is required, however. It may actually suit a landlord or his successors to accept a surrender. It is, therefore, essential for the tenant that there are effective covenants on the part of the landlord.

Finally, if a prospective tenant is at all doubtful of the developer's ability to deliver, he should be seeking additional appropriate guarantees. Any prospective tenant is, accordingly, on enquiry as to the developer's ability to deliver the development, the impact of other prospective lettings, the scope of letting including particularly mix of uses, and inhibitions on the developer imposed by other players including, not least, those prescribed by any superior lease.

Letting agents

There have been a number of statutes affecting the role of agents such as the Property Misdescriptions Act 1989 and the Estate Agents Act 1979. Misdescription apart, and given the role of agents in actually seeking tenants, this chapter cannot pass without considering the role of agents in relation to each of the players. The matter may be considered from certain broad viewpoints. First, how many employers and, secondly, how many agents? From that stems, hopefully, establishment of commitment and duty and in whose favour.

How many employers? Consider, for example, a developer seeking to comply with his letting obligations and, for such purpose, employing a firm of agents. A funding institution, keen to ensure that, as ultimate investor, its own interests are protected will probably have appointed surveyors to monitor the development. They may also have a role as letting consultants, both in supervising the developer's performance as regards lettings and also to ensure that lettings are actually achieved both as part of the development process and, no doubt, thereafter so soon as construction has been concluded in line with the letting policy agreed between developer and fund. Alternatively the fund may have other agents for this particular function. The fund's interests must be protected at all times.

Clearly it is desirable for the respective firms to work to a common policy. The letting policy prescribed by the funding agreement is intended to fulfil that role. However, who is employing those agents? It is unsatisfactory if each firm produces, quite independently for its own separate master, a tenant for the same unit of accommodation. Will the fund choose the tenant introduced by its own agent merely because of its 'superior' position? Such a scenario cannot be allowed to arise. If it does, it means not just that the developer is prospectively frustrated in the performance of his contractual obligations to the fund, but that his own agenda may not be realised. It follows that, while the developer is so obligated, the role of the agents must be *clearly* distinguished. It should, therefore, usually be provided that, if there are to be two or more agents involved, they will in the first instance be the servants of the developer as regards that particular function. Once the developer's obligations have ceased, for whatever reason, whether because those obligations are fulfilled (or perhaps because they are not fulfilled and the developer's entitlement to perform them has been forfeit) the fund can if it wishes reconstitute the relationship itself either with both agents or its own appointees alone. (Where the developer is in default, if the developer continues to have some kind of interest thereafter (see Chapter 9), the role of the fund's agents many need careful definition.)

However, for the present, while the developer's obligations are proceeding, if there is more than one firm of agents they should be jointly instructed by the developer alone with a common aim based upon the prescribed letting policy. It is vital that the terms of engagement set this out clearly because, otherwise, the developer may lack the means to control all the activities of those agents. They may indeed produce different tenants, it may be found that the letting policy has not recognised fully or has failed to comprehend the competing agendas (something which is probably impossible to avoid entirely but which should be avoided so far as possible).

Ultimately, the developer has got to be placed in a position where he is in direct control of the letting obligations, (including, one is reminded, securing a fund's commitment to enter into leases which satisfy the criteria set out in the development finance agreement). That is not to say that one of the firms of agents, having an advisory role for the fund, cannot also assist the fund in reaching a view as to whether the developer has performed its development obligations. The agent is entitled to its view and should be capable of distinguishing its roles accordingly, not simply by choice but through clear terms of engagement. The lesson for the agent is that if he feels that his role has not been sufficiently defined, it is in his interests to ensure that the other players recognise that he has an agenda as well, and that his terms of engagement are suitably drawn.

A fund's agent will naturally be concerned about the impact of his respective roles on the ability to earn commission but this boils down to the terms of engagement between him and the developer, assuming the developer is his master for letting purposes.

How many agents? Once the identity of the employer is clear, and precisely which master an agent is serving and for which purpose, the matter of how many agents is a little easier. At least, it should be, except that over the years a substantial body of case law has built up distinguishing agents' roles and in particular the consequences of employing more than one agent, who has the right to negotiate and so on. As with everything else in this life, the presence of so much conflict and uncertainty is borne entirely of the lack of clarity in the relationship.

It is foolish to imagine that the appointment of an agent, particularly in a development scenario where a number of firms may be involved having underlying subsidiary commitments to various principals, can be achieved with minimum formality. Uncertainty is inexcusable because it is, from the outset, avoidable. Once the employer (for the purposes of the agency) is clearly identified then it is for him to enter into clear terms of engagement with his agent (or agents). That was always so and agents should not regard themselves any differently simply because they are working in the context of new development.

Therefore, it follows that a properly advised developer will identify at the outset those agents who are to be instructed to market the (completed) development. If the bank or fund require that other agents be appointed as well, perhaps the same firms as their respective surveyors monitoring the development, they may become joint agents, but in that role they should be agents of the developer (until the bank or fund steps in and, as between developer and bank/fund it may be prescribed that the appointment can be novated in case of developer default). Nothing in the foregoing prevents an agent, like any professional, from being required to give collateral warranties to a landowner, bank or fund, in the case of the last two mentioned with an agreement that the appointment may be transferred to or novated with the bank or fund or other nominated appointee. Through this mechanism, in case of developer default, there can be continuity. Flexibility should be built into appointments to allow for replacements, additions and so on. Each agent should be appointed on the basis that he may not be acting alone.

Agency collaterals are not normally contemplated but for anyone with a financial interest in the development, they are certainly draftable. After all, agents are seen to be keen to impress on the property world that they have a professional role.

In turn, the right to negotiate has long been a source of legal difficulty. Thus, where an agent had a sole right to negotiate but another agent was appointed and earned a commission, the first agent was still entitled to his commission. It is beyond the scope of this book to examine these questions in more detail but the underlying message is that such conflict can and should be avoided by the simple expedient of clear terms of engagement. The agents will obviously have views about entitlement to commission, sharing of commission and so on, but all of these things must ultimately be accommodated in a workable agreement.

In the final analysis, it must be made clear in the relationship precisely who will be entitled to commission as a result of successful letting, how much and when, whoever has actually introduced the tenant. On experience, and as a glance through any legal textbook on agency will show, lax procedures over appointments and terms of engagement, and particularly as to termination of appointments, have time and time again given rise to unexpected claims for commission. The reality is that, with care and thought, they *should not* have been unexpected.

Clarity is required not just in terms of with whom an agent may be sharing a commission, whether he is entitled to it alone or with others, whether the commission rate increases or decreases depending upon with whom and how many other agents are involved but also, very particularly, it depends upon the present and future status of the agent in relation to his employer and, very particularly again, the basis upon which he *ceases* to be so entitled.

A consequence of a carelessly defined relationship has often been that an agent who has perhaps not performed has been forgotten about only to arise to make a legitimate claim so soon as a letting is actually achieved. Again, it is a simple matter of defining the relationship.

Terms of engagement should, therefore, also include clear rules as to disengagement and the basis upon which entitlement to commission ceases. The two are clear and distinct scenarios. It should be possible, in every case, to look at the appointments and determine precisely who is entitled to how much, and *when*, and indeed if at all.

'When?' is an area of difficulty, again wholly susceptible to clarification. It is a simple matter, for example, for a developer to prescribe that commission will only become payable upon completion of the lease itself. It is for agents to negotiate a basis for earlier entitlement: that is their privilege, but whenever the entitlement arises it should be completely possible for the developer to know precisely his commission commitment and between which agents. Because this is entirely a contractual matter, in the final analysis any doubt is inexcusable on any grounds and reflects directly upon the terms of engagement themselves.

Finally, it should be observed that so long as the terms of engagement of agents are correctly prescribed, any conflict over interpretation of letting policy should be properly be removed, from a squabble between joint agents having additional and separate professional responsibilities to those players having different interests, to the definition of the relationship between the developer and those players. In other words it is a matter for principals, with or without evidence in support from their advisers. In the case of the example given at the beginning of this chapter, where conflicting views of respective agents impaired the letting of a city centre shopping development, it was open to the developer under carefully defined terms of engagement of both of those agents to steer the agents towards the agreed goals set by the fund in the letting obligations of the developer contained in the development finance agreement. If, for example, the consent of the fund was not to be unreasonably withheld to a letting meeting certain criteria, that was in the final analysis entirely between the developer and the fund. The conflicting views of agents, given their respective secondary roles, may have been used in evidence in determining that issue, as between principals, but not as a means of thwarting their primary role as agents for the developer.

All the foregoing sounds trite and simplistic, it is not: it points to the need for clarity of purpose and the imposition of discipline in implementation.

Checklist

1. Which of the players will benefit directly, and in what way, from a letting policy?
2. Consider the impact of letting on other players.
3. Which of the players will or should decide upon the letting policy?
4. Where the major interest is or will be leasehold, what are the letting criteria in terms of:
   4.1 the lettings themselves.
   4.2 the (head) landlord's prospective rent?
5. Is the (head) landlord to share the income and if so, how may this inhibit:
   5.1 lettings at all.
   5.2 use of the premises.
   5.3 alterations or replacement of buildings.
   5.4 redevelopment?
6. In case of redevelopment, what factors may inhibit redevelopment even where there is tenant co-operation?
7. What provisions of the headlease may inhibit a head tenant (developer) from reaching a bargain with his tenants?
8. Long leaseholds apart, what are the requirements of an investor? Will the investor's criteria withstand pressure from an adverse market? What are the fall backs? Can the letting obligations be frustrated entirely?
9. Will the developer be required to give an income commitment meanwhile?
10. What is the proposed mix of uses? How will this be judged? Are the issues confined by the planning permission or is some latitude afforded, eg within a shopping development?
11. How may the interests of a bank conflict with a landowner or investing institution?
12. How may the interests of a bank conflict with those of the developer? Compare the bank's desire to let at a rate which will at least see disposal sufficient to repay the bank, and a developer's desire to maximise the investment value.
13. If the bank's consent is required for a letting, and is duly given, is this enough for the tenant?
14. How may the needs of individual tenants serve to modify a letting policy?
15. What safeguards should a tenant require to be incorporated to preserve his interests, particularly his ability to trade without

undue or any competition from other tenants within the same development?
16. Does an agent have more than one role? How may these be reconciled? What are the appropriate terms of engagement?
17. Who employs the agents? If the developer, what is the fall back in case of developer default?
18. What provisions will be made as to rights to negotiate? Will the terms of an agent's appointment survive a further appointment to give to an unexpected entitlement to commission? How may this be avoided?
19. When has commission been earned and when will it become payable and to whom?
20. Has there been sufficient lawyer input to ensure that any provisions of the letting policy are not self-contradictory, leave questions unanswered or invite conflict?
21. How far are the players satisfied that the terms of engagement will effectively translate any differing views between agents into a matter for determination between principals alone? Does the letting policy suffice and will the operative provisions in the relevant development agreement(s) serve to determine the matter between the players?

8 Funding

> 'Neither a borrower, nor a lender be;
> For loan oft loses both itself and friend,
> And borrowing dulls the edge of husbandry.
> This above all: to thine own self be true,
> And it must follow, as the night the day,
> Thou canst not then be false to any man.'
>
> *Polonius, Hamlet, Prince of Denmark: Act I Scene III*

A developer using his own money is operating in an essentially two-dimensional landscape. He makes his own decisions, and conceives and executes the development according to his own perception of how it should be achieved and how he may, thereby, attract his prey, the unsuspecting tenant. However, as soon as he becomes dependent upon another player to help him achieve his objectives, his mind is no longer entirely his own. He has not only the views of another to consider but, depending upon what is required of that player, there may be more than one agenda. In Chapter 1 we said:

> 'It should be appreciated from the outset of a development transaction that the various players are approaching the matter from different standpoints. Their interests are as diverse as their contributions. Their priorities and needs must be understood as also the statutory and other legal constraints in which they are working'.

Accordingly, joining forces with perhaps another developer who may be bringing additional development skills may suggest some commonality of approach. Their joint venture, perhaps in partnership, will set a common agenda but perhaps different duties. In reality, every joint venture, partnership, etc has an element of separate agenda as well. The landowner requiring the skills of the developer may have a long term interest to be encapsulated in the reversion to a long headlease of a completed development. The developer's interest may be transient, concerned only with fulfilling his role, earning his profit, and moving on to the next project. Those providing finance may have transient interests too, or long term interests, or in their own way a combination of both, and an investor's interest speaks for itself.

Accordingly, as soon as the developer joins forces with a financier, the exercise becomes three dimensional and may develop, with the participation of other players, into a multi-faceted model. By looking into the prism thus constructed, the different and possibly conflicting agendas of the players are reflected, depending upon the angle of view and the manner in which they are placed in relation to each other, by different combinations of patterns and colours. Our attention must be directed, as always, to the interaction between the players which is dictated by each of their respective agendas.

Security

Security itself is a multi-dimensional concept. For the moment, we must put out of our minds any association of the term with mortgages and consider it simply as a factor against which to balance risk. Risk and security go hand in hand in any business, so what is security in the context of development?

It is not just land, or even bricks and mortar upon it. Unless there is, or will be, a use or function, land has no value, except in the negative sense that without it land deprives the provider of the land as formal security of the opportunity of exploiting it for his own benefit. Security is thus not in land alone but in obligation, of commitment, skill, financial strength and even hope, ie that this combination will bring about the particular reward which each agenda seeks to derive.

It is not just the developer, or the project itself, which will attract the financier but also the commitment of the other players and the impact of every player's agenda.

The land itself must be capable of development. There must also be a market or at least a prospective market for the finished product. Unless there is a pre-let, or a prospective buyer of the product, someone who will actually use the property and who wishes to pay for the privilege, to embark thus upon the provision of finance is prospectively hazardous. It is said to be 'speculative'. There is nothing wrong with speculative development, to embark upon it is a matter of judgment, and we can leave it for others to debate how and in what way that judgment may be said to be 'professional'.

Starting with the land itself, the green field site, or perhaps the derelict or even contaminated site, is the raw material and the focus of the financier's attention upon which every aspect of the feasibility ultimately rests. From the lawyer's point of view, land is a far more abstract concept. It is not, for example, a mere rectangle of ground. It is represented by legal estates, legal interests and equitable interests. Before the reforming legislation of 1925 there were even equitable estates and the variety of estates and interests was infinitely more complex than those we have today.

However, it is in the nature of estates and interests that they represent not only the land but also what may be done with the land. The effect of restrictive covenants apart, land comprises not merely ground but also what is affixed to it. A lease of a penthouse suite at the top of a skyscraper block comprises as much a legal estate in land as the freehold of the site upon which the skyscraper was erected. Moreover, a legal agreement prior to the conferring of an estate creates an equitable interest in land. Thus, the development process may also be reflected in subsidiary or transient interests in land which in turn bear upon financial viability.

From a financier's point of view, a pre-let agreement is a vital component in his security because it will lead, when the development is completed, to the grant of a lease and, in turn, a rent, premium, or a combination of both. In reality, he is now looking to the financial covenant of the tenant, the right in effect to 'put' a lease onto the tenant in due course and to extract a financial benefit. Security is containment of risk, financial strength, covenant: land is but one manifestation of security.

This is not an essay in valuation: that is for valuers. But what we are concerned with here is the *utilisation* of devices and mechanisms, ultimately reflected in binding legal obligation, as part of the provision and realisation of security.

Development agreements and major interests

In considering funding media, and combinations of funding media, for simplicity we shall, later, work off the platform of an essentially unencumbered site. Meanwhile, however, in the case of major development, it is frequently the case that there will be a landowner who is seeking to exploit the potential in land by hiring development skills which may afford to him a benefit not just in cash but also of a certain kind, as we have already seen. From the point of view of every player who stands to gain in some way from participation in the development, we have also seen that both the agreement itself and the major interest to be granted pursuant to it, whether freehold or leasehold, or other reward, should not be so framed as to inhibit attainment of the objectives for which it was set up.

A local authority landowner, committing assets in this way, starts from a statutory base in relation to maximising its returns: it is not just a matter of commercial prudence. That maximisation may be measurable in cash but by no means necessarily defined in cash. The provision of facilities at no expense to the local authority is a simple example.

Moreover, the commitment it requires of the developer should be capable of being performed. Where there is default it should be capable of remedy. The ability to remedy, and to retrieve one's position, goes to the root of every development agreement because, not least in the case of a financier, his investment in the project is otherwise worth nothing, or may be wasted.

Alienation

Against the background of feasibility of the scheme and practicality of each of the development obligations, the reasonableness (in context) of approvals, time scales, certification, letting, etc the introduction of a financier by a developer necessarily implies that the interests of the developer are no longer merely personal between him and the landowner. If they are, the exercise is inherently unfundable, from independent resources.

First, if the major interest to be granted in due course is completely alienable, as in any event a freehold and also, except to the extent of preserving essential interests of the landowner, a prospective leasehold, the development agreement should also provide (if only for stamp duty purposes) that the developer can call for the *grant* of that major interest direct to a third party, say a purchasing institution or whoever. By that time the development will have been completed and the identity of the person owning the major interest is largely (or may be) a secondary consideration.

The implementation of the agreement itself, as opposed to the entitlement to a major interest on completion of the development enshrined within it, is another matter. A burden in contract cannot move except by fulfilment, release or novation, although an assignee of the benefit can be called upon contractually to indemnify an assignor for the former's contractual obligations. In practice the agreement itself will not usually be freely alienable, despite no legal impediment as such if the parties so desire.

In practice, it will usually provide that it is expressly inalienable except to an assignee, from a bank or institution, who meets essential performance related criteria, and whereby the assignee enters into direct covenants with the landowner.

The developer himself is not usually permitted to alienate, as being contrary to the underlying intention. A landowner, having struck a bargain with the developer, expects to stick with that developer and it is essentially the needs of a financier which dictate the added flexibility to ensure that the bank or fund can either procure that the development is carried out in case of developer default (thus avoiding the prospect of forfeiture (see Chapter 9)) and that its financial burden can be relieved (see below).

As a matter of contract, the obligations of the developer, *qua* developer under the development agreement, are paramount. They will be framed to survive grant of the major interest, for example remedial works and, subject to legal rules of limitation, will continue if breach of the development obligations be subsequently found. By contrast the choice or identity of the person taking the major interest in due course will be inhibited as well by the constraints imposed by the obligations he may in turn owe to the landowner under that major interest alone. Particularly, the burden of the covenants on the part of the tenant contained in a headlease may be a factor in determining the identity of the tenant. For example, if there is a financial commitment, eg rent, grant of (or free alienation under) a headlease to a mere nominee entity may be entirely inappropriate. For the most part, such inhibitions will be readily recognisable and, for a financier, so long as the requirements are reasonable in context and enable him to retrieve his own position, the development agreement with the landowner may to this effect be considered to be fundable.

A financier will also see the security afforded by the development agreement not merely in terms of what can be delivered as between landowner and developer but also in terms of how he may protect his financial input. First, he must be able to embrace the agreement as security of a certain kind. For the moment, we are not yet concerned with the intricacies of debt finance, institutional investment or any combination of the two. The issue is not just the nature of the relationship between the financier and the developer but how that relationship can be brought to fruition. The agreement itself must be alienable, at least to the extent suggested above. It is not just a matter of ensuring that the developer can meet his contractual commitments but that, if necessary, the financier can secure his own position by performing those commitments himself so as to secure, in due course, grant of the major interest, or by procuring someone of suitable standing to satisfy the proper concerns of the landowner, and thus realise his security.

This presents an immediate dilemma for the landowner (prospective head landlord). If the development agreement is used as security, it is implicit that a default on the part of the developer in relation to the financier, but not necessarily in relation to the landowner, must lead to the financier desiring to exercise a remedy. It is axiomatic that a default as between developer and landowner should properly constitute default in the eyes of the financier so that the wrong can be put right. The landowner may have no difficulty with the idea of the financier himself remedying the default under the development agreement (or procuring it) but this implies the prospective interposing of a stranger, perhaps physically, on site.

There must, therefore, be an ability in the development agreement to use it as security; this implies the need to lay down specific ground rules so that the interests of the landowner are not impaired, and this in turn gives rise to a need for limited alienation.

Thus, for example, the development agreement should usually first provide that the developer may use the agreement as security in order to raise finance for the development. It follows that if that security is realised, the developer may be deprived of the ability to proceed but the financier should either himself, or through another, be permitted to carry on the development. It follows again that if, for example, the financier is a lender he must be able to recoup his outlay, if need be by transferring the agreement on again to a new developer who will complete the project, the financier having cut his losses (or made them good) and retired entirely from the project.

The agreement must, accordingly, expressly provide for all of this and it is reasonable for the landowner to prescribe certain criteria for any permitted transfer. Such criteria may include being satisfied as to financial status, skill and so on. It must always be possible for someone to carry the torch to enable the agreement to be fulfilled. The alienation provisions should, in addition, properly prescribe for direct covenants to be given by the new developer to the landowner and for the development agreement to be reconstituted between them accordingly.

It follows that a purely personal agreement, incapable of alienation, is inherently unfundable because it presents no security. Any landowner has to recognise that the provision of finance can take a variety of forms. It may not necessarily be a bank or an investing institution which provides the finance. It may be a joint venture partner who wishes to take some kind of stake in the development. It is more usually, as between a developer and his financier, that the latter will be concerned with the constitution of the developer. However, the developer's ability to perform may subsequently be impaired through a change of constitution, and landowners should consider imposing inhibitions as well.

Where the skills of the team comprised in the developer are a recognised feature of what that particular developer has to offer, the landowner would do well to consider whether there should not be some inhibition on change in share ownership and other aspects of the constitution of the developer. These are always legitimate concerns of a financier (which are less frequently in focus as between landowner and developer): it is rare for public sector landowners to make such provision–perhaps they should consider it. (It should be remembered that ownership of a company does not burden the owner with any implied guarantee. The fact that a company is a subsidiary of so and so is itself of no comfort. At best it suggests the possibility that the parent may provide support, but there is no inherent legal obligation to do so.)

For the most part, a landowner will welcome the added strength which the addition of financial interests will bring to the development scene. A bank will not commit its own covenant to the development process. That is not its function. Its function is to lend and to secure development obligations although it may appoint a receiver to carry on the business of the developer in case of default under a loan agreement. A receiver stands in the shoes of the developer and, indeed, will act as its agent. Where the developer is insolvent, apart from any other breach giving rise to an act of default under the development agreement, the mechanism by which the bank retrieves its position is by way of permitted alienation (under the development agreement) or by otherwise selling on the development (where the major interest already exists, eg a freehold) in its part built state. In the case of the former the development agreement should have been made expressly alienable to this limited extent subject to appropriate criteria surrounding the prospective assignee of the development agreement.

On the other hand, a purchaser intending to acquire the investment particularly at an early stage through forward funding may, by complete contrast, be prepared to give a direct contractual commitment on the basis of securing the ability to control the development while re-appointing the developer in that role under a forward funding agreement. (If the fund is introduced after the agreement is entered into, chances are that the landlord will not wish to release the developer from its original obligation.) If the developer fails, the fund can either complete the development itself (and some funds do so anyway without the intervention of a developer) or appoint a fresh developer. As between landowner and fund, the latter thus becomes directly responsible for the development (and looks forward to receipt of the major interest if relevant in due course).

Bank funding

Long term bank finance apart, development loan finance has been a major plank of development activity, particularly over the last ten years or so. Not that it was not a major factor before but, during the 1980s, a relatively more cautious institutional family began to retreat from development finance. Again, that is not to say that institutional funds ceased to be deployed: they were heavily utilised right up until the recession. However, the diminution in institutional activity was filled by an expanding banking sector which hurriedly filled the increasing vacuum. A wide variety of techniques was devised to reflect the different interests and strengths of the players in a particular piece, including the participating bank (or a consortium of banks).

It is perhaps an over-simplification that clearing banks tend to lend against a more established security than a green field site, although this did not always deter speculative ventures. However, where development finance is involved, the more usual medium is a layer cake of various kinds of security, of which the bottom layer comprises a first legal charge on the site itself. That document, as an entity in itself, cannot deliver the completed development. Essentially, apart from its inherent charging mechanisms, equity of redemption and so on, it requires the borrower to observe all obligations relating to the title to the site and regulates its use and enjoyment. It then goes on to prohibit dealings, including lettings, alterations, building, indeed just about every aspect of the property with which the developer will be concerned. It is the very antithesis of a development agreement, hence the distinguishing role of the latter discussed above.

It will also enable, in case of default on part of the developer, the bank to exercise its rights as mortgagee and, if need be, to dispose of the land: the practicalities of so doing are quite another matter.

A first legal charge will further contain express provisions concerning the appointment of a receiver. He will be a receiver appointed under the Law of Property Act 1925 and will essentially be required to act as agent for the borrower, and not the bank. It is a characteristic of an 'LPA receiver', as he is known, that although he can receive rents, grant tenancies, etc he cannot himself, as of right, execute dealings with the property. This can only be achieved either by the bank exercising its powers as mortgagee, or by attorney provisions incorporated in the legal charge whereby the receiver, in his capacity as attorney for the developer, may deal with the property. A receiver, once appointed, must realise the security essentially to best advantage, but because his role is centred upon the borrower he is vulnerable to attack if he merely does the bidding of the bank. His appointment will usually, however, be hedged with a number of exclusions of personal liability to his putative master, the developer, but he is unlikely to be excused liability to the developer (borrower) in negligence.

The problem with fixed charge receiverships is that, since the Insolvency Act 1986, while the underlying security is not impaired, the successful appointment of an administrator may give rise to a moratorium upon enforcement measures and thus effectively thwart the bank's intentions at least in the short term. The legislation is so constructed, however, that if the bank can also take security (for example a debenture by way of fixed and floating charge) over all the assets of the company, the rules for the appointment of an administrative receiver can thus be satisfied, that is to say if the bank enjoys security over the whole or substantially the whole of the assets of the developer. Both administrators and administrative receivers enjoy their particular capacities in respect of a company, not a partnership although the latter may have, as a partnership asset, a company which can give such security.

The single asset company, perhaps a subsidiary of a development company, has, therefore, become the common medium for development since the Insolvency Act 1986 because, thereby, it can more easily satisfy the rules for the appointment of an administrative receiver and the bank can be satisfied that, with the ability to appoint an administrative receiver, the appointment of an administrator can be avoided through operation of the procedures laid down in the Act.

Whether the bank will actually wish to exercise its powers as chargee will be determined, not so much by the security afforded by a first legal charge or, indeed, by a fixed and floating charge but principally by a development loan agreement which will be so drawn as to be directly related to the principal security documents, development agreement (if any), legal charge and so on. The development loan agreement will prescribe the true underlying relationship between developer and bank, approvals, draw downs, construction, supervision, delay, completion, letting *et al*. It will also, crucially, define events of default which may give rise to the bank exercising its rights as mortgagee—under its principal security.

Needless to say, as between development loan agreement and principal security documents, it should be made clear that, where there is conflict, the loan agreement will prevail. The apparently contradictory relationship is not a contradiction at all. It is, more accurately, a definition of the relationship according to the circumstances. If there is default, the developer may be required to cease his activities. In that case, he is not at liberty, for example to implement the development loan agreement and the bank falls back upon its rights set out in the security documents. Again, when the development is completed, and perhaps remains as security following first letting, the building and letting obligations may have ceased and, thereafter, the rules laid down in the security documents prevail. It may be expected to be found that as regards day-to-day management of the property a charge will not itself conflict in that respect, but many dealings from alterations to lettings will be effectively prohibited and thus require formal consent.

The development loan agreement, being in every respect a development agreement, will also attract various peripheral or ancillary transactions. First, appointments of professionals, the building contract, etc apart from requiring consent will probably necessitate the giving of collateral warranties to the bank which, because of the bank's position as financier and unless the original appointments so prescribe, may require such persons to accept instructions from the bank in the event of developer default. A wise professional will usually seek to negotiate the payment of outstanding fees as a condition of acceptance. The developer, being a single purpose vehicle and perhaps the subsidiary of a principal development company, the latter may also be required to give guarantees of performance of development obligations. If the developer actually carrying out the development is a joint venture vehicle, then there may be a series of guarantees the ground rules for the offering of which may well have been prescribed in the joint venture.

Non-recourse

This is a term used essentially to denote an element of risk being assumed by the lender. In one sense there is no such thing as non-recourse because the term is usually applied to a lending situation in which security is being given. There is, of course, recourse to the extent of that security. At best, accordingly, a non-recourse facility will provide for the lender to resort ultimately to the security afforded by the land alone and not, for example, to financial guarantees (as opposed to those which are offered in support of the developer's development obligations). At this point a certain measure of confusion may arise. Enter another term, 'limited recourse'. Neither label can or should be given a precise meaning.

The giving of guarantees covers two broad areas, first the indebtedness of the developer and, secondly, the performance of development and other obligations. In terms of indebtedness, ie quite simply what the developer owes the bank at any particular moment, the term 'non-recourse' may simply be applied to the security actually offered, ie the land and whatever forms part of it (fixtures) for the time being. If a loan is made 'non-recourse', any guarantee in support of the developer's debt obligations may be expected to be effectively circumscribed by that limited financial commitment.

However, the differentiation between non-recourse and limited recourse becomes steadily more opaque as soon as one moves away from the simple notion of indebtedness versus available assets. What, for example, of a developer's failure to carry out building obligations? There is a tendency for the non-lawyer to assume that business terminology necessarily has some special (perhaps legal) meaning. It may do as a short-cut to concept but, in this particular area, it is to the underlying contractual obligations one should look, and one should be particularly wary of any assumption about the kind of obligation which is being sought.

Suppose, for example, the bank is looking for a commitment which goes beyond the immediate cover provided by the assets? Suppose, again, that the bank is looking for a measure of return over and above value derived from realisation of security and which is dependent upon developer performance so as to raise the value of the assets towards the level of indebtedness incurred overall? In this scenario, the bank may be looking for a contractual commitment, perhaps by way of guarantee, which goes beyond the mere realisation of assets. Before exploring this idea, suffice it to say that non-recourse may develop into limited recourse if, for example, a guarantor is required to guarantee up to a certain level of financial commitment.

What happens if the underlying security, the indebtedness of the borrower and any guarantees in support are further translated into debt plus an added factor (see below)? It is inherent in our law that there must be no clog or fetter upon the equity of redemption. The notion of a collateral advantage, as it is known, raises the spectre of an arrangement which is 'unfair and unconscionable' and which is inherently inconsistent with the borrower's right to redeem the security. It is, incidentally, well found in law that a lender cannot necessarily wait to realise his security if the borrower is in default. Sale may be the borrower's only redemption, in the literal sense, and in such circumstances the lender need not and possibly must not wait until the time is more propitious.

Profit sharing mortgages

The profit sharing mortgage is not unknown to other jurisdictions and neither is it entirely unknown here in the UK. It does, nevertheless, require careful structuring in order to avoid conflict with underlying basic principles of the law of England and Wales (this book does not attempt to consider the laws of Scotland, Northern Ireland or the Republic of Ireland). As a funding vehicle, the profit sharing mortgage may be seen as an alternative to institutional funding mechanisms. It is not an immediately recognisable banking medium, because of legal constraints although that is not to say that a bank may not have a subsidiary, or create a special subsidiary for the transaction in hand, which will enter into such an arrangement (in that case, such a subsidiary might just as well speculate in the development by becoming a participator in the development vehicle but there are also accounting and taxation mechanisms in play which are beyond the scope of this book) to provide the necessary interface to avoid legal inhibitions. Prospective profit sharing mechanisms include a mortgagee's option to convert his loan into a percentage of equity ('convertible mortgage'), if not in the property then in shares in the owning entity. Again, beware the use of descriptive labels. There are still statutory and other inhibitions in play including for example the possibility of a profit sharing mortgage being considered a collective investment scheme under the Financial Services Act 1986. The subject is discussed in more detail in *Property Development Partnerships* which also highlights difficulties of enforceability.

Institutional funding

Market conditions apart, a developer hoping to let and trade a development will be concerned with short term finance in the first instance. He can combine both the shorter and longer terms if he looks to the institutional market which seeks to invest in property. Having used bank finance to fund his development he may in any case sell on to a financial institution who will simply buy the completed investment, let fully or otherwise at whatever price it will fetch in the market, hopefully in excess of the cost to the developer, thus affording repayment of loans and a prospective profit for the developer.

Early involvement by a financial institution gives rise to the prospect of that institution itself providing the finance or leaving the developer to finance the development himself, initially, with the institution (fund) paying for the completed development in due course.

It is of particular advantage to a developer if he can involve institutional finance from the outset. This implies the institution itself buying the property on day one, thus confining the financial exposure of the developer. The developer's financial risk is thereafter confined to the maximum commitment of the fund in financing the development being exceeded.

Forward funding, as it is known, has been described as the best off-balance sheet funding medium. The risk for the fund is that if the developer fails to perform, even with the benefit of finance advanced by it, then subject to such remedies as the fund can exact in contract against the developer, the problems are essentially for the fund to collect and resolve. The fund does not have this problem if its commitment is confined merely to a completed and let development (forward purchase) save to the extent that, in the event of developer failure, the pre-allocation of funds for the purpose may not be realised. The pre-allocation point is, incidentally, equally felt by a bank in case of developer failure where funds are not utilised for the purpose of which they were allocated, quite apart from such remedies as the bank might have to pursue, and a bank will usually prescribe a charge for failure to draw down.

Forward funding

The essence of forward funding is the acquisition by a fund of development risk from the outset. In considering the proposal, the fund must decide quite clearly in its mind whether it is relying upon the market, the developer, or upon such guarantors as it may require, or perhaps upon some combination of all three, to bring about the desired result.

One of the lessons of the recession, in the case of failed forward funding transactions, has been that some funds failed to look to the consequences, however remotely perceived at the time, of market failure and the recourse which might be had to developer strength. Very large development groups, soundly resourced (and thus still in business today) will have made ideal forward funding partners from whom a financial commitment could have been secured, in addition to development obligations, to support the development until it was income producing in its own right.

Having decided upon the nature of the risk to be assumed, the fund can then devise the forward funding package. First, against the background of the feasibility of the scheme, and particularly the time scale for the completion of the development, and market prospects apart, it will be possible for the fund to look ahead to the resultant investment. All of these factors are for consideration by surveyors and valuers but, at some point, the consequences of the views of such advisers must be encapsulated in a workable agreement. It works thus: first, the site is acquired by the fund. Possibly if it withstands valuation, this may result in an initial profit to the developer simply on disposal. Finance is advanced during the project, and the development and construction is monitored, in the manner earlier described in this book.

Against all advances of development cost (including the purchase price initially paid by the fund and associated costs), there will be a 'roll-up' of notional interest. In one sense, the fund's investment has already commenced because advances will appear to grow. However, the impact can only be felt by the developer if the combined advances and roll-up are subject to a maximum commitment, the attainment of which (or failure to attain) will give rise to certain consequences. (By reason of the fund being owner of the property, the developer's contractual commitments with other players to deliver the finished result may be frustrated if, for some reason, the developer is so in default of the forward funding agreement as to be excluded by the fund from his licence to go on site (see Chapter 9).)

Assuming good behaviour by the developer and assuming also success in letting there may be financial consequences which are beneficial to the developer. (Forward funding can be both speculative and non-speculative or a combination of both. There may be pre-lets or partial pre-lets, but for every pre-let there is the knowledge that, subject to performance by the prospective tenant of its contractual obligations to enter into the lease and to maintain the flow of income thereafter, the true investment will be tangible earlier.)

When the maximum commitment is reached (but so far as the development is not complete) it will be prescribed that the developer must meet the additional cost out of his own resources in the same way as when the entirety of a bank facility has been taken up. Cost over-runs can be treated in a number of ways, whether by general provisions or by specific capping of items of development cost. Whether the maximum commitment is reached or if the development is practically complete before the maximum commitment is reached, a decision has to be made as to the intended financial relationship between the developer and fund thereafter. It is implicit that once maximum commitment has ben reached and, until such time as the development is complete (and even if there are lettings which can then be consummated) the financial commitment will have to be met by the developer in at least two ways. First, he must find the balance of the development cost out of his own resources and secondly, the fund's investment must not be allowed to remain moribund. He must start to pay real interest to the fund *in lieu* of income or the generation of income must be reflected in some other way. There is thus no roll-up of notional interest thereafter because the maximum commitment is a ceiling. Remember that in no sense is forward funding a loan. There is no requirement to re-pay advances. The fund has been investing in its own property.

When the buildings are complete, and in so far as there are lettings in place, the fund will be deriving an income (subject to rent free or rent reduced periods as negotiated). Any income vacuum may have to be met by the developer in some way. The income vacuum, as discussed earlier in this book, may be represented by interest, a notional lease or an actual lease of the unlet portions. In the last case, it should be provided that any such financial commitment must be permitted to give way to proper occupational lettings in due course whether the developer has continuing letting obligations. This is clearly a matter of negotiation and has given rise, in the recession, to some strange consequences. In some cases it has been necessary for developers to seek consent to underlet perhaps on terms less advantageous than their own commitment to the fund, in order to off-set the income commitment, which is otherwise quite beyond the contemplation of the forward funding agreement. Hopefully, post recession, it will be in contemplation so that acceptability of a funding proposal may carry with it an income commitment in any event on the basis of initial recognition that lettings may not meet minimum criteria to trigger an overage payment.

Financial formulae

A conventional pre-recession forward funding agreement, having been based upon certain market expectations (in the absence of pre-lets), naturally prescribed for lettings which laid down certain criteria (see Chapter 7). Those criteria would also be expected to include achievement of a minimum rent and an obligation in any event to maximise rent. This has its own logic: unless such rents were achieved, the scheme was not viable. Therefore, the developer should seek to achieve at least those minimum rents and try to do better. Undoubtedly, as markets regain confidence and memories fade the same thinking will be applied again. If so, the players must understand the risks and the downsides and exercise judgment accordingly.

The frustration of letting obligations is now well rehearsed. If the income commitment of the developer is satisfied by one of the mechanisms suggested above in the meanwhile, the fund has a measure of comfort and it is a small step then for a formula to be devised whereby, upon the attainment of each letting of the development, and diversion of the source of income stream from the developer to the tenant, a payment may be awarded by the fund to the developer. Again, that is a matter for surveyors and valuers and, for the most part, these mechanisms once devised are susceptible to well worn drafting techniques.

Underlying all such formulae are valuation characteristics, but the formula-based developer's overage is dependent on pre-conceived notions of the margin between development cost and the resultant market value, in turn driven by letting expectations.

The difficulty for property professionals, in all of this, lies in risk assessment. The difficulty for lawyers is in the effectiveness with which the nature of that risk is exposed, and what fallbacks should be devised in the interests of both fund and, indeed, developer. *Naiveté* is one of the more charming characteristics of investment surveyors matched only by the lawyer's inability to perceive all the possible downsides of the formulae which he is being asked to set in a contractual context. The answer, one supposes, lies in the need for commercial awareness which is acquired with experience (and, possibly, with a little help from this book).

Profit erosion

The profit erosion deal, again a label not to be too closely defined, suggests a shift of emphasis away from a purely formula based developer's profit towards a recognition of the underlying value of the resultant investment, and then working backwards towards the development cost. The fund should not pay too much for its investment, at least in theory. The greater the development cost, including accumulated notional interest, the smaller the profit margin. Any allowance of income commitment to the developer as well, post-maximum commitment/practical completion, will marginalise that profit still further. However, as suggested earlier, a profit mechanism of this nature is capable of leaving the fund exposed to a financial outlay which is not matched by income, unless the property has been let, and at the desired levels, or unless the developer remains liable for income.

It is not for a lawyer to suggest what the commercial attitudes of funds should be. Long may they do deals and take risks and, hopefully, long may they also prosper, and at least pay their fees if they do not! However, purely in terms of mechanisms, the expedient is always available of ensuring that a loss on an investment can be made good by retaining a developer's commitment to underpin the income at least for a certain period. It is a *sine qua non* as a technical expedient against which will be balanced all other relevant commercial factors including whether the decision to invest is based upon developer strength or scheme viability.

Default versus overage

Finally, if there should have been developer default giving rise to exclusion of the developer from further participation in the development, the question arises to what extent the developer should still be entitled to participate in profit and to what extent the fund should attract a shift of profit away from the developer towards itself. This will be debated more fully in Chapter 9, but it is a subject which merits some consideration in the context of devising a financial formula. In every case it is a matter of initial negotiation and developers would do well to consider the consequences of default, and exclusion from participation, at different stages of the development.

It is easy to consider the extremes: on the one hand, the developer may have performed all of his obligations in relation to the development itself but may still be in the process of seeking lettings. Perhaps the developer then becomes insolvent (a prescribed event of default in the forward funding agreement) for unrelated reasons. Is he to be deprived of an overage payment upon subsequent letting by the fund which meets the criteria laid down in the forward funding agreement and which would otherwise give rise to a payment? Again, if the developer has defaulted heavily in the earlier stages of the development, leaving to the fund the substantial burden of completing the development in order to gain a return on its investment, what is the position then? The answer, subject to any particular characteristics of the deal which necessarily implies that the whole package must be analysed in order to draw conclusions, lies in terms of mechanisms within the default procedures which require careful negotiation. It should not be ignored, if only for the two examples given above, and is yet another factor in determining whether the development is, in fact, covenant driven or deal driven.

Forward purchase

This topic has been substantially covered. Forward purchase has so many of the characteristics of forward funding, in terms of development obligations, as to be seen largely in parallel. The underlying risks for developer and fund are, however, fundamentally different, deriving from the developer's need to secure interim finance, the attitude which a lender may strike towards the package presented by the forward purchase agreement, and, with both bank and fund according to their respective interests, their respective attitudes to timing of draw down, allocation of funds, loss of business elsewhere and so on. Moreover, an obvious event of default under a forward purchase agreement will be failure to meet a final date by which the completed development is delivered, and the purchase may thus never be completed. Overage payments are a feature of forward purchase so far as pre-lets are not already in place.

Leaseback

Leaseback finance is a familiar long term vehicle. As a straightforward investment medium it is frequently used by owner occupiers, freeing up capital assets in return for an income commitment. The full impact of the Landlord and Tenant (Covenants) Act 1995 has yet to be experienced and considered. For example, in the case of new leases granted from January 1996, a tenant's rental liability will be circumscribed by tenure as also, to an extent, a landlord's liability. The debate which gave rise to the legislation apart, leaseback is a mechanism which still has a role to play in development finance. Indeed, many shopping centres and other major developments of the 1960s and 1970s were borne of leaseback finance combined with a forward funding agreement and, as with the modern day development agreement, the lease was granted on practical completion, leaving the management with the developer who still had a marketable headlease. The popularity of leaseback is gathering momentum again today but in a slightly different form.

For today's 'borrower', perhaps concerned with owner occupation, a mortgage backed transaction may not suit him for a variety of reasons, perhaps tax or accounting based. He can, instead, consider not a mortgage but a sale of his property in return for a leaseback package. This may be combined with an agreement in the case of development to be carried out and under which, instead of the full value of the completed development, development finance is advanced. When the buildings are completed a lease is granted. However, *unlike* older forms, it does not have to be a long lease, indeed it can be a conventional institutional form of lease. However, it does not necessarily have to prescribe for conventional rent review criteria: the rental pattern can be couched in terms much more akin to payments under a repayment mortgage by reflecting the initial advances, with a rental payment period to accord.

The result is that, at the conclusion of the lease term, the tenant can probably be allowed to exercise an option to purchase the reversion, perhaps for a nominal sum. The difference is that the transaction is based upon the law of landlord and tenant and not that of mortgages, and accounting treatment will in turn be different. When he disposes of the lease, the developer is dispensing, not with the underlying reversion, but with a rental commitment which is alleviated by the benefit of an option to acquire the reversion in due course. Accordingly, the closer the term expiry, the greater the prospective capital reflected by the reversion to the lease.

Overview

The focus of this chapter is upon factors in play when considering different funding techniques. As a treatise on development finance media, it must give way to the formal education of financiers and their professional advisers. Consideration of tax aspects has been carefully avoided and it suffices only to say that, for every mechanism considered, the tax consequences must be considered in parallel. Security apart, they are usually the driving force behind the structuring of any funding proposal.

It is not intended to suggest that the drawbacks to certain funding techniques were not understood before the recession. The judgment in prescribing financial formulae was not, however, always correctly placed. Assessment of downside risk is not the exclusive preserve of those who are initially packaging the proposal. It is helpful to them to understand that it is equally the role of the experienced lawyer to look critically at what is proposed and to consider in that context the legal consequences of failure, and in particular at least to allow him to do so before drawing conclusions. In so doing, it so often happens that practical consequences, other than those first perceived, are brought to light.

Moreover, it should never surprise the developer's and fund's surveyors negotiating a package to find that heads of terms do not necessarily bring about the desired result. On experience, time and time again, analysis of the proposals upon attempt to document them leads to disclosure of unwelcome side effects. Sometimes such difficulties do not materialise until the deal is documented in draft and is in course of intensive negotiation, and it is then necessary to re-analyse the proposal and frame it in a way which avoids the perceived difficulty. Once the deal is concluded, it may be too late, and the fall-back of going to the court for rectification on grounds of mistake is an extreme and hazardous measure.

Funding   151

In turn, a lawyer is to some extent inhibited by his training, and it requires perhaps as much commercial experience as enjoyed by those instructing him to perceive the hidden downside risks. At the end of the day, the resultant financial package reflects the thoughts of a variety of disciplines each with its overlapping parameters. In encapsulating the package in legal documents, the lawyer is at all times on enquiry and must, at least to some extent, be indulged. It may be perceived, correctly, that his enquiry has gone too far or too wide. If that perception is incorrect, it does not necessarily follow that the resultant disaster is due to the negligence of the lawyer. It has been said that the best defence to negligence is incompetence, not least but not exclusively on the part of the alleged negligent. (Again, this book can only hope to draw attention to the dilemma and to underline that not every disastrous product of the 1980s boom was the result of negligence, incompetence or a combination of both.)

Checklist

1. Consider the assets in play, and the security they represent, not just in the sense of security for a mortgage but as a factor in the development.
2. Is the development deal driven or covenant driven, or some combination of the two? What features make the development financially attractive?
3. How far should a developer be permitted to alienate (dispose) of the benefit of his development agreement in order to raise money?
4. Why else should the developer alienate? What are his needs?
5. Under what circumstances should a landowner countenance alienation of a development agreement?
6. What tests need to be satisfied in order to show that a development agreement can be used as security for advances (debt finance) or institutional funding (forward finance)?
7. What are the strengths of the proposed/present developer? How is it constituted? Will any guarantees be forthcoming?
8. Can the bank secure the whole or substantially the whole of the assets of a company? In what circumstances, if any, will a lesser standard be required? Is there any reason why a special purpose vehicle ('SPV') cannot be created for the development?
9. What collateral agreements are required by the financier? What else is required beyond a duty of care? How far should ancillary players, eg professionals, be required to give collateral agreements and should their relationship be prospectively novated

with a fund or the bank or its nominee?
10. If the lender is participating in more than mere repayment, what mechanisms are to be deployed, and how may a 'clog or fetter' on the equity of redemption be avoided?
11. When a deal is forward funded, what is the maximum commitment? What is the roll-up rate for it? What is the true interest rate/income commitment thereafter?
12. In the final analysis, who is exploiting whom? Do the fund's circumstances allow it to undertake the development itself, or will it have to employ another developer? (See Chapter 9 also.)
13. In forward purchase, can the fund rely upon the developer's covenant to deliver (given that because the fund's purchase is conditional, it will not be able to 'take over' the development in case of default)? How may it protect its commitment of funds to a certain time scale?
14. Would a leaseback package be appropriate? In addition to the commercial terms and economic consequences, what impact would this approach have in accounting terms compared to say, debt finance or forward funding?
15. Given the accounting treatment of different funding media, what will be the tax impact? Have the developer's tax advisers (and indeed those of the other players) considered the proposal?

9 Default and Disputes

> 'We will bind and hoodwink him so, that he shall
> suppose no other but that he is carried into the
> leaguer of the adversaries, when we bring him to our own tents.
> Be but your lordship present at
> the examination: if he do not, for the promise
> of his life and in the highest compulsion of base
> fear, offer to betray you and deliver all the in-
> telligence in his power against you, and that with
> the divine forfeit of his sole upon oath, never
> trust my judgement in anything.'
> *First Lord, All's Well That Ends Well: Act III, Scene VI*

Mistrust is a peculiar subject for an exercise in collaboration. Yet this simple instinct, instilled into every creature with a will to survive, underlies and, in conjunction with security in the broadest sense, underpins every contract. The best protection from default and disputes is to deal only with those whom one can trust implicitly. In the course of some research into joint ventures, evidence from one developer showed that the reason he would on no account enter into a joint venture was that he could not afford to have a dispute. Uppermost in his mind was the painful truth that whether there is default or dispute under any contract, there will be delay in consequence, and the honouring of parallel or subsidiary contractual commitments may be impaired.

It is beyond the scope of this book to examine in depth the legal concepts behind consequential loss and remoteness of damage. If one is considering the tort of negligence however, the 'Who is my neighbour?' principle determines how far the blame for one's actions may reach. In contract, a breach may give rise to what is known as consequential loss. For example, if a building is not finished on time or is found to be defective such that an intended business cannot be carried on from it, is the default such as to afford a remedy in damages which will extend as far as loss of business? The answer (unhappily) may well be yes. Contractual commitments given in contemplation of specific consequences may produce precisely that result.

Contractual commitments, once given, are hedged by periods of limitation, as indeed are also tortious remedies (there are different periods of limitation within both contract and tort upon which legal advice should be sought in context). The giving of contractual obligations, however, may also give rise to extended limitation as well. Earlier forms of collateral warranty, in particular, sometimes gave rise unexpectedly to fresh limitation periods in favour of those to whom warranties were given and, sometimes, liability for consequential loss as well.

Now, of course, it is to be expected that the documentation will be so drawn as to ring-fence the exposure so as to confine it expressly where necessary both in terms of limitation and also more particularly in terms of consequential loss. Meanwhile, although the thinking is in the course of development, exposure is also being further confined by looking to the contribution of other players, in the case of professional warranties with the view to minimising so far as may be the downside risk, by use of 'net contribution' clauses. (The tide has turned somewhat in favour of the alleged negligent since for example *D & F Estates v Church Commissioners* (1989) (CA) and *Murphy v Brentwood District Council* (1991) (HL) as regards defects unless for example personal injury is caused or other property is damaged. In contract, it depends entirely on the terms, however, and the objective of a person giving warranty must, therefore, be to ensure that exposure to liability, particularly for consequential loss, is contained.)

The above thoughts may seem, at first sight, slightly out of place in relation to the interaction between principal players. However, they are aspects of construction-related documentation, now common to development, which serve admirably to illustrate that, in fact, whatever the contractual commitment, there are possible side effects at all stages. Every player, in entering into a contractual commitment of whatever kind, must learn to think of those commitments not just in terms of positive objectives but also in terms of the consequences which may result from failure. Whatever one's particular agenda, it is not enough to deal with others, particularly those upon whose advice one may rely, on a need to know basis. Whatever the matter in hand, it must be shown to be workable, and in so far as it is not the risks must be measured as closely as may be, including possible underlying consequences.

The sole purpose of the above remarks, in this introduction to default and disputes is to instil, so far as may be, a healthy level of paranoia as a basis for entering into contractual commitments at all. Once this instinct takes root, it becomes much easier, for example, for the lawyer to perform the function for which he is trained. Even if his client is not on enquiry, a lawyer is, and if he is not armed with the relevant facts and circumstances and, so far as necessary, the benefit of others' expertise, the less his client's interests can be protected.

Default and disputes are in any case themselves so conceptually different as to require very different treatment. As a matter of practicality, the resolution of a dispute may nonetheless show that there was an underlying default with the consequence that, prospectively, default mechanisms may require to be implemented. Some of the consequences of default have been hinted at above, but what provisions should developers' agreements of all their various kinds make for the prospects of default and how should default be dealt with?

Default

As a general principle, the court is usually the best medium for dealing with default in the sense that, if there has to be enforcement, then the court is the appropriate enforcing agency. If the remedy lies with a dominant player, say a bank, there may be immediate steps which can also be taken, eg exercise of a power of sale. In the case of a building contract, for example, failure to complete work or a certain section of work by a certain time may give rise to a pre-programmed consequence eg liquidated and ascertained damages.

If the exercise of the power of sale does not deliver the bank's recompense, or in the case of liquidated and ascertained damages becoming payable under a building contract they are not paid, one is left with the 'personal covenant' which—depending upon the resources available, ie whether it is worth powder and shot—will inevitably lead to recourse to the court for enforcement including insolvency proceedings where appropriate. Questions then arise as to the practicalities of enforcement, and the appropriate measures to be taken, and the litigator's art must thus be employed.

In Chapter 6 we considered the interaction between the players in matters of timing and completion, and how particular contractual commitments should be so framed that, at every stage of the development process, the needs of each player might be accommodated. Particularly we considered questions of delay, delay clauses and the desirability of extensions of time. Such extensions, in general terms, ought properly to be afforded contractually by the remaining players also where a particular player, for example the building contractor, fails to perform and, *in extremis*, when perhaps the developer needs to engage another contractor to finish the project or at least the particular stage. Delay clauses are, therefore, an inherent part of every development agreement and, so far as concerns the developer, should properly protect the developer from matters beyond his control.

However, when a matter is within his control, and he has still delayed, or his default is not a matter of delay but simply a breach of contractual obligation, every player in the piece becomes interested in the outcome. In addition, in the same way as a developer should be protected from matters which are beyond his immediate control, parallel and subsidiary development agreements, of whatever kind, may need to contemplate matters which are perhaps in consequence beyond the control of one or more of the other players concerned.

People who are not in direct contractual relationships with each other may yet find that an unrelated contract may result in default of a player. As a matter of contract, default cannot generally be excused: a remedy must be found. Again, it is beyond the scope of this book to consider the doctrine of frustration in any depth, that is to say the legal doctrine by which a party to a contract may be able to show that notwithstanding that he is in breach of his contractual obligations, the ability to perform them was frustrated by the action or default of some third party or event over which he had no control. Add to this the doctrine of notice and the argument begins to trickle in the opposite direction. Again, it is necessary to inject a healthy measure of paranoia and to consider, in formulating every agreement, the possible consequences of default and the fallbacks available.

In the development process, with so many agreements making up the whole, it is once again the idea of interaction which drives the process. As before, unless the developer owns the site outright, we must start with the classic development agreement under which the landowner will grant a major interest upon completion of the development.

The landowner

We have already seen, in Chapter 8, how for example a development agreement should be so framed that not only is the opportunity afforded to remedy a default but that other players, for example a bank or funding institution, can effectively be permitted to intervene either to remedy the default or to deal with the site in such a way that the development can continue in the care of another so that the development agreement can be kept alive, and thus made bankable. Despite these measures, it is still possible for a default to be considered so grave as perhaps to deprive the developer, whoever the developer is for the time being, of his entitlement to a major interest. If the landowner exercises his ultimate right of forfeiture, the whole project is in danger of collapsing. Perhaps a funding institution to whom the benefit of the development agreement has been assigned pursuant to a forward funding agreement may be similarly dismayed as a result of developer default, with the prospect of the entirety of his investment to date being lost to the landowner. Again, a bank may thereby lose the security of the development agreement.

A typical default clause will, therefore, contain measures which prescribe the events upon which the entitlement of the developer (or his successor as the case may be, eg the institution) to the major interest may become forfeit.

The first of these is usually developer insolvency (less of a problem when an institution has become the developer in the eyes of the landowner, but certainly an event the clarity and finality of which can only put matters beyond doubt). The remaining players, particularly a bank, or purchasing institution under a forward purchase agreement, can ringfence this difficulty through the expedient of ensuring that the development agreement can in such an event either be assigned or novated (reconstituted) under contractual provisions in that behalf. In one sense, therefore, developer insolvency is easy to deal with because carefully constructed contractual measures can immediately be brought into play to keep the agreement alive.

Again, the agreement may provide that there will be default where there is a substantial breach which inevitably cannot be remedied. It would be folly to negotiate an agreement which became capable of forfeiture on grounds of matters which could, in the event, be remedied (and were) or which were not significant so far as concerns the landowner. While the development agreement is in course of negotiation, much may turn upon what is material, significant, substantial, etc the degree of severity of default which may give rise to forfeiture and the steps which may be taken to bring about that adjustment in the relationship which effectively restores the *status quo*.

In this chapter we are, however, concerned principally with ultimate default, and the extreme circumstances in which notwithstanding the interests of the other players and the protective provisions which may be built into the agreement to keep that agreement alive, it must still be forfeit.

There is a clear dilemma here which is easily illustrated. As the development progresses, more work is done, more expenditure incurred and value or prospective value built into the outcome, to be deprived of the entitlement to one's major interest becomes progressively unfair. Where, notwithstanding all of this, the breach is so great as to amount to a repudiation, it is perhaps no less unfair upon the landowner.

However, he has the advantage that he has the land and the benefit of such provisions as have been written into the development agreement. It follows that, in the case of extreme default, the prospect may arise of a last ditch stand on the part of the developer to save the day. The developer, in such extreme circumstances, may be minded (particularly if the landowner is of the view that the breach is so great that allowing a bank to dispose and so on will not even begin to remedy the problem) to move the court and challenge the determination. The default is now clothed with the trappings of dispute, but not one to which a disputes procedure can necessarily apply. In such circumstances, one can begin to draw an analogy with the kind of proceedings which may require to be conducted in the case of forfeiture of a lease. Under a lease, for example, s 146 of the Law of Property Act 1925 will protect the tenant from immediate forfeiture unless the appropriate proceedings for breach have been conducted, and the tenant has still been found wanting after such indulgence as is afforded by the court has been exhausted.

It is entirely a matter of negotiation but it seems appropriate, therefore, to build into the default provisions in a development agreement a final series of fallbacks under which, only in the event of failure to comply even then, the agreement may be forfeit.

Forfeiture of a development agreement must usually be seen as a very extreme event. The contractual safeguards which are taken to ensure continued compliance will usually serve to preserve the *status quo* and to secure, if they are properly drafted, that the interests of other players are similarly safeguarded. If they are not, then the prospect is that other players will not have been drawn into the development to start with. It is probably unfundable.

The bank

A development loan agreement, by contrast, sets in train a series of development obligations which may not necessarily touch and concern the interests of the landowner (if ever there was one—the landowner may of course be the developer himself). In a development loan agreement, an event of insolvency will almost certainly be prescribed as an event of default as much as any breach by the developer of his obligations. However, starting with the base of a development agreement, it follows that if a developer is in breach of his obligations to a bank, he may thereby be deprived of his relationship with the underlying landowner. That is the risk he must assume with the consequence that the development may proceed without him and thus he may be deprived thereby of the ability to profit from the development in due course.

The bank will also have provided in its security documentation for the appointment of a receiver to manage and, if need be, to run the business of the developer, ie the development. (If there is a development agreement with promise of a major interest, insolvency will not normally be tolerated by the landowner, and so other expedients must be chosen. However, developer insolvency if expressed as an event of default should be circumscribed by mechanisms to facilitate bank/fund support, and not made a subject of inevitable forfeiture.) In the case of a corporate developer, the receiver will almost certainly be an administrative receiver of the development vehicle. Further, the requirements of banks are usually so tightly drawn that, in all probability, it is true to say that at no time will the developer *not* be in default (in turn this being something of an inhibition upon the developer becoming involved in a dispute). Because the bank's principal aim is the lending of money, its concern with seeing the development through is characterised by that objective and, in turn, the objective of seeing the loan repaid with interest thereon in the meantime. If it can fully realise its security by passing on the site, it will very likely do so. If it cannot do so without concluding the development, or perhaps because the developer's guarantors have ceased to be capable of supporting the commitment, eg again perhaps because of insolvency, the bank will then be faced with a decision of whether to cut its losses and dispose or employ a receiver to continue to build out the development. Whatever the bank's decision, the prospective loss is greater for the developer who thereby loses his opportunity to profit from the venture (unless a receiver is appointed and the receiver is so successful that as formal agent of the developer he achieves precisely the developer's objectives or more!).

In this scenario, no question of fairness arises. It is essentially one of security alone. The bank has not been contracted in any sense to provide a benefit to the developer, unlike a landowner prospectively granting a major interest under a development agreement or even an institution granting overage under a forward funding agreement.

The banker/developer relationship, therefore, represents a clear cut scenario. Every obligation imposed by the loan agreement and security documentation must be scrutinised with care to see that it is capable of being performed, and that a sensible working relationship can be forged.

Forward funding

Here, the consequence of unremedied default is that the developer is deprived of his ability to earn overage. He must, at all costs, be permitted from his point of view to retain the ability to carry out and complete the development.

Developer insolvency is a clear instance of the developer no longer being able to perform that role. A financial institution will not usually countenance a forward funding agreement under which a developer could continue to operate while his affairs were being conducted by an administrator or an administrative receiver (and if the administrator's moratorium threw the whole development programme into disarray). Usually, as with banking documents and a principal development agreement also, a series of insolvency events is written down. The fund will usually expect to deal with a live and wholesome developer or not at all. (Once an administrator is appointed and unless the insolvency event bringing the agreement to an end is presentation of the petition, the moratorium bites! Thus, in the case of administration the relevant insolvency event may be expected to be presentation of the petition rather than the order itself.)

Serious breaches of the development funding agreement may, as with a development agreement with any other landowner, also give rise to licence to go on site to carry out the development being terminated. As to further effects on third parties, see **Third parties** below. There is a similar dilemma for a developer in dealing with an institution as for a landowner where the developer is to be deprived of overage, as opposed to a major interest in land. Depending upon the nature of his breach, there is an implication of progressive unfairness as the development proceeds. However, the difference is that it is the fund's money which has been used to carry out the development. The developer has no interest beyond that of obtaining overage upon grant of lettings in due course and so default provisions in forward funding agreements tend to be harsher and correspondingly less elaborate, allowing little sympathy for the developer.

Insolvency apart, one is still left with the difficulties which may ensue from breach. In the case of forward funding, and leaving aside subsidiary contracts such as the building contract, there are effectively only two major players, ie the developer and the fund. Delay clauses apart, if the developer's default has been so great during the course of the development that he has no realistic prospect of completing on time or indeed at all, it may be necessary for the fund to deprive him of his licence to go on site and terminate the agreement, with all the consequences which this may produce for the developer, including breach of his commitments elsewhere, eg as employer under the building contract.

However, it is easy to see by way of extreme examples how unfairness can still be built in. For example, the developer may have completed the development in all respects in accordance with the development agreement. Perhaps he has even procured the first lettings and the letting programme is well on track. If the developer then becomes insolvent, should the fund profit from the developer's misfortune? More subtly, suppose the developer has been in such breach of the agreement as to be properly excluded from his right to go on the site and his continued entitlement to draw down of finance. In that event, if the fund itself continues to carry out the development, again is it fair that the fund should profit from the developer's misfortune?

The answer, in the latter case, is probably yes to the extent that the fund now assumes the developer's burden and this is matched by the developer's deprivation of the entitlement to overage. However, there may be marginal differences. Suppose the cost to the fund is less than the value of overage ultimately derived. Should the fund actually profit from this? These are all matters of negotiation and one has seen forward funding agreements under which, if the developer is in such breach as to bring his relationship with the fund to an end whatever the circumstances, that is the developer's misfortune entirely.

A developer, properly advised, should always seek to negotiate a fallback provision if he can, and either the fund will see the reasonableness of his arguments or it will not. Commonly, however, provisions will be written in affording the developer some recognition of his efforts once the fund's cost of completing the development is fully covered. This may have included the cost of employing another developer on perhaps different terms and so one cannot lay down any hard and fast rules. If the fund does acquiesce, however, it is implicit that the project account be kept alive and that, in addition to development costs as prescribed, other costs of the fund incurred in consequence of the developer's default will be debited to it, with the prospect of limited overage for the developer upon settlement in due course.

Forward purchase and tenants

For those whose interests are essentially contingent upon the development being carried out, their relationship with the developer is different again. If, for any one of the events of default arising, the developer does not deliver, the prospective purchaser or tenant may simply depart the scene. Worse, he may sue the developer for default. The prospect of the relevant player staying upon the scene and undertaking his commitment in due course is hedged around by his other interests, for example the need to invest money elsewhere or, if a tenant, to open from other premises as soon as possible in order to commence trading.

Third parties

Accordingly, the relationship of the developer with the principal players will be very different, in the event of default, depending on the nature of the relationship. Nevertheless, developer default under a development agreement, giving rise for one reason or another to the developer no longer being able to proceed with the project, necessarily implies that neither will the developer be able to continue to operate his subsidiary contracts, for example the appointments of professionals and, most particularly, the building contract itself. In such cases, the developer will have placed himself in clear default of these contracts and may be liable for damages. Because the default has arisen through the developer's default elsewhere and assuming that the developer was in culpable default, neither can it be said that the contract in question was frustrated. Thus, the prospect is that the developer will accumulate a series of law suits. The other side of this particular coin is that the subsidiary players in question may yet be re-engaged for the purpose of completion of the project. One has yet to see a provision in a warranty agreement under which a building contractor secures the entitlement to novation of his contract *in any event*, say with a bank or fund, if his employer is in default. One is used to seeing, however, provisions allowing for assignment or novation of an original appointment in favour of the party to whom the warranty is given in terms which may include, for example in the case of a bank, an assignee or purchaser from the bank.

Default of major players

As between the developer and each of the principal players, the position is usually more clear cut. If there is significant default on the part of one of the other players there may be entitlement to damages or specific performance. In that event, the developer is also likely to be supported by the other major players who are directly concerned with the outcome. Moreover, where there is such a breach, there may be afforded to the developer the ability to plead frustration of his commitments to remaining players. Suffice it to say for the purpose of this book that any such event, however remote, must be considered on the legal merits at the time.

Disputes

An effect of default or dispute under one agreement may possibly be to give rise to frustration of another. Depending upon the outcome of the dispute it may, equally, be shown that by reason of the dispute having been wrongly joined, the player concerned having suffered the inevitable delay which the dispute brought about may, in consequence, have placed himself or been placed in default of other commitments. The interaction between the players at large can, therefore, become very confused until a dispute is resolved. If a player is in dispute, and the project is being delayed, he may find that his other contractual commitments are progressively collapsing and that he faces proceedings for default under those relationships. Accordingly, the first rule of disputes is not to have them at all, and if one must then one must strive to find the most effective means of dealing with them. In this part of the chapter we consider the practicalities of using experts and arbitrators, and also alternative dispute resolution (ADR).

For many contractual disputes, the court is an acceptable tribunal. In commercial cases there is a long tradition of arbitration, often through the medium of the court, and development and construction are no exceptions. The process of arbitration, whether privately or through the court, affords the ability to deploy specialist expertise and technical knowledge where such matters lie at the heart of the dispute. Of course there may be legal points for reference to the court alone and, under building contracts in particular, the official referee's court can constitute an arbitration for the conduct of such disputes.

All relevant development agreements need to be drawn to accommodate, so far as may be, at least the realisation of the possibility not only of the developer being the victim of default elsewhere (through a carefully drafted delay clause) but also of dispute, and in such circumstances if only by reason of inevitable delay the developer is himself always open to the danger of being found in default of his principal obligations. Disputes can arise between the players to any development agreement, by no means necessarily on a construction related issue and, consequences of delay and the prospects of being considered in default under other agreements apart, dispute resolution needs to be considered in a wider context. If there is an ability to bring the parties together in a forum which more conveniently deals with the issues involved, then it is to be preferred. Well drawn development agreements therefore usually accommodate a disputes clause.

One of the problems with any dispute in development is that it may also give rise to a parallel dispute elsewhere. Most development agreements concentrate upon the issues arising directly between the players to the agreement in question. Nevertheless, if there are disputes under different agreements relating to the same issue or issues then it is perfectly possible for separately constituted tribunals, of whatever kind, to reach conflicting decisions. For the most part, because of the very different interests of the players in each relevant development agreement, this is unlikely to be a problem in practice. There are other areas of the law where the problem is more readily recognisable. For example, in the case of leases, if a head landlord shares in a percentage of rents, one can see immediately that he has a prospective interest in rent reviews arising under underleases and a lease may therefore expressly prescribe that he may be joined as a party to an occupation lease rent review. Such technical niceties apart, what of arbitration and the use of experts?

Arbitration

This is a quasi judicial function with the result that the award of an arbitrator is capable, ultimately, of enforcement through the court without need in the agreement, whereby the arbitration is originated, for any express provision in that particular regard. As to the issues to be arbitrated upon, the arbitrator is nevertheless constrained by the authority conferred upon him. His function is to decide the issues by strict reference to what is prescribed in the agreement, and no further. Indeed, because of the *quasi* judicial nature of an arbitration (which by implication also requires formal submission of arguments and evidence and also affords the ability to subpoena witnesses), an arbitrator is often thought of as being immune from attack. In fact, if there is a formal defect in his award he may yet be found personally liable.

Arbitration is governed by a series of statutes, principally the Arbitration Act 1950. However, that does not mean that the parties cannot by formal agreement modify the arbitrator's powers. Nevertheless, because arbitration is a voluntary procedure, even though contractually prescribed, initiation of arbitration necessarily requires a formal reference to arbitration. There are rules as to who may be an arbitrator and who may be disqualified from being an arbitrator. A point of law can be referred to the court for determination but appeals as such from an arbitrator are rare and, indeed, are governed by provisions of the Arbitration Act 1979 whereby the leave of the court is required to appeal and may be granted if the matter concerns an issue of law of general public importance or is one which the Court of Appeal should consider.

With both arbitration and the employment of an expert, there is a degree of finality which should not be underestimated. The whole point of dispute resolution procedures is that disputes should be resolved, not perpetuated.

Experts

The role of an expert is less formal and, again, may be prescribed by the relevant agreement. An expert is not effectively constrained in the expression of his views but, clearly, if he goes beyond the matters put to him for determination and fails to qualify his views, it is not impossible for him to be held personally liable in negligence. Indeed, it is perhaps the best reason for his giving conclusions alone without reasons (and it may, in turn, be difficult to engage an expert if one has gone to the trouble of setting up a disputes clause which requires that reasons be given in any determination!).

Proceedings before an expert have no special mechanism for enforcement. Accordingly, reference to an expert must be incorporated contractually so that the results of the determination can be enforced by one party against another.

Again, it should not be assumed that the award of an expert can be readily overturned. If he simply gets it wrong, the prospect is that the court will not overturn his mistake. Contrast, however, an expert's implied duty to act fairly and impartially. That is not to say that the determination of an expert may not for some reason find its way before a court. Fairness and impartiality apart, it might for example be shown that the expert has actually answered the wrong question. However, simply getting the answer wrong is not, on its own, likely to constitute grounds for appeal. An expert is, very literally, entitled to his opinion.

Alternative dispute resolution (ADR)

Proponents of ADR can neither look to these pages for support nor disapproval. Parties to a contract having a genuine difference of view have long sought mechanisms for resolving their difficulties. Sometimes, the difficulties arise between players who have worked together well in the past and have every desire to do so in the future. To place themselves in formal opposition is not always conducive to development of the relationship. The award of an arbitrator is inherently enforceable, that of an expert is not, except by contract. To elevate ADR to a formal dispute procedure having the force of law is essentially self-defeating, so it will be found that ADR procedures will be conducted expressly without prejudice to the rights of the parties in any future proceedings, unless the ADR proceedings are themselves concluded by formal legal agreement.

ADR is a developing approach to disputes resolution. A body known as the Centre for Disputes Resolution (CEDR) was set up in 1990 specifically to promote ADR. Through a neutral mediator, the process of mediation can be employed to assist the parties towards a common view. Mediation may be labelled conciliation if, in the process, the neutral mediator expresses his own opinions. A slightly more formal procedure is the mini trial before a panel of representatives of the parties in dispute consisting of decision making executives perhaps assisted by a neutral mediator.

ADR clauses have been and are being developed in order to give shape to the process which, clearly, is essentially simpler than more formal techniques. However, one wonders whether if, in pursuit of perfection, ADR may not be in danger of becoming as complex as more formal procedures. If it does, it may perhaps be seen as self-defeating. To make such proceedings expressly without prejudice to legal rights does raise the possibility of reluctance to share information which might otherwise be privileged in proceedings, and perhaps nothing turns on the point if the information in question would necessarily have to be adduced in formal proceedings. If the information is given confidentially to the neutral mediator, the question arises as to whether he may be required by subpoena to adduce it subsequently. One answer may be to have a legally qualified mediator who is, accordingly, bound by the rules of privilege.

In any event, in the context of development, if ADR is used to resolve a difficulty under one agreement, but not under another, this may itself give rise to conflict. For example, the development agreement between a landowner and a developer may prescribe that the costs of the landowner properly incurred in connection with this and that shall be met by the developer. Under the development loan agreement, the bank is to advance to the developer as part of the development cost sums properly incurred by it in performance of its duties under the development agreement. The landowner and the developer are in dispute which they resolve through ADR. The bank is of the view that the sum was not properly payable. In context, the answer may be that, unless the development loan agreement expressly provides, the bank may not be bound to recognise the ADR result. However, if a formal disputes procedure had been used or the results of ADR were expressly legally binding by virtue of some enabling provision in the development agreement, and unless the bank was properly of the view that the circumstances were such as should be appealed (for which there would probably be limited scope—see above) the bank would very likely be bound.

Accordingly, as a tool of interaction, ADR may be provided for but should be used with care because, by being in essence without prejudice to formal procedures, it may give rise to issues failing to be resolved in other areas.

Other kinds of dispute procedure

It is an unfortunate characteristic of disputes that measures for resolving them are so often given labels which, unless given statutory cognisance, eg arbitration, have as much legal authority as mnemonics.

Thus, for example, 'deadlock' has a variety of meanings. The state of matrimony apart, it might refer, for example, to a company under whose shareholders' agreement, supported if necessary by the articles, there are equal voting rights which—quite deliberately—provide no exit route for the players. If the company has contractual commitments and the deadlock structure represents the joint venture so far as it goes, the absence of a disputes procedure can concentrate minds wonderfully. However, where the deadlock company is in a contractual relationship with another, the building in of certain kinds of exit routes may also be wholly unsatisfactory. If shares are sold so that the company ceases to be characterised by certain qualities or skills, the vehicle may also be unattractive to a funder. Having said that, if the participators, or their holding companies, have already given guarantees to the funder not a great deal may turn on it. A deadlock structure may, again, be circumscribed by a disputes procedure: in that case, is it really a deadlock?

Where players are joined together under a joint venture, various mechanisms can be employed for one to buy out the interest of another or others. These procedures may be inappropriate in funding terms generally, even if commitments have not yet been given, because the buying out of one interest may, through loss of identity, make the package unfundable and thus unattractive for one or more of the remaining players. (In any case, as soon as one adopts a corporate or partnership structure there are critical tax issues to be addressed as well.) A loan or forward funding agreement may in any case prescribe for the development vehicle to maintain the same constitution throughout the development period, notwithstanding the articles or shareholders' agreement, breach of which may give rise to an event of default.

Texas shoot out, piggy back and Russian roulette (otherwise known as Mexican stand off) are mechanisms whereby one party can buy out the other's interest according to different techniques, whether at a predetermined or ascertainable price (a Texas shoot out occurs when the first party to exercise the option to buy draws first), by piggy back (offers to buy matched by incremental responses until someone gives up!) or Russian roulette (failure to accept an offer giving rise to an obligation to buy the offeror's shares at the same price). Further, the oppressed minority rules relating to companies may be relevant where an effective procedure does not provide.

Contrast a default procedure which may deprive a player of his entitlement to dividends or require him to forfeit his shares, whether some or all of them. Such arrangements within a corporate development vehicle need great care in terms of exposure to prospective funders and the terms which they may wish to see imposed.

In all of these circumstances, the ability of one party to buy out the interest of another may be driven by financial strength. Clearly, where the players are of unequal strength it is desirable for the weaker party to negotiate a fairer footing or, if his bargaining position is weak to start with and he must acquiesce in such procedures, that he will be treated fairly in other ways. Failing this, the question arises why he is in negotiation at all!

Overview

At the outset of this chapter reference was made to a developer who did not indulge in joint ventures because they prospectively led to disputes. All contracts, questions of default apart, are capable of giving rise to disputes. Any one development attracts a diversity of skills and interests by no means all of which are in any way committed to a future association, even though this is frequently the case.

Disputes can often be avoided, nevertheless, by the simple expedient of joining together players who have mutual trust, particularly those who have worked closely together before. Experience shows that such trust can only be leavened by communication and dialogue, the absence of which is the very antithesis of trust. In this respect, there is perhaps a limit to what legal documentation can achieve but there is also plenty that legal documentation can impair. Everything that is reduced to writing must have a purpose. The purpose, therefore, requires careful analysis and must be tested so far as may be, whether it be a mechanism, a formula or whatever. The lawyer needs to know and understand precisely what it is the parties are seeking to achieve and to draft critically. If his client fails to instruct fully, or he indulges in 'need to know' he will likely thwart his own intentions.

In an ideal world it is said that, once signed, the documents should be placed in a drawer and left until the deal is done. One can only concur with that but must also add, very cautiously, the rider that if the documents must be looked at to provide guidance, the acid test lies in opening the drawer and reading what is said! If it fails to provide for the point at issue, it is not just a legal matter but whether the principals and/or the lawyers had thought adequately about what it was they were trying to achieve.

Finally, no disputes procedure is capable of resolving a dispute borne of uncertainty or omission, unless that procedure itself contains some mechanism upon which that procedure can bear. At the simplest level, even where the matter in dispute is recognised as being one which, in the absence of agreement, must be subjected to determination in some way, if the document itself gives no clue, a determination may be impossible to achieve. To say, for example, that in case of dispute an issue shall be determined by referral to so and so may give that person absolutely nothing to work on. If it says, for example, that it shall be referred to so and so to determine what in the circumstances is fair and reasonable at least gives one a criterion. If the matter for determination is not contemplated at all, or the objective is unclear, the documents may be found wanting and then any number of factors, beyond the scope of discussion in this book, may be employed to determine what the parties intended. The extreme example is a contract which is thereby so hopelessly flawed as to be shown to be void *ab initio*. The court beckons and the lawyers win!

Checklist

1. Who is my neighbour? How may he be affected by:

Default and Disputes

    1.1 my commitment (in contract), and/or
    1.2 my action or inaction (in tort)?
2. What is the potential for consequential or economic loss? How may it be avoided?
3. How should questions of default be addressed? What is the consequence for the immediate contractual relationship?
4. What is the consequence for ancillary or independent relationships?
5. In the context of the transaction in hand, what ought to constitute an event of default?
6. How far should a particular agreement afford the opportunity to make good the default?
7. Should a player be permitted to profit from the default of another? If all costs can be covered, what then?
8. If there is a dispute, what is the prospective impact on other relationships?
9. What will be the preferred method of dispute resolution under a particular agreement?
10. How may resolution of a dispute under one agreement impact upon the efficacy of another?
11. What is the best medium for dispute resolution in context?
12. How may other players, particularly under separate contracts, be required to recognise the validity of a dispute resolution in the context of their own agreements?
13. Particularly, if ADR is used, and by virtue of being without prejudice to formal rights, how may this be recognised in the context of interpretation of a parallel agreement?
14. If there is a corporate structure, what provisions for default are operative? If the process may deprive a player of his interest, how may this impact on, say, a funder concerned with the constitution of the vehicle?
15. Is there any issue which has been so framed that, by whatever means, it cannot be resolved? If so, does it go to the root of the contract so that, prospectively, it may simply dissolve?

10 Epilogue

> 'Tis ten to one, this play can never please
> All that are here: some come to take their ease
> And sleep an act or two; but those, we fear
> We've frighted with our trumpets; so, 'tis clear
> They'll say 'tis nought: others, to hear the city
> Abus'd extremely, and to cry, 'That's witty!'
>
> *Epilogue: King Henry the Eighth*

For those new to development, the whole process will no doubt seem complicated. It is undoubtedly complex, embracing many skills and disciplines, a vast array of technical knowledge and apparently hedged at every stage by legal constraint. That does not mean, however, that development is necessarily 'complicated'. Complication can be overcome by personal discipline, and intelligent application which, provided one has the will, may be achieved in time with experience. The purpose of this book has been to illustrate some of the practical thinking which goes into the process, albeit seen through the eyes of a lawyer. One's own experience has shown, time and again, that from whatever quarter someone is participating in that process, success, and the prospect of greater success, can be measured directly in these simple principles and also a pro-active approach to 'making it happen'. Order and discipline on their own are not enough, however, and distinguish the rest of the world from those with creative skills, and so these initial remarks may be seen as no more than one manifestation or facet of the art of negotiation.

Negotiation

For the principals involved, face to face negotiation is, at some point, inevitable. That professionals thereupon become involved in the process is a measure of the resulting success. Some professionals (particularly surveyors) are in any case engaged to negotiate from the very outset of a transaction. This process may be lengthy. On personal experience, one truly major scheme had involved the same firm of surveyors for some 25 years, and negotiations between the principals some 11 years, before the development documentation was finally signed. (On a slightly more personal note, the lawyers were involved for only 15 months!)

As a negotiation develops and ideas begin to crystallise, there is a natural tendency for agreed points of principle to be perceived in a certain form. As each part of the jigsaw is put in place, those points of principle may take on a different dimension and require modification. Unfortunately, it is precisely the zeal of the players, and a pro-active approach, which may also give rise to difficulty as the negotiation develops. As further players are introduced to the piece their negotiating positions may, perversely, be strengthened precisely because of a fixation of ideas and an inability on the part of those hitherto involved if not to comprehend then to accommodate the kind of thinking advanced by the new participators.

At one level, this may be seen, for example, in convincing a planning authority that a proposal is desirable and appropriate notwithstanding that it runs contrary to the local plan. At another, the difficulty may lie in working with an adjoining landowner or a prospective joint venture partner whose co-operation is needed. Again, a funder may bring an added dimension, not just by reason of the provision of finance but by reason of the manner in which it is to be applied.

The acid test lies ultimately in the manner in which the negotiation is contractually reflected. In this respect, it is not just that legal inhibition may require a different approach, a different reflection of the thinking, etc: most principals will readily understand that this is an essential part of the lawyer's role and, equally, the same sort of proposition applies in its own way to the roles of other professionals involved. More subtly, the consequences of reflecting a negotiation in a certain manner may not be immediately apparent.

A shiver runs down the spine of lawyers and other professionals some of whose clients would strike a bargain over the lunch table and subsequently announce 'It's all been agreed!'. *Deja vu*? Happily, most of those clients were seen off by the recession and one client in particular, from whom the above remark is recalled most often to have emanated became spectacularly insolvent right in the middle of the 1980s' boom. Indeed, when the accountancy firm handling the liquidation produced its initial statement of affairs, one felt, with the benefit of hands on experience of all the deals which the company had done over the years, that one could have written the statement in an hour or so off the top of one's head without the need for a painstaking forensic examination.

The art of initial negotiation does not lie in careful heads of terms alone. As the negotiation progresses these should be constantly revisited and tested against each new circumstance. Eventually, in the course of the legal process the practicality of each proposition will, or should, in any event be tested. In a complex funding proposal, for example, it is perhaps to be expected that at least some aspect will require to be redefined because the process of drafting will itself identify the flaw. Unhappily, sometimes, the flaw will remain uncovered and the legal drafting will encapsulate the defect. In very complex developments it sometimes cannot be helped that the application of a variety of disciplines, including that of the lawyers, fails to uncover the defect. If there is a mutual recognition that the intention was not served, making the appropriate adjustment will not be difficult to achieve.

If a player had misconstrued its own position, it may have to suffer the disadvantage as an inevitable consequence of the particular negotiation: there may have been no mistake as such. If there is a mistake which is not recognised as such by one or more of the other parties, there may be a thin dividing line between a dispute over interpretation (which can be accommodated by a disputes procedure, if there is one) and a dispute over intention (which may be a matter which can be resolved only by the court). These sorts of difficulties may even find themselves combined in some way with the consequence that a contractual commitment, so far as it went, was itself fully intended but perhaps gave rise unexpectedly to consequential loss.

In the final analysis, perhaps no one is an expert. One can only be certain so far as may be, and the ability as much to analyse and to assess the impact of a proposition on each of the players as on oneself is fundamental to the art of negotiation, without which it may never come to fruition.

Public versus private sectors

In times of ever restricted resources, there has been a sea change in approaches to resourcing development. The idea of pooling resources strengthened its hold on the private sector during the 1980s but, for the public sector, the idea is, in very relative terms, quite new. Traditionally, what may be described as a municipal private finance initiative has taken the form of identifying a developer, say perhaps for a town centre, and using the developer's skill in particular to achieve the desired result. Much of that goes on today. However, for the public sector, and in particular local authorities, there is increasing pro-activity.

Public authorities in search of the means to carry out urban regeneration have needed to attract private sector investment while pursuing a pro-active role for themselves, and to this end have received statutory encouragement to do so. This creates considerable difficulty for local government officers whose tradition has been entirely municipally centred. They now have to live the dichotomy of performing their traditional role, which is hedged around by statutory inhibition and the meeting of requirements of public servants in that capacity, on the one hand, while adopting an entrepreneurial role on the other. Having not been in business as such, they are now thrust into commercial negotiations and to applying commercial criteria to which, in some cases they have rarely, if ever, been exposed. There is already a measure of anecdotal evidence of this elsewhere in the public sector, whether it be through the private finance initiative or the implementation of the grant system, particularly through the single regeneration budget where the underlying criteria for advances have themselves been criticised.

Again, in relation to compulsory competitive tendering the lack of realism in seeking bids for work on behalf of the public sector has met with criticism. There is understandable sensitivity to putting work to outside contractors at all: that said, probably no public sector employee would gamble with the notion of importing expertise which was otherwise lacking, but that is a different point entirely.

However, being a player as such is different from putting out services to tendering save in so far as it points up a relative lack of experience in areas of the public sector in negotiating projects with the private sector. This can only come with experience and understanding and utilising so far as may be outside professionals to provide the appropriate expertise. It was never necessary to be compelled to put work of whatever kind out when specialist skills were actually needed. CCT (Compulsory Competitive Tendering) is about something else entirely.

This book will not seek to justify or criticise compulsory competitive tendering of professional services save to observe, as in all walks of business, that one ultimately tends to get what one pays for. Nevertheless, where a particular function is delegated because it is statutorily required or where outside expertise was required in any event, there must still be those handing down instructions who must ultimately take responsibility for ensuring that the aims of the particular public body have been duly achieved.

With the public sector also being pressed into closer harmony with the private sector, on economic grounds, the experience gap is brought into sharper focus. Once any statutory inhibitions on participation in a project are overcome, as a simple example whether sufficient value is to be derived from disposal of an asset to avoid the unwelcome attention of the district valuer and the prospect of surcharging of councillors, the negotiation of an improved position may for some be a novelty, if not perceived as socially unacceptable (unless it is the developer who is being milked). Accordingly, these are skills on which the public sector must now concentrate given that, whatever the future for the national political scene, the idea of joint ventures between the public and private sectors seems set to stay for the foreseeable future.

Site as a tool of the trade

In Chapter 2 we highlighted aspects of the site itself as a precursor to the project and noted that the site or a component part, or parts, of it might be in negotiation so as to bring one or more landowners into a co-operative venture. We also touched on features of the site which might mould its use, and mechanisms for removing inhibitions.

In the process of site assembly, a number of consequential factors can easily be overlooked. Once the site is assembled, it may be too late and public sector assistance may not be forthcoming particularly if there has been an error. One such difficulty lies in ransom strips.

Land registry filed plans are essentially for identification. They are of fairly small scale albeit of frequently better quality than the plans on unregistered conveyancing documents which gave rise to them. It is always a healthy sign that a lawyer is prepared to walk the site and to understand its features as a way to a better understanding not just of the title deeds produced to him but, more particularly, of the project. Precise dimensions may still not necessarily be inferred, and the absorption of physical characteristics is essentially a matter for principals advised by their property professionals.

From time to time land is disposed of, sometimes by the public sector itself, in such a manner as to leave traps for the unwary. The acquisition of two parcels of land thus apparently removing a right of way, the parcel of land up to which the local highway authority will assume the highway abuts, and so on, may hide the existence—notwithstanding diligent enquiry—of ransom strips, and it by no means necessarily follows that those of whom enquiry was made were necessarily negligent or even dishonest.

The existence of a ransom strip may, quite literally, be hidden from view by plans and documents. On experience, more than 20 years ago, a piece of land had already been bought from one of the new towns and became the subject of a development proposal which, upon presentation of a planning proposal, met with objection from the owner of the true frontage who had, as it turned out, quite deliberately retained a tiny strip along the frontage for the precise purpose of maintaining a measure of control. In the subject case, access lay at the heart of the matter. By that stage, as one had not been privy to the original purchase it could not be said whether more diligent enquiry might have uncovered the truth: the site had already been assembled, indeed from one single parcel of land and from unregistered land as such. In general, lawyers are most attentive to such possibilities: very exceptionally due diligence falls short of providing the appropriate safeguards however well intended and focused.

Accordingly, land which has no practical use in its own right can be used to exact a measure of leverage. Indeed, that is why developers themselves set about acquiring pieces of land which may be pivotal to future development of a wider site in due course.

In recent years, there has been a fundamental relaxation in the rules relating to registration of land. Formerly, the making of a parcels and index search was simply part of the essential enquiry made by a solicitor to see, in the case of unregistered land, whether some interest had already been registered or, indeed, if the land was already known to be registered, what other interests might therein lie. He might have a plan of what he thought his client was wanting to buy only to find that although the title he was being offered seemed similar, the site plan disclosed a different story. Indeed, upon further enquiry of the land registry, he might even have discovered a ransom strip!

Today, however, upon identification of the registered parcels, there is now no inhibition whatsoever on obtaining office copy entries and filed plans of those titles and, indeed, office copies of those legal documents noted on the registers of which copies are said to be filed. (There is, incidentally, one fundamental difficulty outstanding in that the registry does not readily hand out copies of a registered lease and one needs to provide a good excuse to be allowed to have access to a copy.)

Thus it was, for example, in the case of disposal of an investment that somewhere between the mortgagee bank and its appointed receivers, the counterpart leases of all the occupational leases were unfortunately lost: in obtaining office copies of those leases, which will be regarded by the court with the same authority as the originals, one was able to dispose of the investment. On this point, however, there has always been a discretion to disclose on the part of the registry.

However, the more important aspect of this relaxation is that office copy entries will disclose identity of all registered proprietors whether owners as such or mortgagees. Accordingly, there need be no mystery, so long as the title is registered, over who owns what in the context of site assembly and with whom one should be negotiating. In devising a plan of action, it is now very easy to conduct an analysis of current interests in the target site remembering always that not every interest is registrable (eg leases granted for a term not exceeding 21 years, which are expressly prescribed as 'over-riding interests' under s 70 of the Land Registration Act 1925).

Taxation

From one who is avowedly not a tax lawyer, the subject of taxation should be considered circumspectly. However, that is precisely the point because principals in negotiation will, naturally, leave questions of taxation tacitly to one side until they essentially have a deal. Once professionals become involved, however, which suggests that the point has been reached when the proposals must be defined, taxation assumes ever greater importance.

VAT

The days have gone when zero-rating of certain supplies begged the need to reflect and structure commercial development transactions to particular advantage for valued added tax purposes. The emphasis has now shifted to ensuring that the conditions exist whereby there can be a recovery of VAT.

Dealings in land as such are potentially VAT-exempt with certain notable exceptions including in respect of newly built buildings (see below). In order to recover any of that VAT and indeed VAT on other costs incurred in relation to the land, it is essential to make election to waive exemption and thus charge VAT on future supplies in relation to the land. A joint venture vehicle, therefore, entering into the development process will need to register for VAT and then (if appropriate—see below) to make election and it is as well to remember that, as regulations relating to elections have developed, it is essential upon the acquisition of land to make such an election within 30 days of closing the deal. If such an election is not made, the Commissioners have a discretion whether to back date it. If exempt supplies are made meanwhile, consent to elect is still required, and this will not be forthcoming until such apportionment calculations as necessary have been made.

Broadly, sales of freehold land today (and indeed leaseholds within the confines of statutory definition) with new buildings completed or fully occupied within three years before supply (ie sale) (and except where the construction does not involve a qualifying residential or charitable building) will be standard rated (unless the transfer is on a going concern basis). (A purchaser will thus wish to elect to waive exemption unless he intends to make exempt supplies and thus to suffer all the related input tax in consequence.)

Where a developer intends to let on an exempt basis, or occupy while not a fully taxable person before the tenth anniversary of completion of a building his input tax can still be recoverable if he will instead pay the developer's self supply charge, which was repealed with effect from 1 March 1995, but with certain transitional provisions for phasing out until 1 March 1997. The tax point for self supply is the last day of the VAT accounting period in which the developer occupies the building or grants the exempt interest or if later, that in which the building becomes substantially ready for occupation or use.

Reconstruction, extension or enlargement of an existing building and other works were brought into self supply by regulations from 1 January 1992. For self supply to operate, combined land value and construction costs must (with exceptions) be not less than £100,000.00. A developer liable for self supply does not have to be registered for VAT or account for VAT on the self supply if he must pay VAT on his interest in the land, ie because his vendor or landlord has elected to waive exemption. It is advisable at least to notify one's local VAT office, however.

For commencement of construction on or after 1 March 1995 there is no self supply and normal rules will apply in relation to input tax. In case of construction commencing on or after 1 August 1989 but still in progress on 1 March 1995, the developer could have removed it from self supply by making appropriate tax adjustments not later than 31 August 1995.

There are slightly more subtle rules for construction commencing on or after 1 August 1989 (and reconstruction, extension or enlargement as before on or after 1 January 1992) but still in progress on 1 March 1997 which will become liable to a self supply charge on that day whatever the value (except in anticipation of providing wholly taxable supplies where the rules will not apply). Where the works are completed but not put to an exempt use by 1 March 1997, self supply will apply subject to exceptions, eg a qualifying (residential or charitable) use, or where there is a compulsory standard rated disposal of a freehold by reason of the new building rules (disposal within three years of completion ie practical completion or earlier occupation). NB: If there is a self supply charge before 1 March 1997, rents and licence fees will become standard rated and remain so: if the self supply is on or after 1 March 1997 they will be exempt unless the landowner has opted to tax. In a short time, therefore, unhappily not before publication of this book, self supply on development will crystallise in some form or other, and another anomaly of VAT will be removed.

Mention of the above tax points is only made because of their novelty in 1995 and because of their significance to developers, in particular, with developments in hand. VAT is a complex tax and the above notes are too truncated to be more than illustrative of the particular points and professional advice is desirable on all aspects of VAT affecting development.

Stamp duty

This area of the law should not be underestimated. Charges of 1 per cent on any consideration or premium (including upon the amount of VAT thereon payable, ie tax upon tax) are not the only concern. Stamp duty on rents can be as much as 24 per cent of the annual rent. Stamp duty is, in one sense, a voluntary tax. If you have an instrument which is taxable with stamp duty, and you fail to stamp it, you have not at that precise point necessarily offended. Your failure to tax, however, may have adverse consequences. For example, any deed properly registrable at the land registry cannot be so registered unless the duty has been paid. No deed, requiring to be stamped, can be adduced as evidence (except in criminal proceedings) unless it has been stamped. If a deed is presented late for stamping (28 days' grace), a penalty may be exacted. Stamp duty is a complex tax and because of the prospective amounts involved, its consideration is vital to any feasibility.

Corporate and partnership taxation

The existence of a partnership is a matter of substance and not denial. The most meticulous denial of a partnership, if such is to be avoided for tax purposes, cannot alone serve to achieve that objective. Indeed, the very fact of denial may serve to highlight those features of the relationship which give rise to a partnership. Nevertheless, express denial of a partnership, the underlining of the fact that each party is responsible for its own tax and, in particular, that none of the players can bind the other (to be able to do so is an essential feature of a partnership) may together lead to the conclusion that there is no partnership provided, of course, that there are no other features which notwithstanding suggest a partnership.

In some circumstances, it may not matter that the particular exercise has brought about a partnership. A partnership is essentially transparent, tax-wise, so that income and capital taxes reach down directly to the partners themselves.

Sometimes a partnership is operated through a joint venture corporate vehicle whose legal personality nevertheless will attract a tax regime applicable to itself alone (which may be of no consequence if it is only (and demonstrably) a nominee). Whether a trading or an investment vehicle, corporation tax will otherwise be applicable to the profits of a company. Once a joint venture is at an end, this suggests a cessation of trading and a distribution to shareholders, which is itself also taxable.

Every transaction in property prospectively involves taxation. No structure should be settled upon unless the tax consequences have been ascertained.

JV features

There are, obviously, rudimentary principles in play when a transaction is in the course of negotiation. The respective tax positions of each of the players may bear directly upon the manner in which a transaction is structured, and simplicity may not always be available in consequence. Where there is a local authority participator, the need for care is further highlighted in so far as a corporate vehicle is used in which, perhaps, the local authority may become a participator, by reason of regulations for the time being in that behalf relating to local authorities and companies pursuant Pt V of the Local Government and Housing Act 1989.

Wherever the public sector is involved, it is essential for it to appreciate that it is not just ultimate profit but feasibility which depends upon an appropriate tax structure. The private sector players will need to examine the prospective tax consequences of any structure with the utmost care and, when taxation can be avoided by structural measures, it is to be expected that those measures will be taken.

Everyone is entitled to avoid tax and viability of a project may depend upon it. Evasion is another matter entirely and all players in the piece should be equally concerned to ensure that, in some way or another, they are not being drawn into any process of doubtful legality. That is not to say that the players must examine the tax base of each of their opposites. The tax affairs of every player are essentially private to it, but common sense will largely dictate one's acquiescence in a particular strategy, and co-operation in evasion can never be excused.

Negotiating strength and bargaining power

The final paragraphs of this book look down upon the hapless player surrounded by interests far greater, in financial strength, statutory powers and so on, and the difficulties associated with negotiating his position. Whether the player is a minor landowner holding a vital component, or a developer with an idea but lacking the essential financial clout, negotiation may seem intimidating for the newcomer. Until a site or a vital contractual commitment is secured (or perhaps a part of the site or some land adjacent which is vital to viability) a developer's situation is certainly precarious. This was always so and, for experienced developers (to whom this book is not in any case directed) it is part and parcel of the process.

Unless he has already secured some important element, or he has the financial resources, every negotiation starts from some point of weakness. Can the developer justify the acquisition in terms of prospective security, for example? Is his covenant sufficient for his bank simply to take a view without looking alone to the land or its potential? Every negotiation may be liable to failure or to simply being hijacked by a prospective player whose co-operation is required, but again that was always so.

Assuming that the developer has overcome all of these hurdles, and he has a viable project, does it necessarily follow that he must therefore be the weaker party at all stages in the development process as such? Again, it is a matter of negotiation but, through negotiation and contractual commitment, he should be looking to strengthen his eventual position.

In earlier chapters, we looked upon the developer as a central figure feeding off the landowner, bank, institution, tenant and so on. However good a negotiator, the dilemma ultimately lies in the contractual bargaining position of the developer and the extent to which fellow players can dictate how the developer conducts the project. It is essential, therefore, that the respective bargaining positions be adjusted contractually, so far as possible, in order to establish a balance of power.

Certain mechanisms for this were suggested in Chapter 9. The examples given, however, concentrated on, essentially, ultimate remedies not initial bargaining positions. The object of development can only be achieved through a working relationship and, therefore, to underpin this the eventual balance of power will only be achieved through legal mechanisms. These may embrace voting powers (with or without a deadlock) and also benefits. Some default procedures will, for example, deprive a defaulter of his right to dividends, proportion of profit and so on. A disputes procedure based on financial incentive may be no comfort at all.

It is open to each player in the process, in offering his own contribution, to demand in return the acquiescence of his fellow players in a manner which affords him the measure of security and control that he requires. If the player opposing him performs as he is required, the minority player has nothing to fear save the inadequacy of the requirement itself. That, surely, must be a sufficiently glib and naive note on which to end a practical book on development and finance and on which to conclude that the essence of all successful negotiation can be encapsulated in one word, credibility.

Very finally, therefore, how is credibility to be established? A structure has no credibility unless set in the context of a contractual interface between the players. There may be two deals having identical objectives and supported in each case by an identical basic structure. The difference between them is that for one or more related players in each case, success or failure lies in the extent to which the one contemplates the outcome by securing contractual commitments which effectively reach out to the furthest extremities of participation. In other words, the player who secures his position both by obtaining direct commitments and limiting his own exposure in consequence of events over which he has no direct control, protects himself from the economic consequences of failure of part of the stucture or of one or more of the players to perform. The other, leaving matters to chance which could have been contractually secured or limited may yet discover, however financially sound the plan in principle, that his participation was doomed. It is as simple as that.

Index

(All references are to page number)

Access to site, 73–75
Agents role—
   letting, 115–116, 127–131
Alienation, 136–139
Alternative dispute resolution (ADR), 165–166
Appointment of professionals—
   assignment, 46–48
   collateral warranties, 42–43
   generally, 40–41
   novation, 46–48
   termination, 41–42
Approvals—
   planning, 67–69
   works, 80
Arbitration, 163–164
Assignment, 46–48

Bank funding—
   generally, 139–141
   non-recourse, 142–143
   profit-sharing mortgages, 143
Banks interests—
   certification, 104–106
   default and, 158–159
   letting, 123–126
Building contracts—
   completion—
     defects liability, 99–100
     final certificate, 101
     generally, 97
     interim certificates, 97–98
     partial possession, 98
     practical completion, 99
     snagging, 99–100
   construction process, 71–73
   generally, 43–44
   sub-contracts, 45
Building obligations, 77–78
Buildings insurance, 84–85

Capital receipt rules, 6
Certification—
   banks interests, 104–106

Certification—*contd*
   institutional investors interests, 106–107
   landowners interest, 101–104
   local authority's interests, 101–104
   tenants interests, 108
Collateral warranties, 42–43
Completion—
   defects liability, 99–100
   final certificate, 101
   generally, 97
   interim certificates, 97–98
   partial possession, 98
   practical completion, 99
   snagging, 99–100
Consents, 67–69
Construction (Design and Maintenance) Regulations (CDM), 79–80
Construction process—
   access to site, 73–75
   approvals, 67–69
   building contracts, 71–73
   building obligations, 77–78
   consents, 67–69
   delay, 78
   generally, 66–67
   implementation, 75–77
   indemnity, 88
   insurance—
     buildings, 84–85
     contractors, 85–86
     overage of, 86–87
     developers, 88
     generally, 84
     professional indemnity, 90
     reinstatements, 87
     term of, 85–86
   landowners interests, 69
   management, 79
   overview, 90–93
   schedule, 69–71
   supervision—
     defective works, 80–82
     generally, 82–84
     health and safety, 79–80
   tendering process, 71–73
   works approval, 80
Contractors insurance, 85–86

Default—
  banks interests, 158–159
  forward funding, 159–161
  forward purchase, 161
  generally, 155–156, 162
  institutional funding, 148
  landowners interests, 156–158
  tenants interests, 161
  third parties interests, 161–162
Defective works, 80–82
Defects liability insurance, 48–49
Delay, 78, 109–111
Developers insurance, 88
Development agreements—
  alienation, 136–139
  certification—
    banks interests, 104–106
    institutional investors interests, 106–107
    landowners interest, 101–104
    local authority's interests, 101–104
    tenants interests, 108
  construction programme, 69
  funding and, 135–136
  generally, 4
  indemnity clause, 88
Development cost—
  forward funding—
    fund costs, 62–63
    generally, 59–60
    notional interest, 60–61
    separate records, 61–62
  forward purchase, 58–59
  funders interest, 55–57
  generally, 52
  impact on relationships, 63–64
  institutional purchasers interest, 53–55
  interrelationship between parties, 57–59
  landowners interest, 53–55
  overview, 64–65
  profit erosion, 61
  purchasers interest, 57
  tenants interests, 57
  true cost, 53
Development period, 78–79
Disputes—
  alternative dispute resolution, 165–166
  arbitration, 163–164
  experts role, 164–165
  generally, 162–163
  types of procedure, 166–167
Drawdown of funds, 95–97

English Partnerships—
  funding by, 5
  generally, 4–5
  site assembly role, 24–26
Environmental issues, 30–32

Forward funding—
  default and, 159–161
  fund costs, 62–63
  generally, 59–60
  institutional lenders, by, 144–146
  notional interest, 60–61
  separate records, 61–62
Forward purchase—
  construction programme, 70
  default, 161
  development cost, 58–59
  generally, 148–149
Funders interests—
  development cost, 55–57
Funding—
  alienation, 136–139
  bank—
    generally, 139–141
    non-recourse, 142–143
    profit-sharing mortgages, 143
  development agreements, 135–136
  English Partnerships, 5
  forward—
    default and, 159–161
    fund costs, 62–63
    generally, 59–60
    institutional lenders, by, 144–146
    notional interest, 60–61
    separate records, 61–62
  generally, 133–134, 150–151
  institutional—
    default, 148
    financial formulae, 146–147
    forward funding, 144–146
    forward purchase, 148–149
    generally, 144
    overage, 148
    profit erosion, 147
  leaseback, 149–150
  security, 134–135
  Treasury, 5

Health and safety, 79–80

Indemnity, 88
Insolvency—
  effect of, 7–8
Institutional funding—
  default—
    forward purchase, 161
    generally, 148
  financial formulae, 146–147
  forward funding, 144–146
  forward purchase—
    default, 161
    generally, 148–149
  generally, 144
  overage, 148
  profit erosion, 147

Institutional purchasers interests—
  certification, 106–107
  default, 161
  development cost, 53–55
  letting, 119–120
Insurance—
  buildings, 84–85
  contractors, 85–86
  overage of, 86–87
  defects liability, 48–49
  developers, 87–88
  generally, 84
  professional indemnity, 89–90
  reinstatements, 87
  term of, 85–86

Joint venture companies—
  development cost and, 63–64
  generally, 8–9
  interrelationship between parties, 12–13
  profit-sharing arrangements, 20–21
  shareholders agreement, 10
  taxation, 178–179
  use of, 9–12

Landowners interests—
  certification, 101–104
  construction programme, 69
  default and, 156–158
  development cost, 53–55
  letting, 116–119
  site access, 74
Lawyer's role—
  letting, 115–116
Leaseback, 149–150
Letting—
  agents role, 115–116
  banks interests, 123–126
  generally, 113–115
  institutional investors interests, 119–120
  landowners interests, 116–119
  lawyers role, 115–116
  letting agents role, 127–131
  mixed users, 122–1213
  overage provisions, 120–122
  tenants interests, 126–127
Letting agents, 127–131
Limited partnerships, 13–14
Listed building consent, 67
Local authorities—
  capital receipt rules, 6
  co-operation by, 22–23
  set aside rules, 6
  statutory duty, 23–24
  ultra vires transactions, 6

Management of site, 79

Negligence—
  generally, 36–37
  insurance, 88–90
Negotiations—
  generally, 170–172
  strength, 179–181
Non-recourse funding, 142–143
Novation, 46–48
Nuisance, 28–29

Options, 21–22
Overage—
  development cost and, 54
  institutional funding, 148
  insurance, 86–87
  letting, 120–122
  mixed users and, 122–123

Partnerships—
  development by, 13–14
  taxation, 178
Party walls, 28
Planning permission, 67
Practical completion, 99
Pre-emptions, 21–22
Prescriptive rights, 27
Private sector—
  development in—
    insolvency and, 7–8
    role, 6–7
Professional indemnity insurance, 89–90
Professional team—
  appointment—
    assignment, 46–48
    collateral warranties, 42–43
    generally, 40–41
    novation, 46–48
    termination, 41–42
  generally, 34–37, 49–50
  indemnity insurance, 89–90
  role duplication, 37–40
  third party commitments, 45–46
Profit erosion, 61, 147
Profit-sharing mortgages, 143
Property development—
  generally, 14–17
  joint venture companies, by—
    generally, 8–9
    interaction, 12–13
    practical situation, 9–12
  motivations, 1–2
  partnerships, by, 13–14
  private sector, in—
    insolvency and, 7–8
    role, 6–7
  public sector, in—
    English Partnerships, 4–5
    regeneration budget, 5–6
    role, 3–4

Property development—*contd*
  public sector in—*contd*
    set aside rules, 6
    ultra vires transactions, 6
Public sector—
  development in—
    English Partnerships, 4–5
    regeneration budget, 5–6
    role, 3–4
    set aside rules, 6
    ultra vires transactions, 6
Purchasers interests—
  development cost, 57

Reinstatement insurance, 87
Restrictive covenants, 29–30
Rights of light, 27
Rights of support, 27

Security, 134–135
Set aside rules, 6
Shareholders agreement, 10
Site access, 73–75
Site assembly—
  conditional element, 20–21
  considerations, 18
  co-operation of local authorities, 22–23
  English Partnerships, by, 24–26
  environmental issues, 30–32
  generally, 18
  local authorities—
    co-operation by, 22–23
    statutory duty, 23–24
  negotiations, 18–20
  nuisance, 28–29
  options, 21–22
  pre-emptions, 21–22
  restrictive covenants, 29–30
  third party rights, 26–28
Site management, 79

Snagging, 99–100
Stamp duty, 177–178
Sub-contracts, 45
Supervision—
  defective works, 80–82
  generally, 82–84
  health and safety, 79–80

Taxation—
  corporate, 178
  generally, 175–176
  joint ventures, 179
  partnership, 178
  stamp duty, 177–178
  value added tax, 176–177
Tenants interests—
  certification, 108
  default and, 161
  development cost, 57
  letting, 126–127
Tendering process, 71–73
Third party rights, 26–28
Timing of development—
  certificates, 95–97, 101–108
  completion, 97–101
  delay, 109–110
  drawdown of funds, 95–97
  generally, 94
  preliminary stages, 94–95
Treasury funding, 5

Ultra vires—
  local authority transactions, 6
Urban Regeneration Agency, 4–5

Value added tax, 176–177

Warranties, 42–43
Works approval, 80